The
VOCA^{PLUS+}
BULARY

완전 개정판

7

The VOCA✛BULARY 완전 개정판 ❼

지은이 넥서스영어교육연구소
펴낸이 임상진
펴낸곳 (주)넥서스

출판신고 1992년 4월 3일 제311-2002-2호 [2-1]
10880 경기도 파주시 지목로 5
Tel (02)330-5500 Fax (02)330-5555

ISBN 978-89-98454-40-1 54740
        978-89-98454-33-3 (SET)

가격은 뒤표지에 있습니다.
잘못 만들어진 책은 구입처에서 바꾸어 드립니다.

www.nexusEDU.kr

The VOCA^{PLUS}BULARY

완전 개정판

7

넥서스영어교육연구소 지음

NEXUS Edu

1 Essential words for the school test

수능, 토플, 텝스 기본 어휘 625개를 선별하여 수록했을 뿐 아니라 유의어 및 반의어, 파생어, 접미사를 추가하여 다양한 어휘를 폭넓게 학습할 수 있도록 구성했습니다.

2 Sentence-based recognition

각 표제어마다 예문을 제시하여 단어를 보다 효율적으로 암기할 수 있도록 구성했습니다.

3 Synonym / Antonym / Derivative를 통한 어휘 확장

연계 학습을 통해 각 단어와 관련된 유의어 및 반의어, 파생어를 학습할 수 있도록 구성했습니다.

4 A variety of question types

Exercise → Review Test → Accumulative Test로 이어지는 단계적 테스트를 통해 반복 학습 효과를 높일 수 있도록 구성했습니다.

5 Sound-based recognition

학습한 단어를 음성으로 복습할 수 있도록 음성 파일을 제공하여 청취 실력 향상에 도움이 되도록 구성했습니다.

6 학습 리뷰 테스트 온라인 제공

온라인(www.nexusEDU.kr)을 통해 학습 어휘를 테스트해 보면서 다른 학생들과 결과를 비교할 수 있어 자신의 학습 성취도를 모니터링할 수 있습니다.

구성과 특징

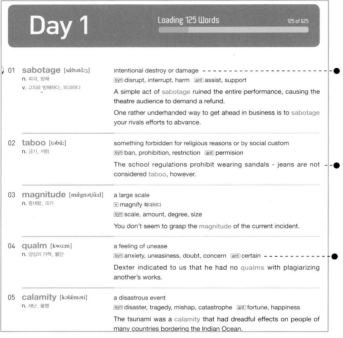

Day Lesson

각 25개씩 단어 목표를 제시하였습니다.

표제어마다 정확한 의미 파악을 위해 영영 풀이를 소개하여 영영 사전으로 학습하는 효과를 얻을 수 있도록 구성했습니다.

Sentence

각 표제어마다 예문을 제시하여 효과적으로 단어를 외울 수 있도록 구성했습니다.

Synonym/Antonym/Derivative

각 단어와 관련된 유의어 및 반의어, 파생어를 학습할 수 있도록 구성했습니다.

Day 1 (속 이미지 내용)

Day 1 — Loading 125 Words — 125 of 625

01 sabotage [sǽbətɑ̀ːʒ]
n. 파괴, 방해
v. 고의로 방해하다, 파괴하다

intentional destroy or damage
[syn] disrupt, interrupt, harm [ant] assist, support
A simple act of sabotage ruined the entire performance, causing the theatre audience to demand a refund.
One rather underhanded way to get ahead in business is to sabotage your rivals efforts to abvance.

02 taboo [təbúː]
n. 금기, 꺼림

something forbidden for religious reasons or by social custom
[syn] ban, prohibition, restriction [ant] permision
The school regulations prohibit wearing sandals - jeans are not considered taboo, however.

03 magnitude [mǽgnətjùːd]
n. 중대함, 크기

a large scale
[v] magnify 확대하다
[syn] scale, amount, degree, size
You don't seem to grasp the magnitude of the current incident.

04 qualm [kwɑːm]
n. 양심의 가책, 불안

a feeling of unease
[syn] anxiety, uneasiness, doubt, concern [ant] certain
Dexter indicated to us that he had no qualms with plagiarizing another's works.

05 calamity [kəlǽməti]
n. 재난, 불행

a disastrous event
[syn] disaster, tragedy, mishap, catastrophe [ant] fortune, happiness
The tsunami was a calamity that had dreadful effects on people of many countries bordering the Indian Ocean.

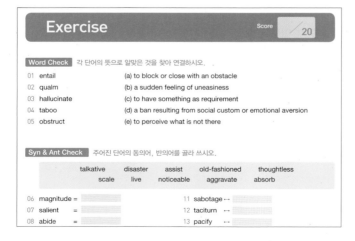

Exercise

Exercise를 통해 학습 단어를 다시 한 번 확인할 수 있습니다.

Exercise (속 이미지 내용)

Exercise — Score / 20

Word Check 각 단어의 뜻으로 알맞은 것을 찾아 연결하시오.

01 entail — (a) to block or close with an obstacle
02 qualm — (b) a sudden feeling of uneasiness
03 hallucinate — (c) to have something as requirement
04 taboo — (d) a ban resulting from social custom or emotional aversion
05 obstruct — (e) to perceive what is not there

Syn & Ant Check 주어진 단어의 동의어, 반의어를 골라 쓰시오.

| talkative | disaster | assist | old-fashioned | thoughtless |
| scale | live | noticeable | aggravate | absorb |

06 magnitude = _____
07 salient = _____
08 abide = _____

11 sabotage ↔ _____
12 taciturn ↔ _____
13 pacify ↔ _____

Suffix

알아두면 유용한 접미사를 선별하여 수록했습니다.

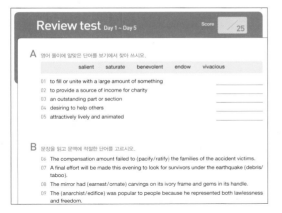

Review Test

5일마다 Review test를 실시하여 앞에서 배운 단어를 한 번 더 검토할 수 있도록 구성했습니다.

Accumulative Test

Accumulative test를 통해 누적된 단어를 다시 한 번 복습할 수 있습니다.

차례

Part 1

01 **sabotage** [sǽbətὰːʒ]
n. 파괴, 방해
v. 고의로 방해하다, 파괴하다

intentional destruction or damage
[syn] disrupt, interrupt, harm [ant] assist, support

A simple act of sabotage ruined the entire performance, causing the theatre audience to demand a refund.

One rather underhanded way to get ahead in business is to sabotage your rivals' efforts to advance.

02 **taboo** [təbúː]
n. 금기, 꺼림

something forbidden for religious reasons or by social custom
[syn] ban, prohibition, restriction [ant] permission

The school regulations prohibit wearing sandals - jeans are not considered taboo, however.

03 **magnitude** [mǽgnətjùːd]
n. 중대함, 크기

a large scale
[v] magnify 확대하다
[syn] scale, amount, degree, size

You don't seem to grasp the magnitude of the current incident.

04 **qualm** [kwɑːm]
n. 양심의 가책, 불안

a feeling of unease
[syn] anxiety, uneasiness, doubt, concern [ant] certain

Dexter indicated to us that he had no qualms with plagiarizing another's works.

05 **calamity** [kəlǽməti]
n. 재난, 불행

a disastrous event
[syn] disaster, tragedy, mishap, catastrophe [ant] fortune, happiness

The tsunami was a calamity that had dreadful effects on people of many countries bordering the Indian Ocean.

06 **obdurate** [ɑ́bdʒurit]
a. 완고한, 냉혹한

refusing to change one's mind
[n] obduracy 고집, 완고
[syn] stubborn, unbending, immovable [ant] flexible, wavering

Even the most obdurate person feels sorry for the child's misery.

---

01 단순한 방해 행위도 공연 관람객의 환불요구를 일으켜 전체 공연을 망칠 수 있다. 다소 공정치 않은 방법이지만 사업에 앞서나가기 위해서는 경쟁업체가 앞서 나아가려는 노력을 방해해야 한다. 02 교칙에는 샌들을 신는 것은 금지하지만 청바지를 입는 것은 금지사항이 아니다. 03 당신은 이번 사건의 중대함을 파악하지 못하고 있는 것 같군요. 04 Dexter는 우리에게 그가 다른 사람의 글을 표절하는 데 대해서 양심의 가책을 받지 않는다고 말했다. 05 쓰나미는 인도양에 접한 많은 나라 사람들에게 끔찍한 영향을 준 재앙이었다. 06 아무리 냉혹한 사람이라도 그 아이의 비참한 상황을 안타까워 할 것이다.

07 earnest [ə́:rnist]
a. 진지한, 진심의

serious and sincere

[ad] earnestly 진지하게

[syn] solemn, sober, serious [ant] frivolous

My mother used to be an earnest Christian before my brother was killed by the car accident in Florida.

---

08 taciturn [tǽsətə̀:rn]
a. 말 없는

tending to say little

[n] taciturnity 말없음, 과묵

[syn] mute, quiet, reticent [ant] fluent, talkative

My taciturn uncle is usually silent, which makes it difficult for me to approach him.

---

09 salient [séiliənt]
a. 두드러진, 눈에 띄는

outstanding

[syn] noticeable, obvious, prominent [ant] unimportant, inconspicuous

There is a salient resemblance between my father and my first child.

---

10 judicious [dʒuːdíʃəs]
a. 사려 깊은, 현명한

showing good judgment and sense

[a] judicial 사법의, 재판의 [n] judiciary 사법부, 사법제도

[syn] careful, thoughtful, astute, sensible [ant] foolish, naive, thoughtless

My mom is always ready to give judicious advice to me.

---

11 wary [wέəri]
a. 조심스러운

cautious or watchful

[v] ware 주의하다, 조심하다

[syn] cautious, suspicious [ant] reckless, inattentive

You should teach your children to be wary of strangers.

---

12 vehement [víːəmənt]
a. 열정적인, 격렬한

expressed with strong feeling

[ad] vehemently 격렬하게

[syn] passionate, fervent, heated, vigorous [ant] apathetic, calm, serene

After a vehement debate both parties agreed to the compromise.

---

13 quaint [kwéint]
a. 예스럽고 정취있는, 색다르고 재미있는

old-fashioned but charming

[syn] old-fashioned, attractive, charming [ant] modern, fashionable

A quaint European castle built out of bricks is surrounded by big trees.

---

07 어머니는 동생이 플로리다에서 교통사고로 죽기 전까지는 독실한 기독교인이었다. 08 말수가 적은 나의 삼촌은 항상 조용하고, 그런점 때문에 내가 그에게 다가가기 어렵다. 09 나의 아버지와 나의 첫째 아이는 눈에 띌 정도로 닮았다. 10 나의 엄마는 나에게 언제나 현명한 충고를 해 줄 준비가 되어 있다. 11 너는 아이들에게 낯선 사람을 조심해야 한다고 가르쳐야 한다. 12 격렬한 토론 이후 양 당은 타협안에 동의했다. 13 벽돌로 만들어진 예스러운 유럽식 성이 커다란 나무에 둘러싸여 있다.

14 debilitate [dibílətèit]
v. 약하게 하다

to lack energy or strength

ⓝ debilitation 허약, 노쇠

syn weaken, drain, enfeeble ant strengthen, empower, gain

The long dry season which begins in July debilitates any creature that relies on water.

15 venerate [vénərèit]
v. 존경하다

to treat someone with respect

ⓐ venerable 존경할만한 ⓝ veneration 존경, 숭배

syn adore, cherish, laud, admire ant condemn, detest, loathe, hate

The elder stateswoman giving a speech at the plaza is venerated by many people.

16 abide [əbáid]
v. 머물다, 살다, 준수하다

to stay, to put up with

ⓝ abode 주소, 거주 ⓝ abidance 지속, 거주

syn live, stay, accept, bear ant leave, migrate, avoid, dodge, escape

Inuit peoples are certainly hearty folk, and they are able to abide even the most treacherous conditions.

The German Socialist Party refused to abide by the conditions of the Treaty of Versailles.

17 entail [entéil]
v. 수반하다, 부과하다

to impose as a necessary accompaniment

ⓝ entailment 세습재산

syn require, necessitate, involve, include ant exclude, prohibit

Learning how to scuba dive entails a number of steps that we have to know.

18 lament [ləmént]
v. 슬퍼하다, 한탄하다

to express sadness or grief

ⓐ lamentable 슬픈 ⓝ lamentation 슬픔, 애도

syn grieve, mourn ant revel, celebrate

Though Tim lamented the loss of his beloved pet, he didn't cry any more.

19 obstruct [əbstrʌ́kt]
v. 방해하다, 막다

to hinder or prevent

ⓝ obstruction 방해물 ⓐ obstructive 방해하는

syn block, hinder, impede ant free, disengage

The demonstrators were arrested for obstructing the police in carrying out their duties.

---

14 7월에 시작되는 긴 건기는 물을 먹고 사는 많은 동물들을 허약하게 한다. 15 광장에서 연설을 하고 있는 저 원로 여성 정치인은 많은 국민들에게 존경받는다. 16 이누이트 족은 강인한 사람들로 가장 혹독한 기후에서도 살아갈 수 있다. 독일 사회당은 베르사유 협약 조약을 준수하기를 거부했다. 17 스쿠버 다이빙을 배우는 데에는 우리가 알아야 할 많은 절차가 수반된다. 18 Tim 은 그의 소중한 애완동물을 잃어서 슬펐지만, 그는 더 이상 울지 않았다. 19 시위자들은 경찰의 공무집행 방해로 체포되었다.

20 hallucinate [həlúːsənèit]

v. 환각을 일으키다

to see things that aren't really there

n hallucination 환각, 환상

syn imagine, dream, fantasize, envision

Michelle began to hallucinate with severe dehydration.

---

21 ignite [ignáit]

v. 불 붙이다

to set something on fire

n ignition 점화, 발화

syn light ant extinguish

Lightning is a leading cause of forest fires because it ignites dry bushes.

---

22 pacify [pǽsəfài]

v. 진정시키다

to appease someone

a pacifistic 평화론적인, 평화주의자의 n pacifism 평화주의

syn placate, appease, calm, soothe ant aggravate

She managed to pacify the angry customer with a calm explanation.

---

23 radiate [réidièit]

v. 발산하다, 방출하다

to send out heat

n radiation 방사, 방사물

syn emit, exude ant absorb, envelope

The heat radiated by the mother bear had a familiar scent the cubs could recognize.

---

24 abdicate [ǽbdikèit]

v. 포기하다, 버리다

to abandon one's right

n abdication 사직, 권고

syn relinquish, abandon ant join, maintain, resist, keep

Mike decided to abdicate smoking cigarettes to save money and improve his health.

---

25 daunt [dɔːnt]

v. 위압하다

to discourage someone

a dauntless 불굴의, 꿈쩍도 하지않은

syn intimidate, overwhelm, deter, scare ant calm, hearten

James was quick to support his team that seemed daunted by the size of the mountain.

---

20 Michelle는 심각한 탈수현상으로 착각을 일으키기 시작했다. 21 번개는 건조한 관목에 즉시 불을 붙이면서 산불을 일으키는 주요 원인이다. 22 그녀는 차분하게 설명하면서 화가 난 고객을 가까스로 진정시켰다. 23 어미 곰에 의해서 발산되는 열에는 새끼곰들이 인지 할 수 있는 친숙한 냄새를 가지고 있다. 24 Mike는 돈을 절약하고 건강을 위해 금연하기로 결심했다. 25 James는 산의 규모에 기가 꺾인 것처럼 보인 그의 팀을 재빠르게 격려했다.

Exercise

Word Check 각 단어의 뜻으로 알맞은 것을 찾아 연결하시오.

01 entail   (a) to block or close with an obstacle

02 qualm   (b) a sudden feeling of uneasiness

03 hallucinate   (c) to have something as requirement

04 taboo   (d) a ban resulting from social custom or emotional aversion

05 obstruct   (e) to perceive what is not there

Syn & Ant Check 주어진 단어의 동의어, 반의어를 골라 쓰시오.

talkative	disaster	assist	old-fashioned	thoughtless
scale	live	noticeable	aggravate	absorb

06 magnitude = _____   11 sabotage ↔ _____

07 salient   = _____   12 taciturn ↔ _____

08 abide   = _____   13 pacify   ↔ _____

09 quaint   = _____   14 radiate   ↔ _____

10 calamity = _____   15 judicious ↔ _____

Sentence Practice 문장을 읽고 빈칸에 알맞은 단어를 고르시오.

16 An innate sense of caution warned him to be _____ of his new employees.

   ⓐ wary   ⓑ earnest   ⓒ taciturn   ⓓ salient

17 A large crowd had gathered to _____ the loss of the popular leader who had done so much to effect successful national development.

   ⓐ abide   ⓑ debilitate   ⓒ radiate   ⓓ lament

18 The hardest task before the parliament is to get the monarch to _____ the throne peacefully.

   ⓐ daunt   ⓑ abdicate   ⓒ venerate   ⓓ ignite

19 He remained _____ in the face of demands from his family and friends to mend his ways.

   ⓐ judicious   ⓑ vehement   ⓒ obdurate   ⓓ salient

20 The Board's proposals to amend the company policy on employee benefits met with _____ opposition.

   ⓐ vehement   ⓑ wary   ⓒ earnest   ⓓ quaint

Day 2

01 debris [dəbríː]
n. 파편

the remains of something broken up
[syn] garbage, remains, waste, rubble

We saw debris covering both sides of the roadway following the crash.

02 knack [næk]
n. 솜씨, 요령

special skill on the ability to do something
[a] knacky 솜씨가 좋은, 교묘한
[syn] flair, talent, ability, skill [ant] inability

His special knack for speaking to people was developed during his years spent leading troops in the World War II.

03 edifice [édəfis]
n. 대건축물, 조직

a large and impressive building
[syn] structure, building, construction

The Hanging Gardens of Babylon is a unique edifice considered one of the seven wonders of the world.

04 remnant [rémnənt]
n. 나머지

a leftover
[syn] remainder, residual

The rugby team made short work of the buffet. The only remnants were the odd vegetable and particularly awful cookies.

05 symbiosis [sìmbaióusis]
n. 공생관계

a relationship between two different things essential for mutual survival
[n] symbiont 공생자
[syn] commensalism

The word symbiosis means living together for the mutual benefit with each other.

06 haphazard [hǽphæzərd]
a. 우연의, 계획성 없는

not arranged according to a plan
[n] haphazardry 우연성
[syn] disorganized, random, jumbled, chaotic [ant] organized, ordered

If you work in a haphazard way, you can not achieve anything.

---

01 우리는 충돌사고 후 파편들이 도로 양쪽에 널려있는 것을 보았다. 02 그의 대중 연설에 대한 재능은 2차 대전시 군대를 통솔하는 동안 발전되었다. 03 Babylon의 공중정원은 독특한 건축물로서, 세계 7대 불가사의 중 하나이다. 04 럭비 팀은 뷔페 음식을 순식간에 다 먹어 치웠다. 남은 거라고는 이상한 야채와 유난히도 맛 없는 과자뿐이었다. 05 공생관계라는 말은 서로 공동 이익을 위해 함께 사는 것을 뜻한다. 06 당신이 일을 계획 없이 처리한다면 아무 것도 이룰 수 없을 것이다.

07 ludicrous [lúːdəkrəs]
a. 우스운, 바보 같은

completely ridiculous
[syn] absurd, bizarre, preposterous [ant] sensible, reasonable, logical

It was ludicrous for you to pay more than twice what was considered standard rate for the three-night stay.

08 sporadic [spəráedik]
a. 때때로 일어나는

occurring from time to time
[ad] sporadically 드물게, 산발적으로
[syn] occasional, infrequent [ant] often, continuous, recurrent

The view from the top of the mountain was obscured by fog and sporadic rain.

09 inimical [inímikəl]
a. 해로운, 불리한

tending to discourage
[syn] hostile, unfriendly, contrary [ant] helpful, friendly, supportive

The agriculture minister stressed that cotton imports were inimical to the farming industry.

10 tactful [táektfəl]
a. 재치 있는, 세련된

having or showing skill and sensitivity
[n] tact 재치 [a] tactless 재치 없는, 무뚝뚝한
[syn] diplomatic, discreet [ant] tactless, thoughtless

The tactful politician tried to avoid answering the sensitive question from a reporter.

11 nocturnal [nɑktə́ːrnl]
a. 야행성의, 밤의

active at night
[n] nocturne 야상곡 [ad] nocturnally 야간에, 매일밤
[syn] late, night [ant] daytime

Cats are nocturnal creatures, and they feel far more comfortable being active at night than in the daytime.

12 eccentric [ikséntrik]
a. 별난
n. 별난 사람

having habits or opinions which are different from what is usual
[n] eccentricity 남다름, 별남
[syn] strange, daft, crazy, odd [ant] stable, common, normal

The eccentric behavior of the male deer is related to the rutting season.

13 hamper [háempər]
v. 방해하다, 막다

to stop the progress or movement of a person
[syn] delay, impede, obstruct [ant] assist, help, catalyze

Rescuers were hampered by the high level of the river.

---

07 3일 체류하는데 기본 숙박료의 2배 이상을 지불한 것은 바보 같은 짓이었다. 08 산 정상으로부터의 경치가 안개와 산발적인 비로 인해 잘 보이지 않는다. 09 농림부 장관은 면화 수입은 농업에 해가 된다는 점을 강조했다. 10 그 재치 있는 정치가는 민감한 질문에 대답을 회피하려고 했다. 11 고양이는 야행성 동물이라 낮보다 밤에 활동하는 것을 훨씬 더 편안해 한다. 12 사슴의 이상한 행동은 발정기와 관련이 있다. 13 구조대원들은 강의 수위가 높아 방해를 받았다.

14 quarantine [kwɔ́:rəntìːn]
v. 격리하다
n. 격리, 차단

to isolate a person or an animal to prevent the spread of any infectious disease

syn isolate, confine, remove   ant integrate, join

Exotic animals entering the United States must be quarantined until they are proven to be free of infectious diseases.

The practice of quarantine has begun since the 14th century to protect coastal cities from plague epidemics.

---

15 coalesce [kòuəlés]
v. 하나가 되다

to come together

n coalescence 합병, 연합

syn blend, connect, join, combine   ant separate, split, divide

The area where three rivers coalesce is termed "the Golden Triangle".

---

16 ventilate [véntəlèit]
v. 환기하다

to allow fresh air to get in

n ventilation 환기, 통풍

syn circulate, freshen   ant close, stifle, smother

This machine factory is relatively clean and well lit, but not adequately ventilated.

---

17 endeavor [indévər]
v. 노력하다
n. 노력

to effort

syn strive, intend, venture, attempt   ant neglect, abandon

A person must endeavor to find the meaning of his/her life.

The ship's first endeavor of sailing around the cape ended in failure as high winds pushed the boat leeward.

---

18 endorse [indɔ́:rs]
v. 인정하다, 시인하다

to support or approve something publicly

n endorsement 배서, 보증

syn approve, recommend   ant disapprove, oppose, reject

Manufacturers often look to celebrities to endorse their products.

---

19 absolve [əvzálv]
v. 면제하다, 사면하다

to set free, or release from some obligation

n absolution 면제, 방면

syn free, discharge, excuse   ant blame, condemn, sentence

Absolved from his charge of robbery, James Dobson wanted immediately to return to his daily life.

---

14 미국으로 들여오는 외래 동물들은 전염병에 걸리지 않았다고 판명될 때까지 격리되어야 한다. 격리 관행은 전염병으로부터 해안 도시를 보호하기 위해 14세기부터 시작되었다. 15 세 개의 강이 모이는 지역을 'the Golden Triangle'이라고 한다. 16 이 기계 공장은 비교적 깨끗하고, 조명도 밝지만 통풍이 잘 안된다. 17 누구나 자신의 인생의 의미를 찾기 위해 노력해야 한다. 갑 주의를 항해하려는 그 배의 첫번째 시도는 사나운 바람이 배를 밀어 실패했다. 18 제조 회사들은 종종 그들의 상품을 인정 받기 위해 유명인들을 의지한다. 19 강도 혐의가 풀렸을 때, James Dobson은 즉시 일상생활로 돌아가고 싶었다.

20 barter [báːrtər]
v. 물물교환하다
n. 물물교환

to exchange something for other goods

[n] barterer 물물교환자

[syn] trade, exchange, swap

Finding his wallet in his pocket gone, Delman was forced to barter his watch for a place to sleep.

Primitive men of the Stone Age used a barter system instead of money.

21 endow [indáu]
v. 기부하다, 기증하다

to provide with a source of income

[n] endowment 기증, 기부

[syn] award, grant, donate, give [ant] deprive, divest

His grandparents endowed the hospital with a lot of money.

22 spawn [spɔːn]
v. 낳다
n. 알

to lay eggs

[n] spawning (물고기의) 산란

[syn] create, hatch, produce, parent [ant] destroy, ruin, raze

We can see fish spawns stuck to the stones in a stream.

When I was in the forest last Sunday, I saw some frogs spawn in the pond.

23 squander [skwándər]
v. 낭비하다, 마구 쓰다

to spend wastefully

[syn] misuse, lose, consume [ant] manage, save, use

When you prepare for an examination, it is important not to squander your time.

24 mourn [mɔːrn]
v. 슬퍼하다, 한탄하다

to feel sad for the loss of someone

[n] mourner 애도자 mourning 슬픔, 비탄 [a] mournful 슬픔에 잠긴

[syn] grieve, lament, agonize [ant] rejoice, exalt, celebrate

My mother has mourned for over 10 years for my father's death.

25 stagger [stǽgər]
v. 비틀거리다
n. 비틀거림

to move unsteadily

[a] staggering 비틀거리는

[syn] reel, sway, teeter [ant] steady, steadfast, stand

The boxer fell back into the ropes, staggering from a devastating blow from his opponent.

I saw the drunken man walk with a stagger last night.

---

20 그의 주머니에 있던 지갑이 사라진 것을 알게 되자 Delman은 잠잘 곳을 위해 어쩔 수 없이 시계를 줘야 했다. 구석기 시대 사람들은 화폐 대신 물물교환 제도를 이용했다. 21 그의 조부모는 병원에 많은 돈을 기부했다. 22 우리는 시냇물 속의 돌에 붙어 있는 물고기 알을 볼 수 있다 . 내가 지난 일요일 숲에 있었을 때 연못에서 개구리들이 산란하는 것을 보았다. 23 시험을 준비할 때 시간을 낭비하지 않는 것이 중요하다. 24 어머니는 아버지의 죽음에 10년 이상 슬픔에 잠겨 있다. 25 권투 선수는 상대편의 파괴적인 펀치에 비틀거리며 링 쪽으로 물러났다. 지난밤 나는 술 취한 남자가 비틀거리며 걸어가는 것을 보았다.

Exercise

Word Check 각 단어의 뜻으로 알맞은 것을 찾아 연결하시오.

01	endeavor	(a) living together of two dissimilar organisms
02	symbiosis	(b) to make an effort
03	nocturnal	(c) doing or coming at night
04	haphazard	(d) without planning or system
05	edifice	(e) a large size building

Syn & Ant Check 주어진 단어의 동의어, 반의어를 골라 쓰시오.

normal	remains	skill	isolate	sentence
rejoice	donate	join	disapprove	sensible

06	debris	= _____		11	eccentric ↔ _____
07	endow	= _____		12	endorse ↔ _____
08	coalesce	= _____		13	absolve ↔ _____
09	quarantine	= _____		14	mourn ↔ _____
10	knack	= _____		15	ludicrous ↔ _____

Sentence Practice 문장을 읽고 빈칸에 알맞은 단어를 고르시오.

16 He has a(n) _____ for anticipating staff needs and providing for them.

ⓐ debris ⓑ knack ⓒ symbiosis ⓓ edifice

17 The _____ of the plane crash are expected to be discovered amidst the dense foliage on the hillside.

ⓐ edifices ⓑ knacks ⓒ trade ⓓ remnants

18 You cannot expect to do well in this class with your _____ attendance and casual study attitude.

ⓐ sporadic ⓑ inimical ⓒ haphazard ⓓ eccentric

19 The village will be placed under _____ to prevent the malaria from spreading further.

ⓐ ventilation ⓑ quarantine ⓒ barter ⓓ symbiosis

20 He is realizing too late that he is _____ all his money on impractical business schemes.

ⓐ hampering ⓑ endorsing ⓒ spawning ⓓ squandering

01 symmetry [símətri]
n. 균형, 좌우대칭

exact similarity in shape
ⓐ symmetrical 균형이 잡힌, 대칭의 ⓥ symmetrize 균형을 잡다
syn balance, similarity, conformity ant imbalance, disorder

Deterrence was a military theory based on symmetry that was popularized during the Cold War.

02 parable [pǽrəbəl]
n. 우화, 비유담

a story in order to convey a moral or religious lesson
syn story, fable, tale, allegory ant history, fact, truth

Plato used the parable of the cave and the shadow to make it easier for the readers to understand his arguments.

03 frenzy [frénzi]
n. 흥분, 격분, 열광
v. 격분하게 하다

extreme agitation
ⓐ frenetic 열광적인, 미친
syn fury, agitation, craze ant calm, tranquil, serene

When the diplomat found his passport missing at the airport, he shouted in a frenzy.

The girls became frenzied when they saw a movie star walking down the street.

04 remorse [rimɔ́:rs]
n. 양심의 가책

a feeling of guilt or regret
ⓐ remorseful 후회의, 양심의 가책을 받은
syn guilt, sorrow, anguish, regret ant indifference, apathy

A judge or jury may look sympathetically on a person who expresses remorse for his actions.

05 plumage [plú:midʒ]
n. 깃털

a bird's feathers
syn feathers

I was told that a bird's plumage is often the key to attracting a mate.

06 placid [plǽsid]
a. 조용한, 고요한

very calm or peaceful
syn calm, tranquil, serene ant rough, choppy, unstill

It is easy to train my dog because it has a placid temperament.

---

01 전쟁 억제론은 냉전시대 동안 인기가 있었던 균형론에 근거한 군사 이론 이었다. 02 플라톤은 독자들이 그의 주장을 더 쉽게 이해하도록 동굴과 그림자 우화를 사용했다. 03 외교관은 공항에서 여권이 없어진 것을 알고 격분했다. 그 소녀들은 거리를 걷고 있는 영화배우를 보자 흥분했다. 04 판사나 배심원들은 자신의 행동에 대해 뉘우치는 사람을 동정적으로 바라볼지도 모른다. 05 나는 새 깃털이 짝을 유혹하는데 중요한 역할을 한다고 들었다. 06 내 개는 성격이 조용하고 온화해서 훈련시키기 쉽다.

07 mandatory [mǽndətɔ̀ːri]
a. 강제의, 필수의

not allowing any choice

[n] [v] mandate 명령, 명령하다

[syn] required, compulsory, forced [ant] optional

Shareholders who could not attend the mandatory meeting were asked to provide a legitimate excuse for their absence.

08 ambivalent [æmbívələnt]
a. 양면적인, 상반하는 감정을 가진

exhibiting opposing feeling

[n] ambivalence 양면의 가치

[syn] unresolved, uncertain, wavering [ant] settled, certain, resolved

After initially indicating he wanted to return to the graduate school, he now seems ambivalent.

09 charitable [tʃǽrətəbəl]
a. 자비로운, 관용적인

willing to give to others

[n] charity 자선, 자비

[syn] philanthropic, generous, humane, giving [ant] miserly, stingy, selfish

His most charitable gesture was that he donated all of his salary to provide hunger relief in West Africa.

10 exorbitant [igzɔ́ːrbətənt]
a. 터무니없는

too high

[n] exorbitance 엄청남, 과대

[syn] expensive, costly, pricey, unreasonable [ant] fair, modest, reasonable

The food price of the restaurant where I went with my friend yesterday was exorbitant.

11 susceptible [səséptəbl]
a. 영향 받기 쉬운

easily affected by something

[n] susceptibility 감수성 [a] susceptive 감수성이 강한, 민감한

[syn] liable, vulnerable, exposed [ant] protected, resistant, invulnerable

The young are most susceptible to an advertisement.

12 pliant [pláiənt]
a. 유연한, 유순한

easily influenced or bent

[a] pliable 유연한, 유순한 [n] pliancy 유연, 유순

[syn] flexible, pliable, adjustable [ant] inflexible, intractable, unbending

The pliant twig that the monkey was gripping broke, and the monkey fell down to the ground.

---

07 의무적으로 참석해야 할 회의에 참석하지 않는 주주들은 불참에 대한 합당한 이유를 제시해야 했다. 08 그는 처음에는 대학원에 가고싶다고 말했지만, 지금은 마음이 바뀐것 같다. 09 그의 가장 자비로운 행동은 서아프리카 기아 구제를 위해 그의 월급 전부를 자진해서 기부한 것이었다. 10 내가 어제 친구와 갔던 레스토랑의 음식값은 터무니없었다. 11 젊은이들은 광고에 쉽게 영향을 받는다. 12 원숭이가 잡고 있던 약한 나뭇가지가 부러지면서 원숭이가 땅으로 떨어졌다.

13 pious [páiəs]
a. 종교적인, 신앙심 깊은

very religious

ⓝ piety 경건, 신앙심

syn holy, priestly, religious, spiritual　ant unholy, secular

Pious figures are willing to sacrifice their own personal needs for the good of the many.

14 relentless [riléntlis]
a. 끊임없는, 가차없는

without stop

syn determined, stubborn, unstoppable　ant yielding, acquiescing

The rain was relentless, pounding incessantly on the tin roof of the old home.

15 renowned [rináund]
a. 유명한, 저명한

well known

ⓝ renown 명성

syn famous, well known, celebrated　ant unknown, anonymous

Few of his admirers were aware that the renowned writer was a frequent critic of the government.

16 mock [mɑk]
v. 조롱하다, 흉내내다

to mimic someone

ⓝ mockery 조롱, 놀림　ⓐ mocking 조롱하는

syn ridicule, deride, needle　ant respect

Her son was being disrespectful to her when he mocked her accent.

17 remunerate [rimjú:nərèit]
v. 보상하다, 보답하다

to pay someone for work

ⓝ remuneration 보수, 보상　ⓐ remunerative 보수가 있는, 수지 맞는

syn reimburse, compensate, pay

Someday you'll be remunerated for what you do to the poor.

18 ingest [indʒést]
v. 먹다, 섭취하다

to take in

ⓝ ingestion 섭취

syn swallow, eat, consume　ant eject, repel

The pill, once ingested will be digested in the stomach and absorbed into the blood stream.

19 relinquish [rilíŋkwiʃ]
v. 포기하다, 그만두다

to give up

syn abandon, vacate, withdraw　ant keep, retain, hold

Nearly out of money, he relinquished his property rights in return for a cash settlement.

---

13 신앙심이 깊은 사람은 많은 사람들의 행복을 위해 자신의 개인적인 욕구를 기꺼이 희생한다. 14 오래된 집의 양철 지붕을 두드리면서 비는 계속 내렸다. 15 그 유명한 작가가 자주 정부를 비판했다는 것을 아는 그의 팬들은 거의 없다. 16 그녀의 아들은 그녀의 억양을 흉내내며 무례하게 행동했다. 17 언젠가 가난한 사람을 위해 당신이 한 일에 대해 보상을 받을 것이다. 18 일단 삼킨 알약은 위에서 소화되어 혈관으로 흡수될 것이다. 19 돈이 거의 떨어져서 그는 합의금을 받고 그의 재산권을 포기했다.

20 saturate [sǽtʃərèit]

v. 흠뻑 적시다, 담그다

to be full of liquid

ⓐ saturated 속속들이 스며든

syn drench, soak, immerse, fill   ant dry

The 1989 Exxon Valdez oil spill saturated the coast of Alaska with crude oil.

---

21 loathe [louð]

v. 몹시 싫어하다

to detest intensely

ⓐ loathsome 싫은   ⓝ loathing 혐오, 질색

syn detest, hate, abhor, despise   ant love, like, adore

The mayor loathed spending time away from his speaking engagements.

---

22 effervesce [èfərvés]

v. 거품이 일다

to give off bubbles

ⓐ effervescent 거품이 이는

syn boil, bubble, foam   ant calm, still, flat

Beer should be poured directly into the center of the glass, which allows the liquid to effervesce.

---

23 enact [enǽkt]

v. 제정하다, 규정하다

to make into law

ⓝ enactment 법령, 법규

syn authorize, pass, institute, proclaim   ant abolish, repeal, veto

A special rule enacted by the court made it illegal to wear inappropriate clothing while in court.

---

24 ratify [rǽtəfài]

v. 승인하다, 비준하다

to give formal approval

ⓝ ratification 비준, 인가, 승인

syn pass, approve, accept   ant revoke, reject, disapprove

Both North Carolina and Rhode Island initially refused to ratify the U.S. Constitution.

---

25 indulge [indʌ́ldʒ]

v. 빠지다, 탐닉하다

to enjoy something excessively

ⓝ indulgence 관대, 탐닉   ⓐ indulgent 멋대로 하는, 관대한

syn pamper, spoil, satisfy   ant deny, withhold, abstain

She indulged herself in drugs, and as a result, she became an extremely spoiled woman.

---

20 1989년 Exxon Valdez 오일 유출로 Alaska 해안이 원유로 완전히 덮였다. 21 시장은 강연으로 시간을 보내는 것을 싫어했다. 22 맥주는 거품이 일도록 잔 중앙에 바로 따라야 한다. 23 법원에 의해 실행된 특별법칙으로 재판시 적절하지 않은 옷을 입는 것은 불법이 되었다. 24 North Carolina와 Rhode Island는 처음에 미국 헌법을 승인하지 않았다. 25 그녀는 약에 빠져 있었고 그 결과 완전히 망가진 여자가 되었다.

Exercise

Score / 20

Word Check 각 단어의 뜻으로 알맞은 것을 찾아 연결하시오.

01 plumage   (a) to pay a suitable equivalent in return for goods

02 susceptible   (b) to act or perform something

03 ambivalent   (c) a bird's feather, colorful clothes

04 enact   (d) uncertainty or fluctuation to two opposite feelings

05 remunerate   (e) capable of being affected by strong feelings

Syn & Ant Check 주어진 단어의 동의어, 반의어를 골라 쓰시오.

story	calm	adore	religious	respect
balance	stingy	abandon	unknown	reasonable

06 parable =   11 renowned ↔

07 pious =   12 mock ↔

08 symmetry =   13 loathe ↔

09 relinquish =   14 exorbitant ↔

10 placid =   15 charitable ↔

Sentence Practice 문장을 읽고 빈칸에 알맞은 단어를 고르시오.

16 Police brutality resulting in the death of the prisoner caused local citizenry to erupt in a violent _____ of rioting, burning and looting.

     ⓐ plumage   ⓑ remorse   ⓒ parable   ⓓ frenzy

17 His innate sense of competitiveness does not permit him to be _____ towards his business rivals.

     ⓐ charitable   ⓑ loathe   ⓒ placid   ⓓ ambivalent

18 I am grateful for the opportunity to listen to the most _____ classical pianist in the world.

     ⓐ renowned   ⓑ relentless   ⓒ pious   ⓓ exorbitant

19 The cabinet appears to be in no hurry to _____ this particular law because of strong opposition from various political parties.

     ⓐ indulge   ⓑ mock   ⓒ loathe   ⓓ ratify

20 Certain medical tests require patients to _____ admittedly distasteful substances like dyes and chemical elements like barium.

     ⓐ remunerate   ⓑ ingest   ⓒ effervesce   ⓓ relinquish

01 misconception
[mìskənsépʃən]
n. 오해

an incorrect understanding of something
v misconceive 잘못 생각하다, 오해하다
syn error, misunderstanding, mistake, fault

Many have the misconception that they would get AIDS merely by touching someone with the disease.

02 novice [návis]
n. 초보자, 풋내기

someone new in a field or activity
syn beginner, amateur, newcomer, rookie ant veteran, expert

Boris Yeltsin, a novice tennis player, played a number of amateur events to raise money for charity.

03 standpoint [stǽndpɔ̀int]
n. 관점, 시각

viewpoint
syn position, perspective, angle

The town elders' standpoint was clear - they would not sell their sacred land.

04 slander [slǽndər]
n. 비방
v. 비방하다

untrue spoken statement about someone
a slanderous 중상적인, 비방하는
syn disparage, belittlement ant praise, acclaim

The country is known for the most punitive laws regarding libel and slander.
He was accused of slandering the leader of the party.

05 pertinent [pə́ːrtənənt]
a. 적절한, 관련된

relevant to something
n pertinence 적절, 적당
syn relevant, appropriate, applicable ant irrelevant, inappropriate

Her comments were not pertinent to the debate over whether we should deploy our soldiers or not.

06 coarse [kɔːrs]
a. 조잡한, 거친

lacking refinement
v coarsen 거칠어지다, 조잡해지다
syn rough, unrefined, rugged, harsh ant smooth

In the past, pig's coarse hair was used extensively as hair brushes.

---

01 많은 사람들은 에이즈에 걸린 사람과 접촉만 해도 에이즈에 걸릴 거라는 오해를 하고 있다. 02 초보 테니스 선수인 Boris Yeltsin은 자선사업을 위한 돈을 모으기 위해 수많은 아마추어 경기를 가졌다. 03 마을 노인들의 입장은 분명했다. 그들은 그들의 신성한 땅을 팔지 않을 것이었다. 04 그 나라는 중상모략에 가장 무서운 처벌을 내리는 것으로 알려졌다. 그는 당 총재를 비방한 혐의로 고소되었다. 05 그녀의 의견은 우리가 군사를 파병 할 지에 대한 논쟁에 적절하지 못했다. 06 과거에는 돼지의 거친 털이 빗으로 광범위하게 사용되었다.

07 inanimate [inǽnəmit]
a. 생명이 없는, 활기가 없는

not living, lifeless

n inanimation 무기력

Jason appeared inanimate and tired before the lecture.

08 benevolent [bənévələnt]
a. 인정 많은, 너그러운

showing or involving kindness

n benevolence 자비심, 박애

syn generous, gracious   ant malevolent, selfish, unkind

Colleges expect their benevolent alumni associations to give them regular donations.

09 pervasive [pərvéisiv]
a. 널리 퍼져있는, 만연한

spreading everywhere

v pervade 널리 퍼지다, 보급하다   n pervasion 보급, 침투

syn extensive, omnipresent   ant limited, narrow, restrictive

The firefighters thought that the pervasive smoke was coming from the air ducts.

10 ornate [ɔːrnéit]
a. 화려한, 잘 꾸민

very adorned

n ornamentation 장식

syn showy, ostentatious, adorned   ant plain, unadorned, basic

Rather than wearing an ornate wedding dress, she chose a much simpler design.

11 imperious [impíəriəs]
a. 권위적인, 거만한

able to do authoritatively

syn overbearing, authoritative, tyrannical   ant meek, timid, submissive

The king's imperious style of rule was evidenced in his mandates to the people.

12 perpetual [pərpétʃuəl]
a. 끊임없는

enduring forever

v perpetuate 불멸하게 하다, 영속시키다

syn continual, permanent, constant   ant temporary, transitory

Her perpetual throat-clearing interfered with a science class.

13 severe [sivíər]
a. 엄한, 엄격한

very strict toward others

n severity 격렬, 혹독   ad severely 심하게, 엄하게

syn strict, intense

She got severe punishment for her cheating during the final exam.

---

07 Jason은 강의 전에 활기가 없고 피곤해 보였다. 08 대학들은 인정 많은 동창회들이 정기적으로 그들에게 기부금을 줄거라고 기대하고 있다. 09 소방관들은 자욱한 연기가 통풍구에서 나온다고 생각했다. 10 화려한 웨딩 드레스를 입기 보다는 그녀는 훨씬 더 심플한 디자인을 선택했다. 11 왕의 권위적인 통치 스타일은 백성들에게 지시한 명령에서 분명히 드러났다. 12 그녀의 끊임 없는 기침은 과학 수업에 방해가 되었다. 13 기말고사 시험에 저지른 부정행위로 그녀는 엄한 처벌을 받았다.

14 amorphous [əmɔ́ːrfəs]
a. 무정형의, 비결정질의

without clear shape or structure
[syn] formless, vague   [ant] defined, shaped, distinctive

In the dim light of the evening, the figure at the end of the driveway appeared amorphous.

15 reciprocal [risíprəkəl]
a. 호혜적인, 상호간의

doing something to each other
[v] reciprocate 보답하다, 답례하다
[syn] exchanged, matching, equal, corresponding   [ant] dissimilar, unequal

Joint custody is a reciprocal agreement that enables divorced parents to enjoy their children's time equally.

16 atrocious [ətróuʃəs]
a. 극악한, 지독한

extremely bad
[n] atrocity 잔악, 포악
[syn] offensive, foul, awful, repulsive   [ant] benevolent, good, virtuous

Upon entry, he found the source of the atrocious smell - a half eaten tuna sandwich that was well on its way to rotting.

17 ample [ǽmpl]
a. 충분한, 풍부한

more than enough
[v] amplify 확대하다, 확장하다
[syn] plenty, sufficient, enough, abundant   [ant] meager, scant, inadequate

The CEO was fired for failing to provide ample leadership for the company.

18 vile [vail]
a. 몹시 나쁜, 지독한

very unpleasant
[v] vilify 비방하다, 중상하다
[syn] offensive, horrid, foul, nasty   [ant] gentle, pure, nice

The Indians used a vile smelling remedy made of bitterroot and water for reducing infection.

19 lenient [líːniənt]
a. 자비로운

not severe, tolerant
[n] lenience 관용, 관대함
[syn] permissive, tolerant, compliant   [ant] firm, stern, strict

Some thought that Gandhi's teachings on non-violent protest were too lenient to be productive.

---

14 희미한 저녁 불빛에서 도로 끝에 있는 사람의 모습이 잘 보이지 않았다. 15 공동 보호권은 이혼한 부모들이 동일하게 그들의 자녀와 시간을 보낼 수 있도록 한 상호 협약이다. 16 입구에서 그는 지독한 냄새의 원인을 발견했다. 그것은 반만 먹다 남은 썩어가고 있는 참치 샌드위치였다. 17 그 사장은 회사를 위해 충분한 지도력을 발휘하지 못해 해고되었다. 18 인디언은 감염을 예방하는 데 다년초와 물로 만든 역겨운 냄새가 나는 치료 약을 사용했다. 19 어떤 사람들은 비폭력 투쟁에 대한 간디의 가르침은 너무 자비로운 것이라 실질적이지 않다고 생각했다.

20 ominous [ámənəs]
a. 불길한

looking threatening or ill-fortune

n omen 전조, 징조

syn foreboding, worrisome, threatening, gloomy   ant promising, hopeful

The dream he had last night was so ominous that he decided to stay home today.

21 replenish [ripléniʃ]
v. 보충하다

to restock something

syn refill, refresh, stock, fill   ant empty, drain, exhaust

The dam needed a day or two of heavy rain to replenish the water supply.

22 stammer [stǽmər]
v. 더듬거리다

to speak haltingly

a stammering 말을 더듬는

syn hesitate, stumble, falter, stutter

Raymond is a bright child, but he stammers when he speaks.

23 rehabilitate [rìːhəbílətèit]
v. 원상복구하다, 사회 복귀시키다

to restore to good condition

n rehabilitation 사회복귀, 갱생

syn renovate, improve, refurbish, mend   ant destroy, hurt

It is an organization for rehabilitating rivers that are contaminated by the chemical factory.

24 ascend [əsénd]
v. 올라가다, 상승하다

to move up

a ascendant 상승하는, 떠오르는   n ascendancy 우세, 패권

syn rise, soar   ant descend, drop, fall

They suddenly started to ascend the mountain more quickly.

25 elicit [ilísit]
v. 이끌어내다, 유도하다

to cause something to happen

syn evoke, extract   ant hide, suppress, cover

In an effort to avoid groupthink, he tried to elicit opinions from each of his advisors.

---

20 어젯밤에 꾼 꿈이 매우 불길해서 그는 오늘 집에 머물기로 했다. 21 물 공급량을 보충하기 위해 하루나 이틀 정도의 강우가 내려야 한다. 22 Raymond는 똑똑한 아이지만 말을 할 때 더듬거린다. 23 이 단체는 화학공장에 의해 오염된 강을 살리기 위한 조직이다. 24 그들은 갑자기 산을 빨리 올라가기 시작했다. 25 집단 순응사고를 피하기 위해 그는 각 고문들로부터 의견을 이끌어 내도록 노력했다.

Exercise

Word Check 각 단어의 뜻으로 알맞은 것을 찾아 연결하시오.

01 standpoint   (a) to restore to a condition of good health, or life

02 stammer   (b) a point of view

03 lenient   (c) to speak something in a faltering or hesitant way

04 rehabilitate   (d) mild and tolerant in punishing

05 coarse   (e) rough or lumpy

Syn & Ant Check 주어진 단어의 동의어, 반의어를 골라 쓰시오.

| misunderstanding | plain | expert | appropriate | permanent |
| sufficient | hopeful | formless | nice | malevolent |

06 perpetual = _____

07 ample = _____

08 pertinent = _____

09 amorphous = _____

10 misconception = _____

11 vile ↔ _____

12 novice ↔ _____

13 ornate ↔ _____

14 benevolent ↔ _____

15 ominous ↔ _____

Sentence Practice 문장을 읽고 빈칸에 알맞은 단어를 고르시오.

16 Newspapers are constantly facing charges of _____ for allegedly publishing false reports.

ⓐ novices   ⓑ slander   ⓒ standpoints   ⓓ misconception

17 He shows a marked preference for the company of _____ objects like computer hardware rather than living things.

ⓐ benevolent   ⓑ pertinent   ⓒ inanimate   ⓓ amorphous

18 This campaign is being launched to counter the _____ influence of alcohol in the neighborhood.

ⓐ pervasive   ⓑ ornate   ⓒ serene   ⓓ ominous

19 Truly _____ arms reductions between our two nations are the key to ensuring peaceful relations over the long term.

ⓐ reciprocal   ⓑ atrocious   ⓒ vile   ⓓ imperious

20 Loud cheers were heard when the plane _____ into the skies on its maiden flight.

ⓐ replenished   ⓑ stammered   ⓒ rehabilitated   ⓓ ascended

01 buffer [bʌ́fər]
n. 완충지
v. 완화시키다

a place helping to lessen the shock of something
[syn] cushion, defense, shield, screen

This region is a buffer zone between the two countries which have been in conflict for decades.

I couldn't do anything to buffer his shock of the news about his son's death.

02 hypocrite [hípəkrìt]
n. 위선자

a person who feigns oneself to be what he is not
[n] hypocrisy 위선
[syn] imposter, actor, pretender, fraud

A hypocrite pretends to possess value he doesn't really have.

03 metaphor [métəfɔ̀:r]
n. 은유, 비유

comparing something with another object that has similar characteristics.
[a] metaphoric 은유의
[syn] allegory, symbol, image, comparison

The translator is likely to be unable to perceive metaphor and irony.

04 anarchist [ǽnərkist]
n. 무정부주의자

someone opposing law, order, and government
[n] anarchy 무정부 상태 anarchism 무정부주의
[syn] nihilist, terrorist [ant] loyalist

The Red Army Faction, an anarchist group aimed at destabilizing the German government.

05 sly [slai]
a. 교활한, 은밀한

cunning or tricky
[n] slyness 교활함 [ad] slyly 교활하게
[syn] clever, devious, tricky, crafty [ant] straightforward, clear

It is not easy to catch a sly fox alive with this simple trap.

06 articulate [á:rtíkjələt]
a. 분명한, 명료한

able to express thoughts well
[n] articulation 또렷한 발음 [a] articulated 똑똑히 발음되는
[syn] coherent, lucid [ant] mumbled, inarticulate

Though just 16, he was quite articulate in his plans for the future.

---

01 이 지역은 수십년간 충돌해온 두 나라 사이의 완충지대이다. 그의 아들 사망 소식에 그가 받을 충격을 더 이상 완화시킬 수 없었다. 02 위선자는 자신이 실제로는 가지고 있지 않은 가치 있는 것을 가지고 있는 체 한다. 03 그 번역가는 은유나 반어법을 인식하지 못하는 것 같다. 04 무정부주의자 그룹인 독일적군파는 독일정부를 동요 시키는 것을 목표로 했다. 05 이런 단순한 덫으로 교활한 여우를 생포한다는 것은 쉽지 않다. 06 16살이지만 그는 자신의 미래에 대한 확실한 계획이 있다.

07 vivacious [vivéiʃəs]
a. 활발한, 생기 있는

attractively active
ⓝ vivacity 생기, 활달
syn lively, animated, vibrant, upbeat   ant stiff, slow

The vivacious and colorful streets of New York are a tourist attraction in themselves.

08 eminent [émənənt]
a. 유명한, 뛰어난

high in ranking
ⓝ eminence 저명, 명성
syn renowned, prominent   ant unremarkable, undistinguished

The world's most eminent mountains, Mt. Everest and K-2, are found in this region.

09 secluded [siklú:did]
a. 격리된

remote and private
ⓥ seclude 차단하다, 격리하다 ⓝ seclusion 격리
syn hidden, remote, isolated, private   ant public, open, accessible

Islamic law does not allow unmarried men and women to be secluded together.

10 tedious [tí:diəs]
a. 지루한, 따분한

very boring
ⓝ tedium 권태, 지겨움
syn repetitive, dull, boring   ant exciting, interesting, entertaining

All of the students had to sit through the headmaster's tedious speech.

11 aesthetic [esθétik]
a. 미의, 미학적인
n. 미학

having a sense of the beautiful
ⓝ aesthete 유미주의자, 심미가   aesthetics 미학
syn beautiful, artistic, gorgeous   ant ugly, unattractive, displeasing

I think that the new building fits in with the aesthetic scene of the skyscrapers in New York.

Much of the discussion about beauty since the Eighteenth century had deployed a notion of the 'aesthetic'.

12 lethal [lí:θəl]
a. 치명적인, 죽음의

causing death
ⓝ lethality 치명적임
syn deadly, fatal, harmful, noxious   ant safe, harmless

Lethal injection is the most common method for implementing a death sentence in the U.S.

---

07 뉴욕의 활기 넘치고 다채로운 거리는 그 자체로 관광 명소이다. 08 세계에서 가장 유명한 산인 에베레스트산과 K-2는 이 지역에 있다. 09 이슬람 법은 미혼인 남자와 여자가 함께 있지 못하도록 한다. 10 모든 학생들은 앉아서 교장 선생님의 지루한 연설을 들어야 했다. 11 나는 저 새로운 건물이 뉴욕 마천루의 미학과 잘 어울린다고 생각한다. 18세기 이후 미에 대한 대부분의 이야기가 "미학"에 대한 관념을 전개 시켰다. 12 치사 주사는 미국에서 사형 선고를 행하는 가장 흔한 방법이다.

13 **elongate** [ilɔ́ːŋgeit]
v. 늘이다, 늘어나다

to lengthen or stretch
[n] elongation 연장, 늘어남
[syn] lengthen, prolong, extend   [ant] shrink, shorten, abbreviate
Rather than elongating his stay with the firm, he was actively pursuing other opportunities.

14 **beleaguer** [bilíːgər]
v. 포위하다, 괴롭히다

to surround with an army
[syn] encompass, bother, harass
The castle beleaguered by the enemy will run out of food soon.

15 **flinch** [flintʃ]
v. 움츠리다, 움찔하다

to withdraw in response to fear or pain
[syn] duck, wince, recoil, shrink
He flinched when the needle pricked his arm.

16 **implement** [ímpləmənt]
v. 이행하다, 실행하다
n. 도구, 기구

to carry out a plan
[n] implementation 이행, 실행
[syn] apply, perform, execute
The Marshall Plan was implemented in part to help European countries rebuild after World War II.
Man's earliest implements were stones and bones.

17 **denounce** [dináuns]
v. 비난하다, 비방하다

to condemn publicly
[n] denunciation 비난
[syn] castigate, vilify, condemn   [ant] compliment, praise, commend
In his sermon, he denounced the current state of society.

18 **smother** [smʌ́ðər]
v. 불을 끄다, 숨 막히게 하다

to extinguish a fire, to kill from lack of air
[a] smothery 질식시키는, 숨막히는
[syn] extinguish, suffocate, muffle, suppress   [ant] stoke, fan
Students were reminded that rolling on the ground helps smother a fire on their clothes.

19 **smuggle** [smʌ́gəl]
v. 밀수출하다

to ship illegally
[n] smuggler 밀수입자
[syn] bootleg
Contraband is often smuggled by being hidden in something else.

---

13 법률회사에서 계속 근무하기 보다 그는 다른 기회를 찾고 있었다. 14 적에 의해 포위된 그 성은 곧 식량이 떨어질 것이다. 15 바늘이 그의 팔을 찔렀을 때 그는 움찔했다. 16 Marshall Plan은 2차 세계 대전 이후에 유럽 나라들의 재건을 돕는 일환으로 실행되었다. 인간의 최초의 도구는 돌과 뼈였다. 17 그의 강론에서 그는 사회의 현상태에 비난했다. 18 학생들은 바닥에 구르는 것이 옷에 붙은 불을 끄는데 도움이 된다는 것이 생각났다. 19 밀수품은 종종 다른 데 숨겨져서 밀수입된다.

20 berate [biréit]

v. 호되게 꾸짖다

to scold someone severely

[syn] scold, criticize, chide [ant] praise, laud, compliment

My mother berated me for entering a stranger's car.

---

21 implore [implɔ́:r]

v. 간청하다, 애원하다

to plead for something to occur

[a] imploring 애원하는

[syn] beg, appeal, plead, urge

Party representatives have long implored their constituents to support their agenda.

---

22 fortify [fɔ́:rtəfài]

v. 강화하다

to make strong

[n] fortitude 굳건함, 강건함 fortification 방어시설

[syn] secure, brace, gird, reinforce [ant] weaken, wane

Most breakfast cereals are fortified with vitamins and minerals.

---

23 capitulate [kəpítʃəlèit]

v. 굴복하다, 항복하다

to give in formally

[n] capitulation 무조건 항복

[syn] submit, surrender [ant] defend, fight

Samurai warriors were trained to end their own lives before they would capitulate to an opponent.

---

24 indict [indáit]

v. 기소하다, 비난하다

to accuse someone of a crime

[n] indictment 기소, 고발

[syn] accuse, prosecute, charge, arraign [ant] acquit

Though indicted on five counts of robbery, he was formally charged with only one.

---

25 condescend [kàndisénd]

v. 겸손하게 행동하다

to behave as one is inferior

[n] condescension 겸손, 겸양

[syn] humiliate [ant] respect, revere, value

We have to condescend to the poor when we serve them.

---

20 엄마는 내가 낯선 사람 차에 올라 탔다고 엄청 야단치셨다. 21 당 대표는 그들의 결정 사항을 지지해 달라고 선거 구민들에게 호소했다. 22 대부분의 아침 시리얼에는 비타민과 미네랄이 강화되어있다. 23 사무라이 전사들은 그들이 적에게 항복하기 전에 목숨을 끊으라고 훈련 받았다. 24 그는 강도죄로 5번이나 고소되었지만 공식적으로는 한번만 처벌을 받았다. 25 우리가 가난한 자들을 위해 봉사를 할 때 그들에게 겸손하게 행동해야 한다.

Exercise

Word Check 각 단어의 뜻으로 알맞은 것을 찾아 연결하시오.

01 sly   (a) keeping oneself away from other people

02 buffer   (b) to accuse someone of

03 secluded   (c) secretively cunning or dishonest

04 indict   (d) an apparatus designed to absorb shock

05 flinch   (e) to make a sudden movement in pain

Syn & Ant Check 주어진 단어의 동의어, 반의어를 골라 쓰시오.

exciting	mumbled	appeal	pretender	shrink
extinguish	fatal	weaken	scold	compliment

06 implore   =   11 fortify   ↔

07 berate   =   12 articulate ↔

08 smother   =   13 denounce   ↔

09 hypocrite =   14 elongate   ↔

10 lethal   =   15 tedious   ↔

Sentence Practice 문장을 읽고 빈칸에 알맞은 단어를 고르시오.

16 The _____ World Times photo journalist Paula Thompson has traveled to the most remote areas of the world.

ⓐ eminent   ⓑ secluded   ⓒ lethal   ⓓ aesthetic

17 Most people are captivated by her _____ nature as well as her charming innocence.

ⓐ buffer   ⓑ articulate   ⓒ vivacious   ⓓ flinch

18 He was quick to _____ the president for his regressive policies that would negatively impact low income earners.

ⓐ implement   ⓑ flinch   ⓒ smuggle   ⓓ denounce

19 Captain Lim angrily _____ the cadets for their indiscipline during joint combat drills.

ⓐ smothered   ⓑ indicted   ⓒ elongated   ⓓ berated

20 Sometimes it requires more courage to _____ than to carry on a fight.

ⓐ capitulate   ⓑ condescend   ⓒ implore   ⓓ beleaguer

suffix

명사 suffix Ⅰ

성질, 상태: -ment, -tion, -sion, -ance, -ence, -ness
사람, 집단: -ade -(e)or, -cant, -ce, -cy, -ty, -gy, -ant, -ent
지소사(작은): -ee, -ette, -kin, -let, -ling
상태, 지위 : -ship, -hood, -osis

동사 → 명사

-ee : interview ⇨ interviewee, employ ⇨ employee
You have to be punctual and suited when you are an interviewee.
면접을 볼 때에는 항상 시간을 지키고 정장을 입어야 한다.

-ive : detect ⇨ detective, relate ⇨ relative
Detective stories are stories whose main theme is the solving of a crime.
탐정소설은 범죄의 실마리를 풀어가는 이야기들이다.

-ant : assist ⇨ assistant, attend ⇨ attendant
The initial assignment of assistant professor is to help professors or collect research papers.
보조교수의 주 업무는 교수를 돕거나 연구 자료를 수거하는 것입니다.

-ion, -sion, -tion : (상태) object ⇨ objection, educate ⇨ education,
permit ⇨ permission
Most of students have no objection to the new school policy on the dress code.
학생들 대부분은 학교의 새로운 복장규정에 대해 불만이 없었다.

-ment : (상태) achieve ⇨ achievement, excite ⇨ excitement
The sentence 'If you dream it, you can do it.' is carved on the Ladder of Achievement in Orlando.
미국 올랜도 성취의 다리 위에는 '꿈꾸면 이룰 수 있다'라는 문장이 새겨져 있다.

형용사 → 명사

-ness : fearful ⇨ fearfulness, friendly ⇨ friendliness
Patients who suffer from thyroid deficiency have symptoms of fearfulness or phobias.
갑상선 결핍으로 고생하는 환자들은 두려움과 기피증의 증상을 보인다.

-ance, ancy : absent ⇨ absence, important ⇨ importance
Absence without leave is one of the major infractions of the school regulations.
무단결석이 학교 규칙 중 가장 중요한 위반 중 하나이다.

Review test Day 1 ~ Day 5

Score / 25

A 영어 풀이에 알맞은 단어를 보기에서 찾아 쓰시오.

salient	saturate	benevolent	endow	vivacious

01 to fill or unite with a large amount of something _____

02 to provide a source of income for charity _____

03 an outstanding part or section _____

04 desiring to help others _____

05 attractively lively and animated _____

B 문장을 읽고 문맥에 적절한 단어를 고르시오.

06 The compensation amount failed to (pacify/ratify) the families of the accident victims.

07 A final effort will be made this evening to look for survivors under the earthquake (debris/taboo).

08 The mirror had (earnest/ornate) carvings on its ivory frame and gems in its handle.

09 The (anarchist/edifice) was popular to people because he represented both lawlessness and freedom.

C 표시된 부분과 뜻이 가장 가까운 것을 고르시오.

10 Korean culture venerates traditional customs and knowledge passed on from one generation to another.

ⓐ abdicate   ⓑ admire   ⓒ endow   ⓓ ingest

11 Most tourists find it pleasurable to go boating on the placid waters of Lake Ramona.

ⓐ vehement   ⓑ quaint   ⓒ tranquil   ⓓ tactful

12 It will be entertaining to watch dignified citizens parade in ludicrous costumes at the fancy dress ball.

ⓐ absurd   ⓑ judicious   ⓒ imperious   ⓓ tedious

13 Our army has worked all night to fortify the post with heavy machine gun emplacements and antitank cannons.

ⓐ hamper   ⓑ obstruct   ⓒ reinforce   ⓓ debilitate

D 표시된 부분의 반대말로 가장 알맞은 것을 고르시오.

14 Lieutenant Wells stood quietly to mourn his departed friend while the other soldiers continued their victory celebrations.

ⓐ entail ⓑ hallucinate ⓒ barter ⓓ rejoice

15 The fire was caused by a small spark which ignited the pure oxygen aboard the space capsule.

ⓐ extinguished ⓑ stammered ⓒ implored ⓓ flinched

16 Sales novices like Jason have little experience but are nevertheless able to handle even fumingly irate customers.

ⓐ hypocrites ⓑ anarchist ⓒ veteran ⓓ buffer

17 I loathe the idea of sharing my dormitory quarters with students who are loud and brash.

ⓐ daunt ⓑ adore ⓒ coalesce ⓓ smother

E 주어진 단어를 알맞은 형태로 바꿔 빈칸에 쓰시오.

18 Everyone at the party seemed annoyed by the _____ behavior of the child. (atrocity)

19 The window right here would _____ this stuffy room by allowing in summer breezes. (ventilation)

20 The families of the hostages tearfully entreated the hijackers for mercy with _____ eyes. (implore)

21 Our neighbor's family has _____ their keeping of specific lunar New Year's tradition. (perpetuate)

F 빈 칸에 알맞은 단어를 보기에서 찾아 쓰시오. (필요한 경우 형태를 바꾸시오.)

ingest	quaint	ominous	smother	indulge	tactful	flinch	smuggle

22 Customs and Border Patrol are both responsible for interdicting criminals attempting to _____ drugs into the United States.

23 The company capitalized on his ability to be _____ by sending him to complete business negotiations in Berlin.

24 It is always a(n) _____ sign when an enemy as fearsome as the one at our borders appears to be unusually accommodating.

25 His desire is to _____ in his favorite sporting activities when he recovers.

Accumulative test Day 1 ~ Day 5

A	B	C	D
120~101	100~81	80~61	60 이하

영어를 우리말로 옮기시오.

01 venerate _____

02 perpetual _____

03 debris _____

04 effervesce _____

05 stagger _____

06 vivacious _____

07 susceptible _____

08 benevolent _____

09 earnest _____

10 loathe _____

11 secluded _____

12 charitable _____

13 quarantine _____

14 debilitate _____

15 smother _____

16 vehement _____

17 pervasive _____

18 relinquish _____

19 lenient _____

20 inimical _____

21 berate _____

22 pliant _____

23 implore _____

24 abdicate _____

25 fortify _____

26 ample _____

27 elongate _____

28 endow _____

29 renowned _____

30 endorse _____

31 ventilate _____

32 obstruct _____

33 ascend _____

34 salient _____

35 frenzy _____

36 remnant _____

37 reciprocal _____

38 sabotage _____

39 pertinent _____

40 eminent _____

41 saturate _____

42 denounce _____

43 judicious _____

44 atrocious _____

45 placid _____

46 sporadic _____

47 rehabilitate _____

48 articulate _____

49 lament _____

50 remunerate _____

51 condescend _____

52 absolve _____

53 vile _____

54 tedious _____

55 pacify _____

56 serene _____

57 endeavor _____

58 daunt _____

59 relentless _____

60 mourn _____

우리말을 영어로 옮기시오.

61 솜씨, 요령 _____
62 재치 있는 _____
63 좌우 대칭, 균형 _____
64 오해 _____
65 생명(활기)없는 _____
66 치명적인 _____
67 발산(방출)하다 _____
68 이끌어내다 _____
69 기소(비난)하다 _____
70 완충지 _____
71 낳다, 알 _____
72 양심의 가책 _____
73 비방하다, 비방 _____
74 은유, 비유 _____
75 완고한, 고집 센 _____
76 화려한, 잘 꾸민 _____
77 우스운 _____
78 수반(부과)하다 _____
79 관점, 시각 _____
80 탐닉하다 _____
81 무정형의 _____
82 보충하다 _____
83 불길한 _____
84 환각을 일으키다 _____
85 양면적인 _____
86 이행(실행)하다 _____
87 움츠리다 _____
88 굴복(항복)하다 _____
89 밀수입하다 _____
90 하나가 되다 _____

91 야행성의 _____
92 우화, 비유담 _____
93 조롱하다 _____
94 대건축물 _____
95 금기, 꺼림 _____
96 승인(비준)하다 _____
97 낭비하다 _____
98 위선자 _____
99 깃털 _____
100 중대함, 크기 _____
101 공생관계 _____
102 포위하다 _____
103 재난, 불행 _____
104 말 없는 _____
105 우연의 _____
106 머물다, 살다 _____
107 물물교환하다 _____
108 초보자, 풋내기 _____
109 더듬거리다 _____
110 제정(규정)하다 _____
111 조심스러운 _____
112 강제의, 필수의 _____
113 조잡한, 거친 _____
114 예스러운 _____
115 터무니 없는 _____
116 불 붙이다 _____
117 미학적인 _____
118 교활한, 은밀한 _____
119 별난 _____
120 먹다, 섭취하다 _____

Part 2

01 configuration
[kənfìgjəréiʃən]
n. 배치, 배열

the way something is laid out

v configure 형성하다, 배열하다

syn arrangement, formation, framework

The wagons assembled in a defensive configuration to stave off the anticipated attack.

02 congestion [kəndʒéstʃən]
n. 혼잡, 정체

a jam with vehicles or people

v congest 혼잡하다, 정체 시키다

syn blockage, crowding, profusion, jam ant emptiness

A traffic congestion was particularly bad on Friday evenings.

03 condolence [kəndóuləns]
n. 애도

sympathy for another's grief

v condole 위로하다, 문상하다 a condolent 위로하는

syn sympathy, consolation, solace ant congratulation, gladness

He decided to meet him later to offer his condolences in person.

04 sovereign [sávərin]
n. 통치자

a country's ruler in a monarchy

syn chief, emperor, king, monarch

Elizabeth I, Queen of England from 1558-1603, was one of the most popular sovereigns in English history.

05 candor [kǽndər]
n. 솔직함, 정직

being honest in attitude and speech

a candid 솔직한, 숨김없는

syn honesty, frankness ant deception, indirectness, dishonesty

General Scott was admired for his candor in speaking with his troops.

06 sober [sóubər]
a. 술 취하지 않은, 냉정한
v. 술이 깨다

not having alcohol

n sobriety 술 취하지 않음, 맑은 정신

syn abstinent, steady ant drunk

The police encourage people to drive sober through the holiday season.

He took some medicine which could help him sober up.

---

01 마차들이 예상되는 공격을 막기 위해 방어태세로 모였다. 02 교통체증은 금요일 저녁에 특히 심하다. 03 그는 개인적으로 애도하기 위해 나중에 그를 만나기로 했다. 04 1558년부터 1603년까지 영국의 여왕이었던 엘리자베스 1세는 영국 역사상 가장 인기 있는 통치자 중 한 사람이었다. 05 Scott 장군은 그의 부하들과 솔직한 대화로 존경을 받았다. 06 경찰은 휴가시즌 동안 음주운전을 하지 말 것을 사람들에게 당부하고 있다. 그는 술깨는 데 도움이 되는 약을 먹었다.

07 **incessant** [insésənt]
a. 끊임없는

never-ending
ad incessantly 끊임없이
syn relentless, perpetual, eternal ant occasional, intermittent
A nearby baby's incessant crying made it difficult to talk with him.

08 **meticulous** [mətíkjələs]
a. 세심한, 신중한

doing carefully
ad meticulously 꼼꼼하게
syn detailed, accurate, thorough, precise ant sloppy, careless
Anthropologists must be meticulous when they are at a dig site.

09 **indignant** [indígnənt]
a. 화난, 분개한

angry with something
n indignity 모욕, 경멸 indignation 분개, 분노
syn annoyed, livid, displeased ant content, happy, calm
Jaguars will become indignant if their meal is interrupted, and absolutely livid if it is stolen.

10 **indigenous** [indídʒənəs]
a. 토착의, 원산의

growing in a particular area
syn native, local, domestic, aboriginal ant foreign, migrant
Aborigines are indigenous to Australia and make up just about 2% of the island's population.

11 **translucent** [trænsljú:sənt]
a. (반)투명한

allowing light to pass through
a translucid 반투명의
syn transparent, clear ant blocked, cloudy, opaque
We can see the beautiful scenery of the mountain through the translucent windows.

12 **treacherous** [trétʃərəs]
a. 위험한, 믿을 수 없는

full of peril
n treachery 배반
syn perilous, risky, difficult, unsafe ant harmless, easy, safe
However treacherous our adventures are, we'll reach the destination.

13 **palpable** [pǽlpəbəl]
a. 명백한

easily seen, obvious
n palpability 명백함
syn clear, noticeable, evident, glaring ant hidden, veiled, ambiguous
Certain varieties of snakes have vestigial legs under their scales, barely palpable by the human eyes.

07 가까이서 아기가 계속 울어서 그와 대화를 할 수가 없었다. 08 고고학자들은 발굴 지점에 있을 때는 신중해야 한다. 09 재규어들은 먹이를 먹는 데 방해를 받으면 짜증 내며, 먹이를 빼앗기면 매우 격분을 한다. 10 애보리지니는 호주 원주민으로 호주 인구의 2%정도 차지한다. 11 우리는 산의 아름다운 경치를 투명한 창문을 통해 볼 수 있다. 12 우리의 모험이 위험할지라도 우리는 목적지에 도착 할 것이다. 13 어떤 뱀은 육안으로는 거의 보이지 않지만 비늘 아래에 다리가 있었다는 흔적을 가지고 있다.

14 wholesome [hóulsəm]
a. 건강에 좋은, 유익한

good for health

syn healthy, decent, sanitary ant dirty, soiled, indecent

The wholesome food is rich in fiber, protein, and vitamins, and bereft of excessive fats and sugars.

15 somber [sámbər]
a. 침울한, 흐린

sad or gloomy

syn sad, bleak, depressing, dark ant cheerful, happy, bright

Adonais was a somber-toned poem written by Percy Shelley about John Keats, a fellow poet.

16 malicious [məlíʃəs]
a. 악의 있는

intended to harm people or their reputation

n malice 악의, 원한

syn wicked, hateful, mean, nasty ant nice, gentle, kind

There were a number of malicious rumors that emerged after the death of Marilyn Monroe.

17 congruent [káŋgruənt]
a. 일치하는, 조화된

fit together in size and shape

n congruity 조화, 일치

syn compatible, conforming, harmonious ant incongruent, disparate

The two edges of the picture frame had warped over time and were no longer congruent.

18 solicitous [səlísətəs]
a. 걱정하는, 염려하는

worrying about something or someone

n solicitude 걱정, 근심

syn worried, anxious, concerned, troubled ant assured, relaxed, calm

His family was always solicitous toward his grandfather who suffered from colon cancer.

19 sanction [sǽŋkʃən]
v. 허가하다
n. 제재

to approve formally

syn authorize, approve, allow, grant ant prohibit, ban, refuse

The parade scheduled to take place in March was sanctioned by the government.

The United States is working on the issue of sanctions against Iraq.

---

14 건강에 좋은 음식은 섬유소, 단백질, 비타민이 풍부하지만 지방과 당분이 과도하게 들어있지 않은 음식이다. 15 'Adonais'는 동료 시인인 John Keats에 대해 Percy Shelley가 쓴 슬픈 어조의 시이다. 16 Marilyn Monroe가 사망한 이후 많은 음해성 루머가 나타났다. 17 액자 틀의 두 모서리가 시간이 흐르면서 뒤틀려서 더 이상 맞지 않는다. 18 그의 가족은 직장암으로 고생하는 할아버지 건강을 항상 걱정했다. 19 정부는 3월에 열릴 퍼레이드를 허가했다. 미국은 이라크에 대한 제재 문제에 관여하고 있다.

20 congregate [kɑ́ŋgrigèit]
v. 모이다, 군집하다

to gather together
[n] congregation 모임, 집회 [a] congregative 집합적인
[syn] gather, assemble, muster, mass [ant] disperse, separate, scatter

A large crowd was congregating outside the hotel because they had heard that a movie star was about to arrive.

---

21 seep [si:p]
v. 새다, 누출되다

to leak very slowly through small openings
[n] seepage 누출(액) [a] seepy 물이 스며 나오는
[syn] leak, drain, trickle, flow

Oil is seeping out through a crack in the tank.

---

22 distort [distɔ́:rt]
v. 왜곡하다, 비틀다

to twist or change somehow
[n] distortion 왜곡, 뒤틀림 [a] distorted 비뚤어진, 왜곡된
[syn] warp, twist, falsify, alter [ant] correct, right

By distorting the facts, a commercial can often confuse even the simplest issue.

---

23 persecute [pə́:rsikjù:t]
v. 박해하다, 괴롭히다

to treat unfairly
[n] persecution 박해, 학대
[syn] tyrannize, harass, oppress, bother [ant] defend, help, nurture

Persecuted for their religious beliefs, many people decided to leave their homeland.

---

24 diverge [divə́:rdʒ]
v. 다르다, 갈라지다

to differ or to go in different directions
[n] divergence 분기, 일탈
[syn] dissent, deviate, differ [ant] converge, meet, unify

In most matters, their opinions were not in conflict but tended to diverge on the politics.

---

25 persevere [pə̀:rsəvíər]
v. 참다, 인내하다

to continue despite hardships
[n] perseverance 인내, 참을성
[syn] endure, withstand [ant] quit, end

They persevered through hardships such as a lack of food, poor water, and relentless insects.

---

20 유명한 영화 배우가 도착한다는 말을 듣고 호텔 밖에 많은 인파가 모여들고 있었다. 21 탱크의 갈라진 틈에서 기름이 새고 있다. 22 사실을 왜곡함으로써 상업 광고는 종종 가장 단순한 사실조차도 혼란스럽게 만들 수 있다. 23 종교적 박해를 받자 많은 사람들이 조국을 떠나기로 결심했다. 24 대부분의 문제에서 그들의 의견은 다르지 않지만 정치에 있어서는 다른 경향이 있다. 25 그들은 식량 부족, 식수 오염, 수 많은 벌레와 같은 어려움을 참아냈다.

Exercise

Score ___ / 20

Word Check 각 단어의 뜻으로 알맞은 것을 찾아 연결하시오.

01 sanction

02 wholesome

03 distort

04 malicious

05 configuration

(a) formal or specialized arrangement

(b) feeling or motivated by a desire to cause harm

(c) to twist something out of shape

(d) to allow something to be done

(e) conducive to bodily health

Syn & Ant Check 주어진 단어의 동의어, 반의어를 골라 쓰시오.

| migrant | noticeable | leak | monarch | safe |
| anxious | separate | annoyed | careless | disparate |

06 palpable =

07 sovereign =

08 indignant =

09 solicitous =

10 seep =

11 indigenous ↔

12 congregate ↔

13 congruent ↔

14 treacherous ↔

15 meticulous ↔

Sentence Practice 문장을 읽고 빈칸에 알맞은 단어를 고르시오.

16 Even the most seasoned journalists were taken aback at the leader's _____ in admitting to substance abuse.

ⓐ configuration ⓑ condolence ⓒ candor ⓓ congestion

17 She is _____ at the government's lack of concern for the less privileged rural communities.

ⓐ palpable ⓑ congruent ⓒ indignant ⓓ wholesome

18 He gazed in wonder as the light from the _____ gem revealed a rainbow of colors.

ⓐ indigenous ⓑ translucent ⓒ meticulous ⓓ malicious

19 The soldiers exchanged final handshakes and _____ goodbyes before leaving for the warfront.

ⓐ sober ⓑ candor ⓒ solicitous ⓓ somber

20 Key issues are being debated heatedly as ideological opinions in the party start to _____.

ⓐ diverge ⓑ distort ⓒ sanction ⓓ seep

01 decadence [dékədəns]
n. 타락

a falling from high to low standards

ⓐ decadent 퇴폐적인

syn debasement, perversion, corruption, degeneracy

They say that the moral decadence is one of the factors which led to the fall of Rome.

---

02 nomad [nóumæd]
n. 유목민, 방랑자

people who don't have a permanent home

ⓐ nomadic 유목의, 방랑의

syn wanderer, itinerant, migrant, vagabond

In an effort to discourage nomads from trespassing on their property, farmers set up fences.

---

03 staple [stéipəl]
n. 주요산물, 주요품
a. 주요한, 중요한

key to a diet

syn main, key, primary, basic   ant ancillary, secondary, minor

Oil remains a staple for drawing foreign currency into the country.

Maize is a staple ingredient in making tortillas.

---

04 gist [dʒist]
n. 요점, 요지

main point

syn point, substance, thrust

The gist of her argument was that without some drastic changes, stock holders would begin abandoning the company.

---

05 drawback [drɔ́:bæ̀k]
n. 결점, 단점

a disadvantage

syn shortcoming, disadvantage, difficulty   ant advantage

One drawback in New York City was the high cost of living, which would force me to find a roommate.

---

06 nutrition [nju:tríʃən]
n. 영양분

being nourished

syn nourishment, nutriment

ⓐ nutritious 영양이 많은   ⓝ nutrient 영양분

The UN tries to prevent deaths from the inadequate nutrition.

---

01 그들은 도덕적 타락이 로마제국의 멸망 요인 중의 하나라고 말한다. 02 유랑자들이 그들의 땅에 들어오는 것을 막기 위해 농부들이 담장을 설치했다. 03 오일이 그 나라의 외화를 벌어들이는 주요 상품이다. 옥수수는 또띠야를 만드는 주요 성분이다. 04 그녀 주장의 요점은 급격한 변화가 없다면 주식 보유자들이 그 회사 주식을 팔아버리기 시작할거라는 것이었다. 05 뉴욕에 사는 데 한 가지 단점은 생활비가 많이 든다는 것이었고, 그래서 나는 어쩔 수 없이 룸메이트를 구했다. 06 UN은 영양부족으로 인한 사망을 방지하려고 노력하고 있다.

07 **constellation**
[kὰnstəléiʃən]
n. 성운, 성좌

a group of stars

v constellate 성좌를 이루다, 떼를 짓다

syn collection, assemblage, group

The Orion Constellation is one of the most well known groups of stars.

---

08 **sterile** [stéril]
a. 불임의, 불모의

unable to bear offsprings

n sterility 불임, 불모

syn barren, infertile, dead, fruitless ant fertile, productive

Mules are a combination of donkeys and horses, and they are sterile.

---

09 **complacent** [kəmpléisənt]
a. 만족하는

self-satisfied

n complacence 자기 만족

syn content, satisfied, unworried ant worried, insecure, unsatisfied

The young couple were feeling complacent with their accommodations.

---

10 **languid** [lǽŋgwid]
a. 나른한, 기운 없는

lacking in energy or vitality

v languish 기운이 없어지다, 약해지다

syn lethargic, inert, lazy ant energized, active, robust

Most of the animals appeared to be too languid to even notice our approach.

---

11 **lucid** [lú:sid]
a. 분명한

clear or bright

n lucidity 명료, 밝음

syn clear, distinct, evident, plain ant ambiguous, fuzzy, muddled

A full moon can make an evening walk quite enjoyable as the path is lucid.

---

12 **agile** [ǽdʒəl]
a. 기민한, 재빠른

moving quick

a agility 민첩, 명민함

syn nimble, deft, quick, spry ant slow, lethargic, ponderous

The agile jaguar can take his prey into the tree for safe keeping.

---

13 **distraught** [distrɔ́:t]
a. 정신이 혼란한, 산만한

extremely concerned

syn worried, concerned ant untroubled, calm, relaxed

When you are involved in a traffic accident, it is important to remain calm and not to become distraught.

---

07 오리온성좌는 가장 잘 알려진 성좌 중 하나이다. 08 노새는 당나귀와 말을 교배 시킨 것이고 그들은 새끼를 낳을 수가 없다. 09 그 젊은 커플은 숙박시설에 만족하고 있었다. 10 대부분의 동물들이 지쳐 있어 우리들이 다가가는 것도 알아차리지 못하는 것 같았다. 11 길이 밝아서 보름달은 밤에 산책하는 것을 매우 즐겁게 한다. 12 기민한 재규어는 먹이를 완전히 보호하기 위해 나무로 먹이를 가지고 올라 갈 수 있다. 13 당신이 끔찍한 사고를 당하면 침착해 하고 정신을 차려야 하는 것이 중요하다.

14 obsolete [ɑ̀bsəlíːt]
a. 구식의, 진부한

out of date

v obsolesce 쇠퇴해가다 a obsolescent 쇠퇴해가는, 구식의

syn dated, old-fashioned ant new, modern, contemporary

Considered obsolete by most, the typewriter is still used by some who have not yet fully embraced the "digital" age.

15 compulsory [kəmpʌ́lsəri]
a. 의무적인, 강제적인

required by the rules or law

n compulsion 강박현상, 강제,

syn mandatory, obligatory, forced ant optional, voluntary, elective

In the United States, education is compulsory for children between 6 and 18 years of age.

16 conspicuous [kənspíkjuəs]
a. 눈에 띄는, 뚜렷한

visibly noticed

v conspicuousness 눈에 띔

syn obvious, apparent ant inconspicuous, unseen, unnoticeable

The sickly antelope was a target for the lions as he ran conspicuously slower than the rest of the herd.

17 voracious [vouréiʃəs]
a. 게걸스레 먹는, 탐욕적인

eating food in large quantities

n voracity 폭식, 탐욕

syn insatiable, ravenous, hungry ant satisfied, quenched

People in the restaurant were surprised to see the football players' voracious appetite.

Unfortunately, their voracious quest for riches often led to bloodshed for the Indians.

18 consolidate [kənsálədèit]
v. 통합하다, 합병하다

to bring together

n consolidation 합병

syn mix, combine, fuse, blend ant divide, part, separate

The couple decided to consolidate their possessions when they got married.

19 dissuade [diswéid]
v. 그만두게 하다, 못하게 하다

persuade somebody not to do or believe it

n dissuasion 설득, 만류

syn discourage ant persuade

He would not be dissuaded from his goal of finding employment in the information industry.

---

14 대부분의 사람들이 구식이라고 생각하는 타자기는 디지털 시대를 완전히 받아들이지 않는 몇몇 사람들에 의해 아직도 사용된다. 15 미국에서 6세에서 18세까지 아이들에게 교육은 의무적이다. 16 그 병약한 영양은 나머지 영양들보다 눈에 띄게 느렸기 때문에 사자들의 표적이 되었다. 17 식당에 있는 사람들은 축구 선수들의 완성한 식욕을 보고 놀랐다. 불행하게도 부에 대한 그들의 탐욕스러운 욕구가 인디언들의 학살로 이어졌다. 18 그 커플은 결혼하면 재산을 공동으로 하기로 했다. 19 그는 정보 사업 분야에 취업하려는 목표를 단념하지 않았다.

20 condense [kəndéns]
v. 압축하다, 응축하다

to be shortened
[a] condensed 응축한, 간결한 [n] condensation 응축, 압축
[syn] abbreviate, summarize, curtail [ant] expand, lengthen, enlarge
She had three cans of condensed soup and 5 packets of dried noodles.

21 fathom [fǽðəm]
v. 헤아리다, 간파하다

to come to understand
[a] fathomable 추측할 수 있는
[syn] comprehend, recognize [ant] confuse, misunderstand
He did not fathom the real intention behind her proposal.

22 conspire [kənspáiər]
v. 음모를 꾸미다

to plan something secretly with another
[n] conspiracy 음모, 공모
[syn] plot, scheme, connive, devise
They conspired with Marcus Junius Brutus to assassinate the leader in hopes of restoring Rome to a republican form of government.

23 quench [kwentʃ]
v. 해소하다, (갈증 등을) 가시게 하다

to satisfy thirst
[a] quenchless 억누를 수 없는
[syn] satisfy, satiate, slake [ant] dissatisfy
During the African dry season, the watering hole becomes a dangerous place to quench your thirst.

24 compress [kəmprés]
v. 압축하다, 압박하다

to press together
[a] compressed 압축된, 간결한
[syn] contract, squeeze, shorten [ant] expand, lengthen, broaden
Diamonds are crafted from carbon that has been compressed over a long period of time.

25 disperse [dispə́ːrs]
v. 흩뜨리다, 분산시키다

to scatter in various directions
[n] dispersion 살포, 분산
[syn] scatter, separate, diffuse, disband [ant] collect, gather, congregate
City police used water cannons to disperse the crowd which had gotten more and more unruly as their numbers grew.

---

20 그녀는 농축된 3캔의 스프와 건조된 면 5팩을 가지고 있었다. 21 그는 그녀의 제안 이면에 있는 진짜 속셈을 알아채지 못했다. 22 그들은 로마를 다시 공화정으로 복원하려는 희망을 가지고 부루터스와 공모하여 지도자를 암살 하기로 했다. 23 아프리카 건기동안 물 웅덩이는 갈증을 없애기에는 위험한 곳이다. 24 다이아몬드는 오랜 기간에 걸쳐 압축된 탄소에서 만들어지는 것이다. 25 시 경찰들은 인원이 증가하면서 점점 거칠어지는 군중들을 흩어지게 하기 위해서 방수차를 사용했다.

Exercise

Score / 20

Word Check 각 단어의 뜻으로 알맞은 것을 찾아 연결하시오.

01 gist   (a) to come to understand
02 languid   (b) no longer in use or in practice
03 distraught   (c) in an extremely troubled state of mind
04 fathom   (d) showing little energy and interest
05 obsolete   (e) the general meaning or main point of something

Syn & Ant Check 주어진 단어의 동의어, 반의어를 골라 쓰시오.

| fertile | debasement | advantage | unsatisfied | nimble |
| mandatory | combine | lengthen | congregate | obvious |

06 consolidate = _____
07 agile = _____
08 compulsory = _____
09 decadence = _____
10 conspicuous = _____

11 disperse ↔ _____
12 sterile ↔ _____
13 drawback ↔ _____
14 compress ↔ _____
15 complacent ↔ _____

Sentence Practice 문장을 읽고 빈칸에 알맞은 단어를 고르시오.

16 Rice is the _____ food of most South Asian countries, although wheat is also quite popular.
ⓐ gist ⓑ nutrition ⓒ nomad ⓓ staple

17 At first glance the stark room reminded her of an impersonal and _____ hospital ward.
ⓐ languid ⓑ sterile ⓒ voracious ⓓ lucid

18 Not even the threat to his own life could _____ Steve from completing his dangerous assignment.
ⓐ dissuade ⓑ condense ⓒ conspire ⓓ compress

19 Signboards were put up at _____ places in the city to inform people of the traffic restrictions.
ⓐ conspicuous ⓑ compulsory ⓒ obsolete ⓓ distraught

20 It was so hot and dry that he thought no amount of water would _____ his thirst.
ⓐ fathom ⓑ consolidate ⓒ disperse ⓓ quench

01 monopoly [mənápəli]
n. 독점

the only supplier of a specified product or service

[v] monopolize 독점권을 얻다, 독점하다 [a] monopolistic 독점적인

[syn] dominance, control, cartel

The Sherman Antitrust Act was the first U.S. legislation aimed at limiting corporate monopolies.

02 placebo [pləsí:bou]
n. 위약

a substance with no effects that is administered as a drug

[syn] fake, false, bogus, sham [ant] real, authenticity

Their headache was eased despite the fact that they were given a placebo.

03 alliance [əláiəns]
n. 연합, 동맹

a group that supports the same issues

[v] ally 동맹하다, 제휴하다

[syn] coalition, partnership, union, association

The North Atlantic Treaty Organization(NATO) is a military alliance designed to protect fellow nations from an attack.

04 monotone [mánətòun]
n. 단조로움

no rise or fall in voice, lack of variety

[a] monotonous 단조로운 [v] monotonize 단조롭게 하다

[syn] dullness, lifelessness [ant] melody, harmony

He speaks in a monotone with little inflection in his conversations with people.

05 conventional
[kənvénʃənəl]
a. 전통적인, 틀에 박힌

traditional or normal

[n] convention 집회, 협정, 관습

[syn] common, ordinary, normal [ant] abnormal, unconventional

These days the number of the couples who want a conventional wedding is on the rise.

06 cosmopolitan
[kàzməpálətən]
a. 세계적인, 국제적인

pertinent to the whole world

[n] cosmopolis 국제도시

[syn] worldly [ant] parochial, provincial, rustic

New York is one of the cosmopolitan cities.

---

01 Sherman Antitrust 법령은 기업 독점을 제한하려는 최초의 미국 법이었다. 02 가짜 약을 받았다는 사실에도 불구하고 그들의 두통은 가셨다. 03 NATO 는 우방국을 공격에서 보호하기 위한 군사 동맹이다. 04 그는 다른 사람과 대화할 때 억양이 거의 없이 단조롭게 말한다. 05 오늘날 전통 결혼식을 원하는 커플 들의 수가 증가하고 있다. 06 뉴욕은 국제적인 도시들 중의 하나이다.

07 imperative [impérətiv]
a. 필수적인, 긴요한
n. 필요, 의무

absolutely essential
n imperator 전제군주
syn vital, important, essential ant unimportant, routine, optional

It was imperative that the items he brought to us be proven not to be fakes.

The first imperative is that we make a quick decision.

08 supple [sʌ́pəl]
a. 유연한, 유연성 있는

easily adjusted
n suppleness 유연
syn limber, agile, pliant, flexible ant inflexible, stiff, unbending

Baseball players use a variety of ointments to keep their gloves supple.

09 counterfeit [kàuntərfìt]
a. 위조의
v. 위조하다

made in imitation to deceive somebody
n counterfeiter 위조자
syn fake, copied, fictitious, phony ant real, genuine, actual

The counterfeit money they made circulates widely in the world market.

The criminals who had counterfeited $100 notes were arrested at the hotel in downtown yesterday.

10 exemplary [igzémpləri]
a. 훌륭한, 모범적인

serving as a model
v exemplify 예시하다, 예증하다
syn ideal, representative, laudable ant poor, bad, substandard

Members of the orchestra were congratulated by the conductor who was proud of their exemplary performance.

11 futile [fjúːtl]
a. 헛된, 효과 없는

not being able to produce any result
n futility 무가치, 무익
syn hopeless, vain, useless, ineffective ant effective, fruitful, hopeful

He cleared the streets for hours, but the relentless snowstorm made his efforts futile.

12 deflated [difléitid]
a. 자신감 잃은, 공기가 빠진

taken away one's confidence
v deflate 공기를 빼다, 수축시키다
syn disappointed, disheartened ant encouraged, hopeful, heartened

Deflated by his failure to pass the exam, Mr. Robinson couldn't hide his remorse.

07 그가 우리에게 가져온 물건들이 위조가 아니라는 것을 증명하는 것이 급선무이다. 가장 필요한 것은 우리가 빨리 결정을 내리는 것이다. 08 야구 선수들은 그들의 글러브를 부드럽게 하기 위해 다양한 연고를 사용한다. 09 그들이 만든 위조지폐가 세계 시장에서 광범위하게 유통되고 있다. 100달러 짜리 지폐를 위조한 범죄자들이 어제 시내의 호텔에서 체포되었다. 10 오케스트라 단원들은 훌륭한 연주에 만족한 지휘자에게 축하를 받았다. 11 그가 많은 시간동안 거리를 청소했으나 눈보라가 그의 수고를 헛되이 만들었다. 12 시험에 떨어져 좌절한 Robinson 씨는 슬픔을 감출 수 없었다.

13 vigilant [vídʒələnt]
a. 조심성 있는, 경계하는

giving careful attention to a situation
ⁿ vigilance 경계, 조심
[syn] alert, aware, wary, ready [ant] lethargic, inattentive, asleep
They said the tourists visiting the conflict area should be vigilant.

---

14 prodigal [prádigəl]
a. 낭비하는
n. 방탕자

heedlessly wasteful
ⁿ prodigality 방탕, 낭비
[syn] wasteful, extravagant, uncontrolled [ant] thrifty, economical
It is a prodigal expenditure of your time to watch TV all day.
I don't want my children to be a prodigal who drinks and gambles.

---

15 adjacent [ədʒéisənt]
a. 가까운, 근접한

lying next to something
ⁿ adjacency 인접, 인근
[syn] beside, bordering [ant] detached, distant
A park adjacent to the town will be built for residential use.

---

16 resilient [rizíljənt]
a. 회복하는, 되돌아가는

recovering rightly
ⁿ resilience 탄력, 복원
[syn] flexible, buoyant, bendable [ant] inflexible, rigid, weak
U.S. president George W. Bush insists the American economy will be resilient soon.

---

17 frivolous [frívələs]
a. 사소한, 천박한

trivial
ⁿ frivolity 천박, 경박
[syn] pointless, senseless, foolish [ant] vital, serious, important
Though Alaska might have seemed frivolous at the time, it gave the U.S. a strategic location for defending the continental United States.

---

18 figurative [fígjərətiv]
a. 비유적인

representing something using symbol
ⁿ figure 숫자, 모습 figuration 비유적 표현, 형상
[syn] abstract, metaphoric, symbolic [ant] real, literal, concrete
Poets can use metaphor to write their figurative poems.

---

19 contemplate
[kántəmplèit]
v. 숙고하다, 생각하다

to think about something
ⁿ contemplation 묵상, 명상
[syn] consider, reflect, brood [ant] forget, neglect, disregard
He would often contemplate for a few hours before going to bed.

---

13 그들은 분쟁지역을 방문하는 사람들에게 주의를 당부했다. 14 하루 종일 TV만 보는 것은 시간낭비이다. 나는 우리 아이들이 술이나 마시고 도박이나 하는 방탕아가 되기를 원하지는 않는다 . 15 그 마을 가까이 주민들을 위한 공원이 조성될 것이다. 16 미국 부시 대통령은 미국 경제는 곧 회복할 것이라고 말한다. 17 알래스카는 그 당시에 사소한 것처럼 보였겠지만 미국에게 미 대륙의 방어를 위한 전략기지를 제공해주었다. 18 시인은 비유적 시를 쓰기 위해 은유법을 사용할 수 있다. 19 그는 취침 전에 몇 시간 동안 생각에 빠져 있곤 했다.

20 castigate [kǽstəgèit]
v. 혹평하다, 벌주다

to criticize or punish severely

[n] castigation 혹평

[syn] criticize, scold, punish   [ant] praise, reward, compliment

Wise parents are less likely to castigate their children with people around.

21 erode [iróud]
v. 침식하다, 부식하다

to wear away gradually

[n] erosion 부식, 침식

[syn] disintegrate, corrode, crumble

The bridge might be collapsed when the bridge abutments are eroded by the occasional flood.

22 repel [ripél]
v. 막다, 쫓아버리다

to deter something

[a] repellent 불쾌한, 반발하는

[syn] resist, deter   [ant] attract, welcome

Cats can be repelled from a lawn by the device which emits a sound wave that irritates the creatures.

23 dissemble [disémbəl]
v. 숨기다, 가장하다

to hide or disguise

[syn] conceal, hide, fake, camouflage   [ant] expose, reveal, show

He was a crafty card player and able to dissemble his emotions from the other players.

24 premeditate
[pri:médətèit]
v. 미리 계획하다

to plan beforehand

[n] premeditation 미리 계획함

[syn] plan, orchestrate, develop, construct

The jury deliberated for nearly 12 hours, considering whether the suspect was guilty of premeditated murder.

25 exemplify [igzémpləfài]
v. 예가 되다

to show an example of something

[n] exemplification 예증, 사례   [a] exemplary 모범적인

[syn] illustrate, show, epitomize, typify

The hooliganism demonstrated by the World Cup exemplified some of the problems security officials must deal with in the future soccer contests.

---

20 현명한 부모는 주위에 사람들이 있을 때에는 아이들을 혼내려 하지 않는다. 21 때때로 일어나는 홍수로 인해 다리의 교대가 부식되면 다리가 붕괴 될 수도 있다. 22 고양이를 불안하게 하는 음파를 방출하는 장치로 고양이들을 잔디에 오지 못하게 할 수 있다. 23 그는 영리한 카드 노름꾼으로 다른 사람들에게 자신의 감정을 숨길 수 있었다. 24 배심원들은 거의 12시간 동안 그 용의자가 계획된 살인을 저질렀는지에 대해 심사숙고 했다. 25 월드컵에서 보여줬던 폭력행위는 앞으로 있을 축구경기에 대비해 안전요원들이 다루어야 할 문제점들의 일부를 보여주는 대표적 사례이다.

Exercise

Word Check 각 단어의 뜻으로 알맞은 것을 찾아 연결하시오.

01 monopoly   (a) to be destroyed gradually

02 resilient   (b) the only supplier of a specified commodity

03 erode   (c) able to spring back to former position

04 monotone   (d) belonging to all parts of the world

05 cosmopolitan   (e) a single unvarying tone

Syn & Ant Check 주어진 단어의 동의어, 반의어를 골라 쓰시오.

encouraged	plan	association	conceal	genuine
flexible	inattentive	consider	important	substandard

06 dissemble   = _____   11 counterfeit ↔ _____

07 supple   = _____   12 vigilant   ↔ _____

08 contemplate = _____   13 deflated   ↔ _____

09 alliance   = _____   14 exemplary   ↔ _____

10 premeditate = _____   15 frivolous   ↔ _____

Sentence Practice 문장을 읽고 빈칸에 알맞은 단어를 고르시오.

16 It is _____ that we devise an alternative energy strategy in the face of ever-rising fossil fuel costs.

ⓐ conventional   ⓑ cosmopolitan   ⓒ imperative   ⓓ exemplary

17 All our precautions proved inadequate and _____ in the face of the storm's fury.

ⓐ adjacent   ⓑ resilient   ⓒ futile   ⓓ vigilant

18 We need more funds to pay for the _____ spending of his predecessor.

ⓐ supple   ⓑ prodigal   ⓒ figurative   ⓓ deflated

19 We expected him to _____ us but were surprised instead by his praise.

ⓐ castigate   ⓑ dissemble   ⓒ exemplify   ⓓ erode

20 The smelly fluid secreted by toads when under attack serves to _____ predators.

ⓐ contemplate   ⓑ premeditate   ⓒ dissemble   ⓓ repel

01 denunciation
[dinʌnsiéiʃən]
n. 비난, 탄핵

a public condemnation of someone
ⓥ denounce 비난하다, 고발하다
syn condemnation, accusation, censure   ant advocate, compliment

While he accepted the blame for the incident, he felt humiliated by the denunciation he received by the media.

02 zenith [zíːniθ]
n. 천정, 절정

the highest point
ⓐ zenithal 천정의, 정점의

Dreaming that you have reached the zenith of your profession indicates you are in a dead-end job and need a career change.

03 census [sénsəs]
n. 인구조사

an official count, especially population
syn poll, sample, survey

The government announced that the census of population would be taken for a week next month.

04 grudge [grʌdʒ]
n. 원한
v. 아까워하다, 불평하다

a long-standing feeling of resentment
ⓐ grudging 원한을 품은, 싫어하는
syn bitterness, grievance, resentment, spite

They held a grudge against each other for many years.
He grudged paying 1,000 dollars for just a ring.

05 delusion [dilúːʒən]
n. 망상, 허상

believing things which are not true
ⓝ delude 속이다   ⓐ delusive 기만적인, 거짓의
syn hallucination, illusion, mirage

His rescuers noted that he was suffering from delusions when found.

06 mishap [míshæp]
n. (가벼운)사고, 불행한 일

an unfortunate accident
syn mistake, accident, error, disaster

My parents wish me to finish my military service without any mishap.

---

01 그는 그 사건에 대한 책임을 졌지만 대중매체에서 받은 비난에 수치심을 느꼈다. 02 당신이 직업에서 최고점에 도달하는 꿈을 꾸는 것은 당신이 가능성이 없는 직장에 있고 이직이 필요하다는 것을 나타낸다. 03 정부는 다음달 일주일 동안 인구조사가 실시될 것 이라고 발표했다. 04 그들은 수년 동안 서로 원한을 가지고 있었다. 그는 반지 하나에 1000달러나 내야 하는 것을 아까워했다. 05 그를 구출한 사람들은 그가 발견당시 망상에 시달리고 있었다고 말했다. 06 나의 부모님은 내가 군복무를 무사히 끝마치도록 기원했다.

07 fracture [frǽktʃər]

n. 골절
v. 뼈가 부서지다

a breaking of anything hard, especially bone

a fractural 골절의

syn break, crack, split

His collision with the outfielder seemed harmless, but his coach insisted that he have his sore hand x-rayed in case of a fracture.

My grandmother's bones are likely to fracture against a light strike.

08 limber [límbər]

a. 유연한
v. 유연하게 하다

able to move or bend freely

syn flexible, agile, loose, pliant ant stiff, rigid, fixed

Her limber body can conform to every type of dive no matter what the degree of difficulty.

I do yoga exercises to limber my body three times a week.

09 incontrovertible [ìnkɑntrəvə́:rtəbəl]

a. 명백한

absolutely true

n incontrovertibleness 명백함

syn sure, unequivocal, certain ant questionable, uncertain, unsure

In the face of incontrovertible evidence, he admitted to stealing my car.

10 adverse [ædvə́:rs]

a. 불리한, 반대의

unfavorable, opposing one's interests

n adversity 역경, 불운 adversary 적, 반대자

syn unfavorable, opposing, contrary ant favorable, beneficial

Future homeowners should be careful not to do anything adverse to their credit rating.

11 peripheral [pərífərəl]

a. 중요하지 않는, 주변적인

unimportant to the discussion or not of central importance

n periphery 주의, 주변

syn minor, external, irrelevant, unimportant ant vital, key, central

That was just a peripheral issue that didn't address the heart of the matter at all.

12 frail [freil]

a. 약한, 깨지기 쉬운

not very strong, easily broken

n frailty 약함, 단점

syn weak, infirm, delicate, thin ant strong, thick, firm

Modern lace is usually made of cotton and it is less frail to the touch.

---

07 외야수와의 충돌로 부상당한 것 같지는 않았지만 그의 코치는 골절일 경우를 생각해서 아픈 손을 x-ray 찍어봐야 한다고 했다. 할머니의 뼈는 약간만 부딪쳐도 쉽게 골절될 것 같다. 08 그녀는 유연한 몸으로 난이도 상관없이 모든 다이빙 유형을 할 수 있다. 나는 몸을 유연하게 하기 위해 일주일에 3번 요가를 한다. 09 명확한 증거 앞에서 그는 내 차를 훔친 것을 시인했다. 10 앞으로 주택을 소유할 분들은 신용등급에 좋지 않은 일을 하지 않도록 조심해야 한다. 11 그것은 문제의 핵심을 전혀 언급하지 않은 피상적인 쟁점이었다. 12 요즘의 레이스는 보통 면으로 만들어져서 접촉을 해도 덜 해진다.

13 opulent [ápjələnt]
a. 풍부한, 호사스러운

rich and luxurious

n opulence 풍요, 풍부

syn rich, abundant, luxurious ant spartan

The Eagle's Nest, Hitler's opulent retreat, was occupied by U.S. troops in 1945.

14 pathological
[pæ̀θəládʒikəl]
a. 병적인, 병리상의

being caused by disease

n pathology 병리학

syn created in the mind, fictional

They think that pathological liars are difficult to diagnose.

15 integral [íntigrəl]
a. 절대 필요한, 없어서는 안될

not to be dispensed with

syn vital, essential, critical ant expendable, dispensable

Of all modern conveniences, many think that a refrigerator is the most integral.

16 indomitable [indámətəbəl]
a. 불굴의

unable to be defeated

syn strong, resolute, spirited, determined ant weak, wavering, hesitant

It was his indomitable will that allowed him to walk away from the bitter cold of Antarctica.

17 induce [indjúːs]
v. 유발하다, 야기하다

to encourage something to happen

n induction 유도, 유발 a inductive 귀납의

syn provoke, cause, stimulate, encourage ant discourage

He was induced to fight by his friends who provoked him with a cacophony of jeering and yelling.

18 exert [igzə́ːrt]
v. 쓰다, 노력하다

to put to use

n exertion 노력, 분발 a exertive 노력하는

syn use, apply, strain

The road repairing workers are exerting tremendous energy to pave with asphalt in such oppressive conditions.

19 embed [imbéd]
v. 끼워넣다

to fix something in firmly and deeply

syn implant, sink, bury, ingrain ant excavate

The cathedral had an unexploded mortar shell embedded in its wall.

---

13 히틀러의 호사스러운 은신처였던 "Eagle's Nest"는 1945년 미군에 의해 점령당했다. 14 그들은 병적인 거짓말쟁이는 진단하기 어렵다고 생각한다. 15 모든 현대적인 편리함 중에서 많은 사람들은 냉장고가 가장 필수적이라고 생각한다. 16 남극의 혹한에서 그가 생존 할 수 있었던 것은 그의 불굴의 의지 때문이다. 17 그의 친구들이 그에게 조롱하고 고함을 질러 그에게 싸움을 야기시켰다. 18 도로 보수 노동자들은 그런 힘든 조건 속에서도 도로에 아스팔트를 포장하기 위해 엄청난 힘을 쓰고 있다. 19 대성당에는 벽에 폭발되지 않은 박격포 포탄이 박혀 있다.

| 20 | **trespass** [tréspəs]
v. 불법 침입하다, 침해하다 | to enter someone's property without permission
n trespasser 침입자
syn breach, intrude, invade, encroach
Last night the police arrested the people trying to trespass the border between Canada and USA. |

| 21 | **emulate** [émjəlèit]
v. 모방하다, ~에 필적하다, 경쟁하다 | to try to behave equally
n emulation 경쟁
syn copy, mimic, follow, mirror
As he grew, he emulated many of his grandfather's traits, such as saying less and listening more.
Bear cubs that emulate their mother's hunting techniques stand a better chance of surviving in the wild. |

| 22 | **loiter** [lɔ́itər]
v. 어슬렁거리다 | to stand around or to walk slowly
syn idle, dawdle
The shopkeepers don't like people loitering around their stores. |

| 23 | **mitigate** [mítəgèit]
v. 줄이다 | to make something less severe
n mitigation 경감, 완화   a mitigative 완화하는
syn reduce, lessen, ease, alleviate   ant increase, heighten, exacerbate
The country needs a new measure to mitigate the effects of the inflation. |

| 24 | **reinforce** [rìːinfɔ́ːrs]
v. 강화하다 | to make something stronger or more intense
n reinforcement 보강, 강화
syn strengthen, support, buttress, bolster   ant weaken, lessen
After a blast near U.S. embassy last month they decided to send more troops to reinforce the army. |

| 25 | **dispose** [dispóuz]
v. 처리하다, 처분하다 | to throw something away
n disposal 처분, 처리   a disposable 처분할 수 있는   n 일회용 물품
syn discard, dump   ant obtain, retain, take
Batteries contain toxic metals and should not be disposed of like regular waste. |

---

20 경찰은 어제 캐나다와 미국 국경을 무단으로 넘으려는 사람들을 체포했다. 21 그는 자라면서 말수가 적어지고 더 경청하는 할아버지의 성격을 많이 닮아갔다. 그들의 어미와 필적할 만한 사냥 기술을 가진 새끼곰들은 야생에서 살아남을 확률이 보다 많다. 22 상점 주인들은 가게 주위에서 어슬렁거리는 사람을 좋아하지 않는다. 23 그 국가는 인플레이션의 영향을 줄이기 위해 새로운 정책이 필요하다. 24 지난달 미국 대사관 근처에 폭발이 발생한 후 그들은 부대를 보강하기 위해 더 많은 군인을 파견하기로 했다. 25 배터리는 유독 물질을 포함하고 있어서 일반 쓰레기처럼 버리면 안 된다.

Exercise

Word Check 각 단어의 뜻으로 알맞은 것을 찾아 연결하시오.

01	pathological	(a)	to try hard to equal or be better than someone
02	census	(b)	the breaking or cracking of anything hard
03	emulate	(c)	an official count of a population
04	fracture	(d)	caused by or relating to illness.
05	frail	(e)	easily broken or destroyed

Syn & Ant Check 주어진 단어의 동의어, 반의어를 골라 쓰시오.

strengthen	discard	illusion	invade	abundant
dispensable	favorable	stiff	uncertain	increase

06	trespass =		11	integral	↔
07	delusion =		12	incontrovertible	↔
08	reinforce =		13	mitigate	↔
09	dispose =		14	limber	↔
10	opulent =		15	adverse	↔

Sentence Practice 문장을 읽고 빈칸에 알맞은 단어를 고르시오.

16 I found it impossible to join the crowd's unthinking _____ of the fallen hero.

   ⓐ denunciation   ⓑ census   ⓒ zenith   ⓓ mishap

17 She is too generous and large - hearted to hold a _____ against any person.

   ⓐ grudge   ⓑ fracture   ⓒ delusion   ⓓ frail

18 One of the highlights of the emperor's victory parade was the _____ gold carriage pulled by a team of twelve horses.

   ⓐ frail   ⓑ adverse   ⓒ opulent   ⓓ indomitable

19 Nothing in the world could _____ her to go against her mentor's wishes.

   ⓐ exert   ⓑ induce   ⓒ loiter   ⓓ emulate

20 When the news of the calamity spread, people came out to help _____ the victims' sufferings.

   ⓐ trespass   ⓑ dispose   ⓒ embed   ⓓ mitigate

01 philanthropist
[filǽnθrəpist]
n. 박애주의자

a charitable person
n philanthropy 박애, 인류애
syn altruist, contributor, humanitarian   ant miser, antagonist
One need not have millions of dollars to become a philanthropist.

02 perjury [pə́ːrdʒəri]
n. 위증, 거짓말

crime of making false statements in a legal court
v perjure 위증하다   n perjurer 위증자
syn deception, lie
Former U.S. president Clinton was accused of perjury, but he was never formally charged.

03 ordeal [ɔːrdíːəl]
n. 시련, 고난

a difficult experience
syn difficulty, trial, trouble   ant blessing, solace, consolation
Incidents such as crime, sickness, or injury can be quite an ordeal if you are not adequately insured.

04 antipathy [æntípəθi]
n. 혐오, 반감

a feeling of loathing for someone
a antipathetic 반감을 가진
syn hatred, dislike, animosity, loathing   ant sympathy, love, caring
A good degree of antipathy existed between the Spartans and the rest of the Greek city states.

05 tumult [tjúːmʌlt]
n. 소란, 소동

a violent commotion
a tumultuous 소란스러운, 거친
syn uproar, commotion, turmoil, ruckus   ant quiet, serene, calm
The tornado alarm sounded, causing a tumult in the town square.

06 momentous [moʊméntəs]
a. 중요한, 중대한

of far-reaching important
n momentum 추진력, 힘
syn important, significant, serious   ant trivial, insignificant
The Yalta Conference was a momentous event for the post war international community.

---

01 박애주의자가 되기 위해 수백만 달러가 필요한 것은 아니다. 02 Clinton 전 미국 대통령은 위증을 했다고 비난을 받았으나 정식으로 기소되지는 않았다. 03 당신이 적절한 보험을 들어놓지 않으면 범죄, 질병, 상해와 같은 사고는 매우 힘든 일이 될 수도 있다. 04 스파르타인과 나머지 그리스 도시국가 사이에는 상당한 반감이 존재했다. 05 토네이도 경보가 울리자 마을광장에 소란이 일어났다. 06 얄타 회담은 2차 대전 이후 국제 사회에 중요한 사건이었다.

07 turbulent [tə́:rbjələnt]
a. 거친, 휘몰아치는

violently disturbed
n turbulence 소란, 난기류
syn unsettled, stormy, swirling, disturbed ant calm, placid, tranquil

They needed to arrive at the port quickly in order to avoid the turbulent weather to come.

---

08 picturesque [pìktʃərésk]
a. 그림같이 아름다운

quite beautiful like a painting
n picture 그림
syn beautiful, striking, vivid, colorful⁻ ant drab, dull, ugly

He had heard that Cape May was quite picturesque, so he decided to travel there.

---

09 frugal [frú:gəl]
a. 검소한, 간소한

not spending much money
n frugality 절약, 검소
syn tight, thrifty, economical ant extravagant, wasteful

He learned to be frugal from his grandparents who saved most of their money as a result of lessons learned in the Great Depression.

---

10 trite [trait]
a. 진부한, 흔한

boring because it is overused
syn banal, cliche ant important, relevant, unique

When he was questioned about his loyalty to the company, his response was brief and trite.

---

11 regressive [rigrésiv]
a. 퇴화하는, 회귀하는

opposing progress
n regression 퇴화, 퇴보
syn backward, reactionary ant radical, progressive, forward

The politician's regressive platform was quite popular with some of the people.

---

12 subsequent [sʌ́bsikwənt]
a. 다음의, 수반하는

coming following
n subsequence 다음, 결과 ad subsequently 그 후에, 다음에
syn next, consecutive, following, ensuing ant previous, former, prior

Subsequent crimes proved the accused was not a criminal.

---

13 miniscule [mínəskjù:l]
a. 매우 작은, 하찮은

very small
syn tiny, small, minute, paltry ant large, massive

For fluoride to be applied safely in preventing tooth decay it must be used in miniscule amounts and never eaten.

---

07 그들은 거친 날씨를 피하기 위해 빨리 정박해야만 했다. 08 그는 Cape May가 아름답다는 얘기를 듣고 그 곳을 여행하기로 결정했다. 09 그는 세계 대 공황에서 배운 교훈으로 대부분의 돈을 저축했던 조부모님으로부터 검소해야 한다는 것을 배웠다. 10 애사심에 대한 질문을 받았을 때 그의 대답은 짧고 진부했다. 11 그 정치가의 과거로 회기하는 정책들이 일부 국민에게 인기를 얻었다. 12 그 후의 사건으로 피고인이 범인이 아니라는 것이 입증되었다. 13 불화물이 충치예방에 안전하게 사용되기 위해서는 극소량만 사용해야 하고 절대로 먹어서는 안 된다.

14 subordinate [səbɔ́ːrdənit]

a. 하위의
n. 하급자
v. 하위에 두다

placed to a lower rank

n subordination 종속, 복종

syn lesser, ancillary, secondary, inferior   ant superior, primary, main

Many countries in Asia were once subordinate states of China.

Colonel Scott is always firm but fair to his subordinates.

He always subordinated study to pleasure, so he failed a college entrance exam.

15 agonize [ǽgənàiz]

v. 괴로워하다, 고뇌하다

to worry about something

n agony 고통, 고뇌

syn struggle, suffer, worry, lament

Johnson was said to have agonized over his decision to remain in Vietnam.

16 mimic [mímik]

v. 흉내내다, 모방하다

to imitate the action or voice of a person

n mimicry 흉내   n mimicker 흉내내는 사람

syn parody, copy, imitate, simulate

Young children will copy their older siblings' behavior, mimicking actions both good and bad.

17 rejuvenate [ridʒúːvənèit]

v. 원기를 회복하다(시키다)

to make someone feel young again

n rejuvenation 회춘, 원기회복

syn modernize, renew, restore

The crisp mountain air seemed to rejuvenate the patients.

18 dismiss [dismís]

v. 떠나게 하다, 해고하다

to send someone away

n dismissal 해산, 해고

syn banish, dispel, fire   ant welcome, keep, maintain

Ms. Garrison explained that she needed to be dismissed from jury duty because she had no one to take care of her children.

19 encompass [inkʌ́mpəs]

v. 포함하다, 둘러싸다

to include something

syn include, comprise, incorporate, contain   ant omit, exclude

The desert terrain encompasses nearly all of Nevada and more than half of Utah.

---

14 아시아의 많은 국가들이 중국의 속국이었다. Scott 대령은 항상 엄하지만 부하들에겐 공정하다. 그는 항상 공부하는 것보다 노는 데 치중해서 대입시험에 떨어졌다. 15 Johnson은 베트남에 남겠다는 결정을 내리는 데 많은 고민을 했다고 한다. 16 어린 아이들은 좋은 것이든 나쁜 것이든 손위 형제의 행동을 흉내내면서 따라 한다. 17 신선한 공기가 환자들을 회복시키는 것 같았다. 18 Garrison부인은 아이들을 돌볼 사람이 없어서 배심원 일을 할 수 없다고 설명했다. 19 Nevada 거의 전체와 Utah주의 절반 이상이 사막지역이다.

20 submerge [səbmə́:rdʒ]

v. 잠기다, 가라앉다

to sink under the surface of water

ⓝ submergence 침수, 침몰

[syn] dunk, sink, plunge, descend [ant] surface, emerge, rise

The submarine heading to England submerged to avoid being detected by the enemy ship.

---

21 dismantle [dismǽntl]

v. 분해하다, 떼어내다

to take apart

ⓝ dismantlement 분해

[syn] disassemble [ant] build, erect

After the bomb was discovered, an expert was brought in to dismantle the device.

---

22 perish [périʃ]

v. 멸망하다, 죽다

to die as the result of an accident

ⓐ perishable 죽기 쉬운, 썩기 쉬운

[syn] die, expire, end [ant] live, endure, survive

The Dodo was a flightless bird that perished because it was unable to defend itself from human attackers.

---

23 strain [strein]

v. 잡아당기다, 긴장시키다

n. 접질림, 긴장

to pull something

ⓐ strained 팽팽한, 긴장된

[syn] constrict, extend, sprain, tension, anxiety

The man straining a rope was exhausted and wanted to take a break.

A minor leg strain, for instance, can lead to lifelong injury if left unchecked.

---

24 subdue [səbdjú:]

v. 정복하다, 억제하다

to conquer or control

ⓝ subdued 정복된, 억제된

[syn] control, suppress, detain, overpower

The police fired tear gases to subdue the demonstrators protesting the war in Iraq.

---

25 stumble [stʌ́mbəl]

v. 넘어지다, 비틀거리다

to miss one's step

[syn] stagger, falter, fall, flounder

The first clue that someone has been drinking is that he stumbles when he attempts to walk.

---

20 영국으로 향하던 그 잠수함은 적 군함에 의해 탐지되지 않기 위해 잠수했다. 21 폭탄이 발견된 후에 전문가가 폭탄을 분해하기 위해 왔다. 22 Dodo는 인간의 공격으로부터 자신을 보호할 수 없기 때문에 멸종한 날지 못하는 새였다. 23 줄을 잡아당기고 있던 남자는 지쳤고 휴식을 원했다. 예를 들어 가벼운 접질림도 치료하지 않으면 평생 아플 수 있다. 24 경찰은 이라크 전쟁을 반대하는 시위자들을 진압하기 위해 최루탄을 발사했다. 25 누군가 술에 취했다는 첫 번째 증거는 걸으려 할 때 넘어지는 것이다.

Exercise

Word Check 각 단어의 뜻으로 알맞은 것을 찾아 연결하시오.

01 turbulent   (a) difficult or unpleasant experience

02 tumult   (b) being in a disturbed state

03 trite   (c) a great or confused noise

04 stumble   (d) having no meaning because it has been repeated

05 ordeal   (e) to lose one's balance and trip forwards

Syn & Ant Check 주어진 단어의 동의어, 반의어를 골라 쓰시오.

backward	previous	fire	disassemble	survive
deception	superior	massive	sympathy	sink

06 dismantle = _____

07 dismiss = _____

08 regressive = _____

09 submerge = _____

10 perjury = _____

11 miniscule ↔ _____

12 antipathy ↔ _____

13 subsequent ↔ _____

14 subordinate ↔ _____

15 perish ↔ _____

Sentence Practice 문장을 읽고 빈칸에 알맞은 단어를 고르시오.

16 The courts that are meant to uphold truth are often guilty of condoning _____ instead.

ⓐ ordeal   ⓑ perjury   ⓒ tumult   ⓓ philanthropist

17 Clearly it was the _____ landscape that drew tourists by the thousands to the spot.

ⓐ turbulent   ⓑ picturesque   ⓒ trite   ⓓ momentous

18 Although the meals served at home were _____ they were wholesome and delicious.

ⓐ frugal   ⓑ subsequent   ⓒ miniscule   ⓓ subordinate

19 Our director prefers to _____ over every little detail instead of taking decisive action.

ⓐ strain   ⓑ rejuvenate   ⓒ submerge   ⓓ agonize

20 The trainer's skill and experience were severely tested during his efforts to _____ the rampaging elephant.

ⓐ encompass   ⓑ mimic   ⓒ dismiss   ⓓ subdue

suffix

명사 suffix Ⅱ

small

-ling, -let : lord ⇨ lordling, duck ⇨ duckling, bull ⇨ bullet

The young lordling went out to the well walking full of thought.

그 젊은 왕은 골똘히 생각하면서 우물가로 걸어왔다.

-kin : fir ⇨ firkin, lamb ⇨ lambkins

Firkin is a small wooden vessel or cask of indeterminate size used for butter.

Firkin은 버터를 넣는데 사용하는 작은 크기의 나무통이다.

-ie : dog ⇨ doggie, bird ⇨ birdies

A doggie bag originated from the bag used for wrapping leftover food for dogs.

doggie bag은 남은 음식을 개에게 주기 위해 담았던 봉지에서 유래됐다.

humanize

-ar, -er, -or, -ist, -an : lie ⇨ liar, farm ⇨ farmer, guitar ⇨ guitarist,
magic ⇨ magician

How can we treat the person if he is a pathological liar?

병적인 거짓말쟁이를 어떻게 다룰 수 있을까요?

-ary : adverse ⇨ adversary, mission ⇨ missionary

To succeed in business, you have to be patient though your rivals are ruthless adversaries.

사업에서 성공하기 위해선 상대방이 아무리 무자비해도 참아야만 한다.

-ite : labor ⇨ laborite, Israel ⇨ Israelite,   Seoul ⇨ Seoulite

He was a laborer who supported a labor movement or union.

그는 노동단체 활동을 지원했던 노동 당원이었다.

-ster : trick ⇨ trickster, young ⇨ youngster, song ⇨ songster

This web-site is dedicated to exploring the archetypal figure of tricksters.

이 웹사이트는 전형적인 사기꾼의 형태를 알리는데 목적이 있다.

group

-age, -(e,o,a)ry : leak ⇨ leakage, store ⇨ storage,
machine ⇨ machinery, terra ⇨ territory

This instrument detects air leakage in buildings to reduce energy loss.

이 도구는 빌딩의 공기 누설을 탐지해서 에너지 손실을 줄인다.

A 영어 풀이에 알맞은 단어를 보기에서 찾아 쓰시오.

distort	trespass	integral	submerge	counterfeit

01 an imitation intended to be a genuine article _____

02 to enter without permission _____

03 necessary to complete a whole _____

04 to change the meaning or tone of a statement _____

05 to put or sink below the surface of water _____

B 문장을 읽고 문맥에 적절한 단어를 고르시오.

06 In computer science a "language" seems to become (wholesome/obsolete) almost as soon as it becomes widely accepted.

07 People came in from remote areas to offer (configurations/condolences) at the funeral of the old village patriarch.

08 Being (vigilant/deflated) about our own conduct is the only way to prevent ourselves from falling back into old follies.

09 They were tired of his (trite/agile) comment on the political matter.

C 표시된 부분과 뜻이 가장 가까운 것을 고르시오.

10 The long wait at the doctor's actually gave me time to contemplate the course of my illness.

　ⓐ condense　　　　ⓑ conspire　　　　ⓒ congregate　　　　ⓓ consider

11 Under his loud laughter and strident voice lies a sober and cultured mind.

　ⓐ sterile　　　　ⓑ complacent　　　　ⓒ abstinent　　　　ⓓ indignant

12 The antipathy from his competitors he felt on entering the room went beyond mere professional rivalry.

　ⓐ alliance　　　　ⓑ gist　　　　ⓒ candor　　　　ⓓ loathing

13 The team worked hard on its greatest drawback and eventually won the tournament.

　ⓐ disadvantage　　　　ⓑ staple　　　　ⓒ placebo　　　　ⓓ perjury

D 표시된 부분의 반대말로 가장 알맞은 것을 고르시오.

14 Gymnastics classes were made **compulsory** to encourage all students to pursue some physical activity.

    ⓐ optional   ⓑ incessant   ⓒ voracious   ⓓ frivolous

15 The move to impose user taxes at the new airport has been termed **regressive**.

    ⓐ subordinate   ⓑ progressive   ⓒ opulent   ⓓ resilient

16 We were booked into **adjacent** suites at the hotel for security reasons.

    ⓐ distant   ⓑ exemplary   ⓒ somber   ⓓ supple

17 We complain about the growing **congestion** on the roads without realizing our own share in creating it.

    ⓐ sovereign   ⓑ census   ⓒ ordeal   ⓓ emptiness

E 주어진 단어를 알맞은 형태로 바꿔 빈칸에 쓰시오.

18 To believe that we are supreme masters of our own destinies is to live in a _____. (delusive)

19 True geniuses go against _____ wisdom to make path-breaking discoveries. (convention)

20 The melting snow and ice created muddy roads that were slushy and _____. (treachery)

21 The tiny caterpillar feeds on prodigious quantities of leaves to satisfy its _____ appetite. (voracity)

F 빈 칸에 알맞은 단어를 보기에서 찾아 쓰시오. (필요한 경우 형태를 바꾸시오.)

languid	opulent	incessant	mimic	resilient	ordeal	census

22 The _____ rain kept us indoors and forced us to look for new means of entertainment.

23 Young children are far more _____ than we as indulgent parents imagine.

24 No one realized that her _____ manner was a mask to hide her razor- sharp intellect.

25 Leaf insects _____ their surroundings so perfectly that they are almost impossible to spot.

> 영어를 우리말로 옮기시오.

01 alliance _____

02 subdue _____

03 prodigal _____

04 miniscule _____

05 dispose _____

06 rejuvenate _____

07 congruent _____

08 stumble _____

09 sober _____

10 strain _____

11 imperious _____

12 cosmopolitan _____

13 dissuade _____

14 pathological _____

15 wholesome _____

16 mimic _____

17 dissemble _____

18 diverge _____

19 submerge _____

20 deflated _____

21 conspicuous _____

22 integral _____

23 dismantle _____

24 languid _____

25 contemplate _____

26 induce _____

27 distraught _____

28 frail _____

29 seep _____

30 picturesque _____

31 mitigate _____

32 meticulous _____

33 emulate _____

34 fathom _____

35 momentous _____

36 indignant _____

37 conventional _____

38 reinforce _____

39 incontrovertible _____

40 staple _____

41 opulent _____

42 treacherous _____

43 exert _____

44 compulsory _____

45 persecute _____

46 imperative _____

47 turbulent _____

48 distort _____

49 pious _____

50 resilient _____

51 quench _____

52 sanction _____

53 supple _____

54 peripheral _____

55 disperse _____

56 repel _____

57 drawback _____

58 encompass _____

59 exemplary _____

60 solicitous _____

61	타락		91	독점	
62	비난, 탄핵		92	천정, 절정	
63	유연한		93	요점, 요지	
64	압축(압박)하다		94	모이다, 군집하다	
65	(가벼운) 사고		95	배치, 배열	
66	참다, 인내하다		96	불리한, 반대의	
67	경계하는		97	구식의, 진부한	
68	불법 침입하다		98	어슬렁거리다	
69	위약		99	가까운, 근접한	
70	위증, 거짓말		100	혼잡, 정체	
71	음모를 꾸미다		101	단조로움	
72	사소한, 천박한		102	영양분	
73	애도		103	악의 있는	
74	혹평하다		104	무정부주의자	
75	위조의		105	통합(합병)하다	
76	끼워 넣다		106	비유적인	
77	압축(응축)하다		107	불굴의	
78	골절		108	통치자	
79	퇴화하는		109	불모의, 불임의	
80	검소한, 간소한		110	망상, 허상	
81	끊임없는		111	침식(부식)하다	
82	침울한, 흐린		112	진부한, 흔한	
83	소란, 소동		113	미리 계획하다	
84	괴로워하다		114	명백한	
85	시련, 고난		115	토착의, 원산의	
86	다음의		116	떠나게 하다	
87	만족하는		117	혐오, 반감	
88	원한		118	멸망하다, 죽다	
89	헛된		119	분명한	
90	기민한, 재빠른		120	하위의, 하급자	

Part 3

01 breakthrough [bréikθrù:]
n. 약진, 도약, 돌파구

a new and important development

[syn] progress, development, advance   [ant] regress

When he visited North Korea, many people expected a breakthrough in the stalled six party talks.

02 cessation [seséiʃən]
n. 중단, 정지

an ending or stopping

[v] cease 그치다, 멈추다

[syn] ending, cease, halt   [ant] commencement, beginning, start

Despite the cessation of brain activity, the heart will continue to beat for a limited period of time.

03 innumerable [injú:mərəbəl]
a. 무수한, 수많은

too many to be counted

[n] innumeracy 헤아릴 수 없음

[syn] countless, numerous, many, myriad   [ant] few, scant, little

She purchased an innumerable number of stamps during her lifetime.

04 systematic [sìstəmǽtik]
a. 조직적인, 체계적인

carried our according a fixed plan

[v] systematize 조직화하다

[syn] orderly, methodical, standardized   [ant] chaotic, disorderly

We need a systematic survey to meet what our customers want.

05 monetary [mánətəri]
a. 금전상의, 돈의

relating to money

[n] monetarism 통화주의   [v] monetize 화폐로 주조하다

[syn] financial, pecuniary, budgetary, fiscal

The monetary policy of the Chairman of the U.S. Federal Reserve is essentially a laissez-faire form of management.

06 incredulous [inkrédʒələs]
a. 믿지 않는, 의심 많은

showing disbelief

[a] incredible 대단한, 믿기 어려운   [n] incredulity 믿기 어려움

[syn] unconvinced, skeptical, doubting   [ant] convinced, sure

They were incredulous at Galileo's assertions that the Earth was not the center of the solar system.

---

01 그가 북한을 방문했을 때 많은 사람이 교착상태에 빠진 6자 회담의 돌파구를 기대했다. 02 뇌 활동은 멈췄어도 심장은 일정 기간 계속 뛸 것이다. 03 그녀는 평생동안 수많은 우표를 수집했다. 04 고객들의 욕구를 충족시키기 위해 체계적인 조사가 필요하다. 05 미 연방준비제도 이사회 의장의 금융정책은 본질적으로 자유 방임주의 형태의 관리이다. 06 그들은 지구가 태양계의 중심이 아니라는 갈릴레오의 주장을 믿지 않았다.

07 mortal [mɔ́ːrtl]
a. 죽음을 면할 수 없는, 치명적인

not living forever
n mortality 죽음을 면할 수 없는 운명
syn grave, deadly, dire, extreme

Soldiers who got mortal wounds were common in military hospitals with unsanitary conditions.

08 gullible [gʌ́ləbəl]
a. 잘 속는

easily deceived or persuaded to believe something
a gullish 바보 같은 n gullibility 잘 속음
syn innocent, naive, unsuspecting, trusting ant suspicious, untrusting

His students took advantage of his gullible manner, but only in the most harmless of ways.

09 circumspect [sə́ːrkəmspèkt]
a. 조심성 있는, 신중한

very cautious
a circumspective 주의 깊은, 신중한
syn cautious, vigilant, wary, careful ant bold, rash, reckless

The campers are to be especially circumspect when they cook in the mountain.

10 allocate [ǽləkèit]
v. 배분하다, 할당하다

to give out in designated amounts
n allocation 배당, 배급, 할당
syn assign, give, designate, allot

Revenue sharing enabled the U.S. Federal Government to allocate a set amount of money to each of the States.

11 alleviate [əlíːvièit]
v. 완화시키다, 경감시키다

to relieve pain
n alleviation 경감, 완화
syn relieve, mitigate, allay, ease ant aggravate, intensify, increase

He used meditation to alleviate his daily stress.

12 prosecute [prásəkjùːt]
v. 기소하다, 고소하다

to bring up on charges
v prosecution 기소, 고발
syn indict, summon, sue ant pardon, defend, exonerate

He was being prosecuted for disturbing the peace with his bevy of howling hunting dogs.

13 incorporate [inkɔ́ːrpərèit]
v. 합치다, 법인으로 만들다

to unite into a whole
n incorporation 법인, 회사 a incorporated 법인조직의
syn form, blend, associate, charter ant exclude, end, separate

His latest novel incorporates all the aspects of earlier works.

---

07 비위생적인 병원에서 치명적인 부상을 당한 군인들은 흔했다. 08 학생들은 그의 잘 속는 성격을 이용하지만 악의는 전혀 없다. 09 캠핑하는 사람들은 산에서 취사를 할 때 특히 조심해야 한다. 10 세입 교부는 미 연방정부가 일정액을 각 주에 배분하도록 해준다. 11 그는 일상의 스트레스를 완화시키기 위해 명상을 한다. 12 마구 짖어대는 그의 사냥개들이 평화로움을 방해해서 그는 기소 당했다. 13 그의 최근 소설은 초기 작품들의 모든 것을 다 통합하고 있다.

14 ameliorate [əmíːljərèit]

v. 개선하다, 향상시키다

to make or get better

n amelioration 개량, 개선   a ameliorative 개선의

syn lighten, help, relieve, mitigate   ant exacerbate, worsen, harm

The ointment they made can also ameliorate the effects of other types of skin rashes as well.

---

15 incriminate [inkrímənèit]

v. 죄를 씌우다, 연루 시키다

to charge a crime upon someone

n incrimination 죄를 씌움

syn blame, name, attribute, charge   ant vindicate, exonerate, absolve

He was incriminated in the political scandal based on tapes recording his rivals' conversations.

---

16 coagulate [kouǽgjəlèit]

v. 응고하다, 딱딱해지다

to become clotted

n coagulation 응고, 응고물

syn clot, congeal, thicken, solidify   ant dilute, thin, liquefy

The stew cooled in the refrigerator began to coagulate, leaving a layer of fat at the top of the pot.

---

17 forsake [fərséik]

v. 버리다

to quit or leave entirely

a forsaken 버림받은, 고독한

syn abandon, spurn, jettison   ant keep

A good captain will not forsake anyone on his ship if it is sinking.

---

18 allege [əlédʒ]

v. 단언하다, 우기다, 진술하다

to declare something

n allegation 주장, 진술   ad allegedly 주장 한 바에 의하면

syn claim, declare, testify

They were alleged to have been killed by indigenous people while attempting to cross the river.

---

19 allure [əlúər]

v. 매혹하다, 꾀다

n. 매력

to attract or tempt by something flattering

n allurement 유혹

syn attract, appeal, entice   ant repulse

They allured people to buy their products imported from Japan.

The allure of self-employment is the ability to set your own work hours.

---

14 그들이 만든 연고가 다른 타입의 피부 발진도 개선시킬 수 있다. 15 그는 자신의 경쟁자들의 대화를 녹음한 테이프 때문에 정치 스캔들에 연루되었다. 16 냉장고에서 식힌 스프는 냄비 윗부분에 기름 층을 남기며 응고하기 시작했다. 17 훌륭한 선장은 배가 가라앉고 있어도 배에 탑승한 어느 누구도 포기하지 않을 것이다. 18 그들은 강을 건너려다 원주민에 의해 살해당했다고 전해졌다. 19 그들은 사람들에게 일본에서 수입된 상품을 구매하도록 유혹했다. 자기 사업의 매력은 일하는 시간을 스스로 정할 수 있다는 것이다.

20 enervate [énərvèit]
v. 약하게 하다, 기운을 빼앗다

to deprive of energy or strength

n enervation 원기상실, 쇠약

syn tire, weaken, exhaust　ant strengthen, activate, invigorate

The soldiers were further enervated by poor food and water distribution during the march.

21 allude [əlúːd]
v. 암시하다, 넌지시 말하다

to suggest something

n allusion 암시　a allusive 암시적인, 넌지시 말하는

syn refer, insinuate, suggest, hint　ant advertise, announce, declare

The manager was alluding to several complaints lodged by customers.

22 denote [dinóut]
v. 뜻하다, 의미하다

to mean

n denotation 표시, 지시

syn mean, make, stand for　ant connote, imply

The markers standing on the pavement denoted the number of miles left in the race.

23 detach [ditǽtʃ]
v. 떼어놓다, 분리하다

to separate one thing from another

n detachment 분리, 이탈　a detachable 분리할 수 있는

syn disconnect, separate, sever, divide　ant connect, couple, join

The accident left him blind in one eye as the force of the collision detached his retina.

24 subside [səbsáid]
v. 가라앉다, 진정되다

to settle down

n subsidence 함몰, 침전

syn settle, dip, slip, drop　ant rise, gain, unsettle

After nearly two days, his fever finally began to subside.

25 covet [kʌ́vit]
v. 탐내다

to yearn for something belonging to someone else

a covetous 몹시 탐내는

syn desire, want, crave　ant reject, ignore, spurn

She coveted the old black and white photographs which would help her reminisce about her days in Korea.

---

20 군인들은 행군하는 동안 열악한 음식과 물 배급으로 더욱 지쳤다. 21 매니저는 고객들에 의해 제기된 불만들을 넌지시 말했다. 22 도로 표지판은 경주에서 남은 마일 수를 보여주었다. 23 충돌할 때 충격으로 망막이 떨어져 그의 한 쪽 눈이 실명되었다. 24 거의 이틀 후에야 그의 열이 내리기 시작했다. 25 그녀는 한국에서 보낸 시절을 기억하는 데 도움을 준 흑백사진을 탐냈다.

Exercise

Word Check 각 단어의 뜻으로 알맞은 것을 찾아 연결하시오.

01 mortal   (a) to mention something indirectly

02 breakthrough   (b) to sink to a lower level

03 allege   (c) to claim or declare something to be the case

04 subside   (d) any significant or sudden advance or discovery

05 allude   (e) certain to die at some future time

Syn & Ant Check 주어진 단어의 동의어, 반의어를 골라 쓰시오.

congeal	strengthen	mean	doubting	worsen
reckless	relieve	countless	separate	keep

06 incredulous = _____

07 denote = _____

08 coagulate = _____

09 alleviate = _____

10 innumerable = _____

11 ameliorate ↔ _____

12 circumspect ↔ _____

13 forsake ↔ _____

14 incorporate ↔ _____

15 enervate ↔ _____

Sentence Practice 문장을 읽고 빈칸에 알맞은 단어를 고르시오.

16 As children we are all taught that it is wrong to _____ the possessions of others.

ⓐ allure   ⓑ covet   ⓒ allege   ⓓ detach

17 The trustees pledged their services to the company without any expectation of _____ gain.

ⓐ systematic   ⓑ monetary   ⓒ mortal   ⓓ innumerable

18 Being naive is perhaps excusable compared to the stigma attached to being _____.

ⓐ gullible   ⓑ mortal   ⓒ allure   ⓓ monetary

19 The city council was quick to _____ funds for the ambitious water supply project.

ⓐ coagulate   ⓑ subside   ⓒ forsake   ⓓ allocate

20 The move to _____ the accused was unexplainably delayed and allowed him to escape the trial.

ⓐ covet   ⓑ allude   ⓒ alleviate   ⓓ prosecute

01 intent [intént]
n. 의도, 의향
a. 집중하는

something that is intended

ⁿ intention 의향, 의도 a intentional 인도적인, 계획된

syn purpose, aim, objective, plan

The manager's intent was to completely refurbish the old hotel.

The new president said that he would be intent on reviving the economy.

02 coalition [kòuəlíʃən]
n. 합동, 연합

a group or partnership

syn alliance, merger, consolidation, partnership

The Warsaw Pact created a coalition designed to counterbalance the North Atlantic Treaty Organization(NATO).

03 misgiving [misgíviŋ]
n. 불안, 걱정

a feeling of worry or doubt

v misgive 염려되다, 걱정되다

syn worry, hesitation, uncertainty, doubt ant certainty, confidence

Dr. James had misgivings about promoting his assistant.

04 equity [ékwəti]
n. 공평, 공명

fair condition or treatment

a equitable 공평한, 공정한

syn fairness, impartiality ant discrimination, bias, partiality

The king spoke of equity between all races regardless of their skin color.

05 morbid [mɔ́:rbid]
a. 병적인, 무시무시한

displaying an unhealthy interest in unpleasant things

ⁿ morbidity 병적상태

syn nasty, sick, grisly, abnormal

Stella has a morbid fascination with horror movies.

06 ingenious [indʒí:njəs]
a. 영리한, 재치 있는

showing or having skill, originality and inventive cleverness

ⁿ ingenuity 발명의 재주, 독창력

syn clever, creative, innovative, brilliant

A rain barrel is a simple yet ingenious way to obtain water.

---

01 그 매니저의 의도는 낡은 호텔을 새롭게 개장하는 것이다. 대통령은 경제회복에 전념할 것이라고 말했다. 02 바르샤바 조약은 북대서양 조약기구를 견제하기 위해 형성된 연합이다. 03 James 박사는 그의 조수가 승진하는 것에 불안해했다. 04 왕은 피부색에 상관없이 모든 인종간의 평등함을 말했다. 05 Stella는 공포 영화에 병적인 관심을 가지고 있다. 06 빗물을 받는 통은 단순하지만 물을 얻을 수 있는 영리한 방법이다.

07 lucrative [lúːkrətiv]
a. 득이 되는, 이익이 남는

producing a good profit

n lucre 이득

syn productive, gainful, profitable   ant unprofitable, unproductive

The automobile company has a plan to set up a branch in Spain to enter the lucrative European market.

08 inapt [inǽpt]
a. 적합하지 않은

not appropriate

n inaptitude 적당하지 않음, 부적당

syn inappropriate, unfit, irrelevant   ant appropriate, suitable, relevant

The mower you bought was so small that it was inapt for mowing the company lawn.

09 extrinsic [ekstrínsik]
a. 외부의, 비본질적인

not being a basic part

syn alien, outer, foreign, outside   ant intrinsic, familiar, integral

Most of his motivation for going to medical school was due to extrinsic pressure, especially from his father.

10 enigmatic [ènigmǽtik]
a. 알 수 없는, 불가사의한

hard to understand

n enigma 수수께끼   v enigmatize 수수께끼로 만들다

syn mysterious, puzzling, unfathomable   ant clear, obvious, plain

The diagrams are quite enigmatic and can be perplexing to the engineers.

11 stagnant [stǽgnənt]
a. 고여있는, 발전 없는

not flowing or circulating

v stagnate 흐르지 않다, 썩다   n stagnation 침체, 불경기

syn motionless, standing, inert   ant active, flowing, rushing

Stagnant pools are prime breeding grounds for mosquitoes.

12 mundane [mʌ́ndein]
a. 평범한, 일상적인

very ordinary, pertinent to this world

n mundanity 현세, 속세

syn ordinary, commonplace, basic   ant uncommon, extraordinary

As the newest recruit to the law firm, his first tasks were fairly mundane.

13 preliminary [prilímənèri]
a. 예비의, 준비의

occurring at the beginning

syn first, introductory, initial, opening   ant last, concluding, ending

Preliminary studies suggest the medication has an anti-cancer effect.

---

07 그 회사는 채산성이 높은 유럽 시장에 진출하기 위해 스페인에 지사를 세울 계획을 가지고 있다. 08 당신이 구매한 잔디 깎는 기계는 너무 작아서 회사 잔디를 깎는 데는 부적합하다. 09 의대에 가겠다는 그의 동기는 주로 외부적인 압력, 특히 그의 아빠 때문이었다. 10 그 도표는 정말 이해할 수 없는 것이어서 기술자들에게는 당황스러울 수도 있다. 11 고여있는 웅덩이는 모기들의 주된 번식지이다. 12 법률회사의 신입직원으로 그의 첫 번째 임무는 매우 평범한 것이었다. 13 예비 검사 결과 그 약은 항암 효과가 있는 것으로 나타났다.

14 arbitrary [ɑ́:rbitrὲri]
a. 제멋대로의, 임의의

happening by chance
[syn] subjective, random, erratic [ant] supported, rational, reasonable

To conduct our study, an arbitrary group of people are selected, and they are asked a series of questions related to the study.

15 embody [embάdi]
v. 나타내다, 구체화하다

to stand for
[n] embodiment 구체화
[syn] exemplify, personify, symbolize

It embodies all the rules you have to keep while you are attending the school.

16 esteem [istí:m]
v. 존경하다, 존중하다
n. 존중, 존경

to adore something or somebody
[syn] admire, prize, adore, worship [ant] detest, abhor, hate

We esteemed Ms. Robbins for her devotion to the poor in our community.

He held Mr. James, his basketball coach, in high esteem.

17 rebuke [ribjú:k]
v. 꾸짖다
n. 비난, 질책

to scold for misbehaving
[syn] admonish, scold, reprimand, chide [ant] praise, compliment,

The headmaster rebuked him for failure to recite the school motto when requested.

Tommy got a rebuke from his teacher for being late for school.

18 censor [sénsər]
v. 검열하다
n. 검열관

to examine something
[a] censorable 검열에 걸릴만한
[syn] ban, conceal, edit, delete [ant] sanction, allow, approve

The radio station managers were fired as they failed to properly censor a broadcast against the government.

I am not sure if the film will get past the censor.

19 comply [kəmplái]
v. 응하다, 따르다

to agree to follow something
[n] compliance 응낙, 응함
[syn] agree, adhere, submit [ant] disobey, resist, disregard

Pilots must comply with aeronautical rules if they wish to retain their licenses.

---

14 우리 연구를 시행하기 위해 임의적으로 사람을 뽑아 연구에 관련된 일련의 문제들을 물어 볼 것이다. 15 여러분이 학교를 다니는 동안 지켜야 할 규칙들이 이 곳에 수록되어 있다. 16 우리는 우리 사회의 가난한 사람을 위해 헌신한 Robbins 부인을 존경한다. 그는 그의 농구코치인 James 씨를 매우 존경했다. 17 그는 학교 교훈을 외우지 못해 교장선생님께 혼났다. Tommy는 지각했다고 선생님에게 꾸중을 들었다. 18 정부에 반하는 방송을 제대로 검열하지 못했기 때문에 라디오 방송국 관리자들이 해임되었다. 나는 그 영화가 검열관을 통과할지 확신이 서질 않는다. 19 조종사는 자격증을 유지하기 위해 항공 규칙을 따라야 한다.

20 renounce [rináuns]
v. 버리다, 포기하다

to give something up
n renunciation 포기, 폐기
syn abandon, leave, abdicate   ant acquire, retain, receive

It takes great courage for a member to renounce his or her faith in the religious community.

21 perplex [pərpléks]
v. 당황하게 하다

to puzzle someone with difficulties
a perplexed 당황한, 난처한   n perplexity 당황, 곤혹
syn confuse, puzzle, baffle, stump

Simon studied the math problem for over 5 minutes, and he was perplexed by its difficulty.

22 depreciate [deprí:ʃièit]
v. 가치가 하락하다

to lose original value
n depreciation 가치하락
syn devalue, erode, decay, lessen   ant increase, grow

The U.S. dollar has depreciated markedly against the London pound in recent years.

23 encroach [enkróutʃ]
v. 침해하다, 침입하다

advance beyond the limit
n encroachment 잠식, 침략
syn invade, intrude, trespass, infringe

You should not encroach on the right of another.

24 converge [kənvə́:rdʒ]
v. 한 점에 집중하다, 모이다

to meet at one point
a convergent 점차 집합하는   n convergence 한 점으로 모임
syn concentrate, gather, merge, unite   ant diverge, disperse

Two dogs converged momentarily and tugged on one end of the toy.

25 procrastinate [proukrǽstənèit]
v. 꾸물거리다, 지연시키다

to put off doing something
n procrastination 지연, 연기
syn put off, delay, defer, postpone

She complained to me that he constantly procrastinated when it came to household chores.

---

20 종교 집단에서 구성원이 자신의 신념을 버리는 데는 대단한 용기가 필요하다. 21 Simon은 5분이 넘게 수학문제를 풀어봤지만 어려워서 당황했다. 22 미국 달러는 최근 몇 년 동안 영국의 파운드에 비해 가치가 현저하게 하락했다. 23 너는 다른 사람의 권리를 침해해서는 안된다. 24 두마리 개가 갑자기 몰려와 동시에 한 장난감 끝을 서로 잡아 당겼다. 25 집안일에 있어서는 그가 끊임없이 꾸물거린다고 그녀가 내게 불만을 토로했다.

Exercise

Word Check 각 단어의 뜻으로 알맞은 것을 찾아 연결하시오.

01 embody   (a) something which is aimed at
02 intent   (b) to give a concrete form
03 morbid   (c) occurring at the beginning
04 extrinsic   (d) suggesting an unhealthy mental state
05 preliminary   (e) not a basic part or quality

Syn & Ant Check 주어진 단어의 동의어, 반의어를 골라 쓰시오.

baffle	invade	extraordinary	compliment	delay
fairness	appropriate	mysterious	increase	disobey

06 perplex   = _____   11 inapt   ↔ _____
07 enigmatic   = _____   12 depreciate ↔ _____
08 procrastinate = _____   13 rebuke   ↔ _____
09 encroach   = _____   14 comply   ↔ _____
10 equity   = _____   15 mundane   ↔ _____

Sentence Practice 문장을 읽고 빈칸에 알맞은 단어를 고르시오.

16 Diana was filled with _____ after hearing of the trouble near her husband's office.
    ⓐ misgiving   ⓑ coalition   ⓒ intent   ⓓ equity

17 Children sometimes come up with _____ solutions to the most complex problems.
    ⓐ morbid   ⓑ extrinsic   ⓒ arbitrary   ⓓ ingenious

18 A careful study of the stock market convinced Claire that it was a(n) _____ field of business.
    ⓐ lucrative   ⓑ inapt   ⓒ enigmatic   ⓓ preliminary

19 Many people invest in gold to ensure that their assets do not _____ in times of economic recessions.
    ⓐ perplex   ⓑ converge   ⓒ depreciate   ⓓ esteem

20 Jim's tendency to _____ causes him to be a liability during a crisis of any sort.
    ⓐ censor   ⓑ procrastinate   ⓒ comply   ⓓ encroach

Day 13

01 jargon [dʒáːrgən]
n. 특수용어, 전문어

non-standard language such as slang or descriptive terminology
[v] jargonize 뜻을 알 수 없는 말을 쓰다
[syn] slang, lingo, terminology [ant] standard language

They used a lot of corporate jargon during the meeting which I couldn't understand.

02 anecdote [ǽnikdòut]
n. 일화

a short interesting or funny story
[a] anecdotal 일화의, 일화적인
[syn] story, report, account

Sometimes my uncle told me anecdotes about his childhood in Korea.

03 anesthetic [ænəsθétik]
n. 마취제
a. 마취의, 무감각한

a drug that causes loss of sensation
[v] anesthetize 마취시키다, 마취하다 [n] anesthetist 마취 전문의
[syn] narcotics, painkiller

She took an anesthetic before an operation for colon cancer.

04 avalanche [ǽvəlæntʃ]
n. 눈사태

a large amount of snow sliding from a mountain
[a] avalanchine 거대한, 눈사태와 같은
[syn] snow-slide, landslide

Many people living at the foot of the mountain were killed by an avalanche last night.

05 ebullient [ibuljənt]
a. (열정이) 넘치는, 열광적인

joyously unrestrained
[n] ebullience (감정 등의) 격발,
[syn] joyous, exuberant [ant] lifeless, spiritless

The actress was ebullient when she received the best actress award.

06 precarious [prikέəriəs]
a. 불안정한, 믿을 수 없는

uncertain or not secure
[syn] dangerous, insecure, unsure [ant] secure, stable

His life in a refugee camp was always precarious.

---

01 그들은 회의를 하면서 내가 이해할 수 없는 많은 기업 전문 용어를 사용했다. 02 때때로 나의 삼촌은 한국에서 보낸 자신의 어린시절을 내게 얘기했다. 03 그녀는 대장암 수술 전에 마취제를 맞았다. 04 어젯밤에 산 기슭에 사는 많은 사람들이 눈사태로 사망했다. 05 그 여배우는 여우주연상을 받을 때 매우 활기차 있었다. 06 피난촌에서 그의 삶은 항상 불안했다.

07 prevalent [prévələnt]
a. 널리 퍼져있는, 유행하는

widely existing in a particular place

Ⓥ prevail 널리 퍼지다　ⓝ prevalence 널리 퍼짐, 유행

syn common, general, usual　ant rare

The computer game that my sister is playing now is prevalent among teenagers.

08 medium [mí:diəm]
a. 중간의
n. 수단, 매개물

neither large nor small

syn middle, average　ant extraordinary

This lantern takes three medium sized batteries.

The world becomes smaller due to the development of the medium of communication.

09 avid [ǽvid]
a. 열망하는, 욕심 많은

eager or very enthusiastic

ⓝ avidity 욕망, 탐욕

syn desirous, greedy

People were avid for news of the victory of their soccer team.

10 auspicious [ɔːspíʃəs]
a. 행운의, 길조의

indicating that something will be successful

ⓝ auspice 길조, 전조

syn favorable, bright, fortunate　ant inauspicious, unfortunate

In Korea, the dream about pigs is an auspicious sign.

11 barbaric [bɑːrbǽrik]
a. 야만적인, 야만인의

without civilizing influences

ⓝ barbarian 미개인, 야만인　ⓝ barbarism 미개

syn savage, animalistic, uncivilized　ant civilized, merciful

The way he treats animals is very barbaric and cruel.

12 adept [ədépt]
a. 숙련된, 정통한

very skillful at something

syn expert, skillful, proficient　ant unskilled

They are adept at handling children who are lost in a shopping mall.

13 abstain [əbstéin]
v. 절제하다, 그만두다

to avoid doing something

ⓝ abstention 절제, 금주　ⓐ abstentious 절제하는

syn refrain, desist　ant have, take, take in

The doctor advised him to abstain from eating meat because the level of cholesterol in his blood was very high.

---

07 내 여동생이 하고 있는 컴퓨터 게임은 십대들에게 인기 있는 게임이다. 08 이 랜턴은 중간 크기의 건전지 3개가 들어간다. 통신수단의 발달로 세상은 점점 가까워지고 있다. 09 사람들은 그들 축구 팀의 승리소식을 갈망했다. 10 한국에서 돼지 꿈은 좋은 징조이다. 11 그가 동물을 다루는 방법은 매우 야만적이고 잔인하다. 12 그들은 쇼핑 몰에서 길을 잃은 어린이를 다루는데 능숙하다. 13 혈중 콜레스테롤 수치가 높아서 의사는 그에게 고기를 절제하라고 권유했다.

14 **deride** [diráid]
v. 비웃다, 조롱하다

to laugh at someone
ⓝ derision 비웃음　ⓐ derisive 조롱하는
ⓢⓨⓝ insult, jeer, mock, ridicule　ⓐⓝⓣ compliment, flatter, praise
The colleague you deride today may one day be your supervisor.

15 **kindle** [kíndl]
v. 불 붙이다, 타오르다

to get something to start
ⓝ kindler 불쏘시개
ⓢⓨⓝ rouse, encourage　ⓐⓝⓣ douse, dampen
Happiness kindled in her eyes when she took the diamond ring from her fiance.

16 **entreat** [intríːt]
v. 간청하다, 탄원하다, 부탁하다

ask for or request earnestly
ⓝ entreaty 간청, 탄원
ⓢⓨⓝ plead, implore, beg, urge　ⓐⓝⓣ command, demand, require
He entreated his listeners for donations to the hospital that would be built for the children suffering from leukemia.

17 **enunciate** [inʌ́nsièit]
v. ～을 명확히 발음하다

express or state clearly
ⓝ enunciation 명확한 진술
ⓢⓨⓝ speak, say, voice, utter　ⓐⓝⓣ mumble, mutter, whisper
Tom enunciated each word for his young daughter.

18 **abhor** [æbhɔ́ːr]
v. 싫어하다, 혐오하다

to hate someone or something
ⓝ abhorrence 증오, 혐오　ⓐ abhorrent 질색인, 싫어하는
ⓢⓨⓝ loathe, hate, abominate　ⓐⓝⓣ like, love
My sister abhors mosquitoes disturbing her sleep.

19 **idolize** [áidəlàiz]
v. 숭배하다, 우상화 하다

to admire someone or something too much
ⓝ idolism 우상화
ⓢⓨⓝ worship, revere, admire　ⓐⓝⓣ disparage, condemn, mock
Many teenagers idolize movie stars these days.

20 **hail** [heil]
v. 환호하다, 소리치다

to get someone's attention by shouting
ⓝ hailer 소리지르는 사람, 확성기
ⓢⓨⓝ call, acclaim, cheer
When her car broke down on the highway, she attempted to hail cars as they passed.

---

14 오늘 네가 비웃는 동료가 언젠가 너의 상사가 될 지도 모른다. 15 그녀가 약혼자에게 다이아몬드 반지를 받았을 때 그녀의 눈은 행복으로 빛났다. 16 그는 백혈병으로 고생하는 아이들을 위해 지어질 병원을 위해 기부하라고 청중들에게 간청했다. 17 Tom은 어린 딸에게 각 단어를 명확하게 발음해줬다. 18 내 여동생은 수면을 방해하는 모기를 매우 싫어한다. 19 요즈음 많은 십대들이 영화배우를 우상화한다. 20 그녀의 차가 고속도로에서 고장 나자, 지나가는 차량에게 소리쳤다.

21 avert [əvə́ːrt]
v. 외면하다, 피하다

to prevent something unpleasant, to turn away
ⓐ aversive 피하는, 혐오의
syn avoid, evade, prevent

They averted their eyes from the terrible accident that took place on the road to the airport.

22 camouflage [kǽməflàːʒ]
v. 위장하다
n. 위장

to conceal the identity of something or someone
syn disguise, cover, conceal   ant show, display

Some animals camouflage themselves by changing the colors of their body when they meet their enemy.

A chameleon is known for being good at camouflage.

23 fabricate [fǽbrikèit]
v. 꾸며대다, 제작하다

to make something up or to lie
ⓝ fabrication 제작, 제조   ⓝ fabricant 제조업자
syn manufacture, make-up, invent   ant destroy, be honest

He fabricated a lot of information about the war to avoid his responsibility for killing civilians.

The company fabricates many different types of electronic products and exports them to Europe.

24 censure [sénʃər]
v. 비난하다
n. 비난, 책망

to blame or to express disapproval
ⓐ censurable 비난할만한
syn reprimand, chastise, condemn   ant praise, laud, appreciate

His boss censured him for the negligence of his responsibility.

They expressed strong censure for his taking bribery and asked him to quit office.

25 commence [kəméns]
v. 시작하다, 착수하다

to begin or start
ⓝ commencement 시작, 개시
syn begin, start, initiate   ant end, finish, terminate

The parade commenced with a blast from the cannon sitting in the town square.

---

21 그들은 공항으로 가는 도로에서 발생한 끔찍한 사고 현장에서 눈을 돌렸다. 22 일부 동물들은 적을 만나면 신체의 색을 바꾸어 위장을 한다. 카멜레온은 변장을 잘하는 동물로 알려져 있다. 23 그는 민간인을 살해했다는 책임을 피하기 위해 전쟁에 관련된 많은 정보를 조작했다. 그 회사는 여러 다른 종류의 전자제품을 만들어 유럽에 수출한다. 24 그의 상사는 그가 책임 회피를 한다고 비난했다. 그들은 그의 뇌물수수에 대해 강하게 비난했으며 그에게 사임을 촉구했다. 25 행진은 마을 광장에 있는 대포의 축포와 함께 시작되었다.

Exercise

Score / 20

Word Check 각 단어의 뜻으로 알맞은 것을 찾아 연결하시오.

01 jargon   (a) to love someone or something too much.

02 kindle   (b) to start burning something

03 idolize   (c) something intermediate in nature

04 medium   (d) the specialized vocabulary of a particular profession

05 enunciate   (e) to pronounce words clearly

Syn & Ant Check 주어진 단어의 동의어, 반의어를 골라 쓰시오.

hate	plead	rare	reprimand	disguise
civilized	unfortunate	skillful	terminate	spiritless

06 adept   = _____   11 ebullient ↔ _____

07 abhor   = _____   12 prevalent ↔ _____

08 camouflage = _____   13 barbaric   ↔ _____

09 censure   = _____   14 auspicious ↔ _____

10 entreat   = _____   15 commence ↔ _____

Sentence Practice 문장을 읽고 빈칸에 알맞은 단어를 고르시오.

16 This biography's mix of _____ and advice makes for interesting reading.

    ⓐ anecdotes   ⓑ anesthetics   ⓒ jargons   ⓓ avalanches

17 The firefighting crew went all-out to _____ serious damage by trying to contain the fire.

    ⓐ fabricate   ⓑ kindle   ⓒ deride   ⓓ avert

18 Kelly is a(n) _____ wildlife photographer who devotes many weekends to snapping pictures in shady forests.

    ⓐ avid   ⓑ prevalent   ⓒ hail   ⓓ barbaric

19 Jason was unprepared for the _____ situations he faced during his investigation by the Internal Revenue Service.

    ⓐ auspicious   ⓑ medium   ⓒ precarious   ⓓ adept

20 The residents decided to _____ from voting in the local polls as a mark of protest.

    ⓐ enunciate   ⓑ idolize   ⓒ abstain   ⓓ hail

Day 14

01 contempt [kəntémpt]
n. 경멸, 모욕, 치욕

no respect for someone

ⓐ contemptible 경멸 할 만한

ⓢⓨⓝ hatred, disdain, scorn   ⓐⓝⓣ honor, respect, esteem

She showed her contempt by refusing to respond to his greetings.

---

02 jest [dʒest]
n. 농담, 익살

speaking without serious intention

ⓝ jester 농담하는 사람

ⓢⓨⓝ joke, mockery

Smith makes his students laugh with his jest.

---

03 dignity [dígnəti]
n. 존엄, 위엄

behavior which is calm, formal and admirable

ⓥ dignify 위엄있게 하다

ⓢⓨⓝ pride, self-esteem

Behave yourself if you want to keep your dignity.

---

04 complement [kámpləmənt]
n. 보충물, 보어
v. 보충하다, 보완하다

something that is added to make perfect

ⓐ complementary 보완적인

ⓢⓨⓝ supplement, accompaniment

We need some complements to finish the work by tomorrow.

The two lead actors complemented each other beautifully.

---

05 hypnotic [hipnátik]
a. 최면의, 최면술의

feeling like sleeping

ⓥ hypnotize 최면을 걸다   ⓝ hypnosis 최면

ⓢⓨⓝ narcotic, soporific

The spy who was in a hypnotic state said something to the special agent.

---

06 reticent [rétəsənt]
a. 과묵한, 말이 없는

not tending to talk too much

ⓝ reticence 과묵

ⓢⓨⓝ taciturn   ⓐⓝⓣ voluble, talkative

He decided to remain reticent about the political scandal.

---

01 그녀는 그의 인사에 대꾸하지 않는 방법으로 그에게 모욕감을 줬다. 02 Smith는 농담을 해서 그의 학생들을 웃긴다. 03 너의 품위를 지키려면 행동을 조심해라. 04 우리는 일을 내일까지 완성하기 위해 약간의 보완이 필요하다. 두 주연 배우는 서로를 아름답게 보완해주고 있다. 05 최면 상태에 있는 스파이가 비밀 요원에게 뭔가를 말했다. 06 그는 정치 스캔들에 대해 침묵하기로 했다.

07 myriad [míriəd]
a. 수많은, 무수한

a great number
[syn] countless, numerous [ant] few, scant
A myriad of people have attempted to enter the U.S.A illegally, but most of them have failed to cross the border.

08 stern [stə́:rn]
a. 엄한, 단호한

strict and severe
[syn] strict, authoritarian, tough [ant] friendly, genial
His excessively long lunches brought a stern warning from the boss.

09 legitimate [lidʒítəmit]
a. 합법적인, 정당한

correct according to the law
[n] legitimacy 적법, 합법성
[syn] rightful, accepted, genuine [ant] illegitimate, illegal, unauthorized
Her arguments to review the curriculum appeared legitimate.

10 manifest [mǽnəfèst]
a. 명백한, 분명한
v. 분명하게 하다, 명백히 하다

very clear to see
[syn] obvious, distinct, plain [ant] secret, hidden, undisclosed
His theories on black holes stood as accepted belief for nearly 30 years until a manifest error was found.
She manifested her opinion about the educational reform the new government would carry out.

11 gratify [grǽtəfài]
v. 만족시키다, 기쁘게 하다

to give satisfaction to
[n] gratification 만족감, 희열
[syn] please, satisfy, indulge, content [ant] dissatisfy, displease
Not gratified with his pension from the government, he is looking for a part time job.

12 procure [proukjúər]
v. 얻다, 획득하다

to obtain something
[n] procuration 획득, 조달
[syn] obtain, acquire
After some discussion, the collector procured the painting for an undisclosed sum.

13 constrain [kənstréin]
v. 강요하다, 억지로 ~하게하다

to force someone to do something
[n] constraint 강요, 압박 [a] constrained 강압적인, 강제적인
[syn] compel, restrain, inhibit [ant] free, release
His parents constrained him to join a reading club.

---

07 수 많은 사람들이 미국에 불법으로 입국하려고 하지만 대부분의 사람들이 국경을 넘는데 실패한다. 08 그가 지나치게 오랜 시간 동안 점심을 먹자 그의 상사가 엄중 경고를 했다. 09 커리큘럼을 다시 재고해야 한다는 그의 주장은 정당해 보인다. 10 블랙 홀에 대한 그의 이론은 명백한 에러가 발견될 때까지 30년 동안 사실로 받아들여졌다. 그녀는 새 정부가 실행할 교육개혁에 의견을 분명히 했다. 11 그는 정부로부터 받는 연금에 만족하지 못해서 임시 직업을 찾고 있다. 12 약간의 논의 후 그 수집가는 밝히지 않은 가격에 그 그림을 구입했다. 13 그의 부모는 그가 독서클럽에 가입하도록 강요했다.

14 curtail [kə:rtéil]
v. 줄이다, 생략하다

to reduce something in size, amount or number

n curtailment 단축, 삭감

syn decrease, diminish ant increase

The company has a plan to lay off its employees to curtail expenditures.

---

15 reiterate [ri:ítərèit]
v. 반복하다, 되풀이 하다

to repeat something in order to emphasize it

n reiteration 반복 a reiterant 되풀이 하여 말하는, 반복하는

syn repeat, iterate

They reiterated their claim that they didn't have any responsibility for the accident.

---

16 deceptive [diséptiv]
a. 속이는, 믿을 수 없는

tending to deceive

n deception 속임, 사기

syn dishonest, false, deceitful, sneaky ant honest, forthright, truthful

Home buyers should be careful to avoid falling for the deceptive sales tactics of some realtors.

---

17 comprehend [kàmprihénd]
v. 이해하다, 파악하다

to understand something

n comprehension 이해, 이해력 a comprehensive 이해력 있는

syn understand, apprehend ant misunderstand, misapprehend

They don't seem to comprehend how important this project is.

---

18 comprise [kəmpráiz]
v. 구성되다, 이루어지다

to form something or to consist of something

n comprisal 포함, 함유

syn form, constitute

The preparation committee is comprised of eleven members.

---

19 defer [difə́:r]
v. 미루다, 연기하다

to put off something

syn postpone, put off, delay ant hurry, rush, hasten

We deferred our departure until the hurricane was passed.

---

20 confine [kənfáin]
v. 제한하다, 한정하다

to keep something within a particular place

n confinement 감금, 한정

syn constrain, restrict, limit ant free, release

Let's confine today's discussion to this matter.

---

14 그 회사는 비용을 줄이기 위해 올해 직원을 해고할 계획을 가지고 있다. 15 그들은 사고에 아무런 책임 없다고 반복해서 주장했다. 16 주택 구매자들은 일부 부동산업자들의 기만적인 판매전략에 걸려들지 않도록 조심해야 한다. 17 그들은 이 프로젝트가 얼마나 중요한지 이해하지 못한 것 같다. 18 준비위원회는 11명으로 구성되어 있다. 19 우리는 태풍이 지나갈 때까지 출발을 미뤘다. 20 오늘 의제를 이 문제로 제한합시다.

21 conscript [kánskript]

v. 징집하다

n. 신병, 징집병

to make someone join the army

ⁿ conscription 징병제도

ˢʸⁿ draft

Young men and women are conscripted for as little as one year and as long as two years.

New conscripts will spend one month at a military training camp which is located southeast of Boston.

---

22 disregard [dìsrigá:rd]

v. 무시하다, 경시하다

n. 무시, 경시

not to show respect to someone or something

ᵃ disregardful 무관심한

ˢʸⁿ ignore, overlook, snub   ᵃⁿᵗ consider, regard

The driver disregarded his warning and drove his car toward the river whose level was too high to cross.

Their behavior showed a disregard for the school regulations.

---

23 differentiate [dìfərénʃièit]

v. 구별하다, 차별하다

to make a difference between things

ⁿ differentiation 차별, 구별   ᵃᵈ differently 다르게, 같지않게

ˢʸⁿ separate, discriminate, distinguish   ᵃⁿᵗ integrate

The company has to differentiate its products to survive in a competitive market.

---

24 convince [kənvíns]

v. 확신하다, 설득하다

to make someone believe or realize something

ⁿ conviction 확신

ˢʸⁿ assure, persuade

Jane convinced me that I could lose as much my weight as I want, if I went on a diet.

They made efforts to convince Iran to give up its development of nuclear weapons.

---

25 retaliate [ritǽlièit]

v. 복수하다, 보복하다

to get revenge

ⁿ retaliation 보복, 앙갚음   ᵃ retaliatory 보복의, 복수심이 강한

ˢʸⁿ avenge, revenge

They would retaliate if their military facilities were attacked by a foreign country.

---

21 젊은 남녀들이 짧게는 1년 길게는 2년 동안 군대에 징집된다. 신병들은 보스톤 남동쪽에 위치한 군사 훈련캠프에서 한 달을 보낼 것이다. 22 그 운전사는 그의 경고를 무시하고 수위가 높아 건널 수 없는 강쪽으로 차를 몰았다. 그들의 행동은 학교 규정을 무시하는 처사이다. 23 그 회사는 치열한 시장에서 살아남기 위해 제품을 차별화해야 한다. 24 내가 다이어트를 하면 내가 원하는 만큼 살을 뺄 수 있다고 Jane이 나를 확신시켰다. 그들은 이란이 핵무기 개발을 포기하도록 설득하려고 애썼다. 25 만약에 그들의 군사시설이 외적으로부터 공격을 받는다면 그들은 곧 보복할 것이다.

Exercise

Word Check   각 단어의 뜻으로 알맞은 것을 찾아 연결하시오.

01 manifest   (a) to show or display something clearly

02 curtail   (b) extremely strict

03 stern   (c) to reduce or to cut short

04 reticent   (d) not to speak too much

05 defer   (e) to put off something

Syn & Ant Check   주어진 단어의 동의어, 반의어를 골라 쓰시오.

compel	few	revenge	integrate	respect
misunderstand	supplement	rightful	dissatisfy	ignore

06 disregard   = _____

07 legitimate   = _____

08 constrain   = _____

09 retaliate   = _____

10 complement = _____

11 gratify   ↔ _____

12 myriad   ↔ _____

13 comprehend ↔ _____

14 contempt   ↔ _____

15 differentiate ↔ _____

Sentence Practice   문장을 읽고 빈칸에 알맞은 단어를 고르시오.

16 He feels it would undermine his _____ to accept any kind of charity.

    ⓐ jest   ⓑ dignity   ⓒ complement   ⓓ contempt

17 Katie's normally open and outgoing personality belies the fact that she's surprisingly _____ about her childhood.

    ⓐ myriad   ⓑ stern   ⓒ hypnotic   ⓓ reticent

18 The valley was full of flowers in a _____ of colors that were spread out like an exotic carpet.

    ⓐ reticent   ⓑ myriad   ⓒ legitimate   ⓓ manifest

19 Many countries make it compulsory for young men over 18 to be _____ into the army.

    ⓐ conscripted   ⓑ confined   ⓒ reiterated   ⓓ comprised

20 The recent upgrade of the transportation system will help manufacturers _____ raw materials more easily.

    ⓐ convince   ⓑ curtail   ⓒ procure   ⓓ defer

01 hybrid [háibrid]

n. 잡종, 혼성물

a. 잡종의

a living things produced by two different types of species

n hybridity 잡종성

syn mixture, crossbreed   ant pureblood

The dog my father bought last month turned out to be a hybrid.

We are accustomed to a hybrid culture created by immigrants.

Many car owners have been considering converting to hybrid vehicles in order to reduce fuel costs.

02 subsidy [sʌ́bsidi]

n. 보조금, 장려금, 보상금

money given by a government or other authorities for financial support

a subsidiary 보조의, 부수적인   n subsidiarity 보조적임, 보완성

syn support, backing, funding

A subsidy will only be received if their parents' income is below the minimum cost of living.

03 guile [gail]

n. 교활, 책략

cunning or the way of deceiving

a guileless 악의가 없는, 성실한   a guileful 교활한, 음험한

syn trick, deception

If it had not been for her political guile, he couldn't have become a president.

04 posture [pástʃər]

n. 자세, 몸가짐, 형태

the way in which someone sits, stands or walks

v posturize 포즈를 취하다   a postural 자세의, 마음가짐의

syn attitude, stance

A sleeping posture is essential to keep us healthy.

05 extrovert [ékstrouvə̀ːrt]

n. 사교적인 사람, 외향적인 사람

a person who is very outgoing

a extroverted 외향성이 강한

ant introvert

He preferred to hire extroverts for his sales positions.

Teddy Roosevelt was one of the most extroverted U.S. presidents.

---

01 우리 아버지가 지난 주에 사온 개가 잡종으로 판명되었다. 우리는 이민자들에 의해 형성된 혼성문화에 익숙하다. 많은 자동차 소유자들이 연료비를 절감하기 위해 하이브리드 차량으로 바꿀 것을 고려하고 있다. 02 보조금은 부모의 수입이 최저 생계비 이하일 경우에만 받게될 것이다. 03 그녀의 정치적 술책이 없었다면 그는 대통령이 되지 못했을 것이다. 04 건강을 유지하는데 수면 자세가 중요하다. 05 그는 사교적인 사람을 영업부 직원으로 고용하는 것을 선호한다. 테디 루즈벨트는 가장 외향적인 미국 대통령들 중의 한 사람이었다.

06 maneuver [mənúːvər]
n. 책략
pl. 기동훈련

a military training exercise, a skillful plan to get something
n maneuverer 기동 훈련담당관　a maneuverable 조종할 수 있는
syn tactics

The army holds maneuvers in the Northern area once a month.

---

07 immaculate [imǽkjəlit]
a. 깨끗한, 순결한, 결점 없는

completely clean
n immaculateness 청결함, 티없음　ad immaculately 청결하게, 티없이
syn clean, faultless, perfect　ant dirty, corrupt

My dog sometimes makes a mess in the immaculate kitchen.

---

08 hectic [héktik]
a. 몹시 바쁜, 열광적인

feverish or full of rushed activity
n hecticness 광적임　ad hectically 광적으로, 격앙되어
syn feverish, agitated

Most people living in a big city want to escape their hectic life.

---

09 imminent [ímənənt]
a. 긴박한, 급박한

likely to happen soon
ad imminently 임박하여
syn impending, forthcoming　ant remote, distant

Some scientists said that the demise of the Earth is imminent.

---

10 sanitary [sǽnətèri]
a. 위생의, 청결한

related with keeping things clean
ad sanitarily 위생상, 위생적으로
syn healthful, hygienic　ant unsanitary, unhealthful

The government has a plan to improve poor sanitary conditions in rural areas.

---

11 equivocal [ikwívəkəl]
a. 불확실한, 모호한

unclear meanings
n equivocality 다의성, 애매함　ad equivocally 분명하지 않게, 수상하게
syn vague, ambiguous, unclear　ant unequivocal, clear

They didn't know if he could come to the party because he gave an equivocal answer to the invitation.

---

12 intricate [íntrəkit]
a. 복잡한, 난해한, 얽힌

having many detailed parts
n intricateness 얽힘, 복잡함　ad intricately 얽혀, 복잡하여
syn complex, involved　ant simple

This watch was made by a craftsman through an intricate process.

---

06 육군은 한 달에 한 번 북쪽 지역에서 기동훈련을 한다. 07 가끔 나의 개가 깨끗한 부엌을 어질러 놓는다. 08 도시에 사는 많은 사람들이 그들의 분주한 삶에서 벗어나고 싶어한다. 09 일부 과학자들은 지구의 종말이 임박했다고 말했다. 10 정부는 시골지역의 열악한 위생조건을 개선할 계획을 가지고 있다. 11 그가 초대에 모호하게 답변했기 때문에 그들은 그가 파티에 참석할지 어떨지 몰랐다. 12 이 시계는 복잡한 과정을 거쳐 장인에 의해 만들어졌다.

13 transient [trǽnʃənt]
a. 일시적인, 덧없는

existing for a short time

ad transiently 일시적으로, 단기 체류로   n transience 일시적임, 덧없음

syn temporary, fleeting   ant lasting, permanent

'Gypsy' is a term used to characterize a number of groups of transient people.

He was looking for permanent rather than transient employment.

---

14 exquisite [ikskwízit]
a. 아름다운, 훌륭한, 정교한

very beautiful or delicate

ad exquisitely 절묘하게, 정교하게

syn beautiful, lovely, perfect   ant inferior, flawed, imperfect

All of his works were so exquisite that we were surprised to see them.

---

15 infirm [infə́:rm]
a. 약한, 우유부단한

ill or weak, not strong

n infirmity 허약, 쇠약

syn sick, ill, ailing, unwell   ant healthy, well, fit

His infirm state has made it difficult for him to keep his speaking engagements.

---

16 obstinate [ábstənit]
a. 완고한, 고집 센

unwilling to change one's ideas

ad obstinately 완고하게, 완강하게   n obstinacy 완고함, 완강함

syn stubborn, inflexible   ant compliant

My boss is as obstinate as a mule and he doesn't listen to our opinion about the new project.

---

17 exuberant [igzú:bərənt]
a. 열광적인

filled with cheerful excitement

ad exuberantly 풍성하게, 생기에 가득 차게   n exuberance (활력 · 기쁨 따위의) 충만

syn enthusiastic, passionate   ant depressed, unexcited

An exuberant crowd welcomed the soccer team as they arrived at the airport.

---

18 latent [léitənt]
a. 잠재의, 잠복의, 숨어있는

not active or hidden

ad latently 숨어 있어, 잠재하여   n latency 숨어 있음, 잠재, 잠복

syn inactive, potential, dormant   ant active

If you exercise your latent abilities, you can finish this assignment by yourself.

---

13 'Gypsy'라는 용어는 자주 이사를 다니는 사람들을 묘사할 때 사용된다. 그는 일용직보다는 정규직을 찾고 있었다. 14 그의 작품들이 매우 훌륭해서 우리는 작품들을 보고 매우 놀랐다. 15 그의 병약한 상태 때문에 그가 연설 약속을 이행하는 것은 어렵게 되었다. 16 나의 상사는 정말 완강해서 새로운 프로젝트에 대한 우리의 견해를 듣지 않는다. 17 열광적인 군중들은 축구 팀이 공항에 도착하자 환영을 했다. 18 너의 잠재 능력을 발휘하면 스스로 이 일을 마칠 수 있을 것이다.

19 insolent [ínsələnt]
a. 오만한, 무례한, 건방진

not showing respect or rude
ad insolently 건방지게, 무례하게 n insolence 오만, 무례
syn arrogant, impudent ant modest

Every student is sick of his insolent response to the teacher's questions.

20 extravagant [ikstrǽvəgənt]
a. 낭비하는, 사치스러운

being considered flamboyant
ad extravagantly 낭비적으로, 사치스럽게
syn showy, flamboyant, excessive ant frugal, restrained, reasonable

If you visit the remains of Rome, you will find how Romans were extravagant.

21 parallel [pǽrəlèl]
a. 평행의, 같은 방향의
n. 평행선, 대등한 것

right next to one another
syn alongside, lateral ant opposite

The Olympic road runs parallel with the river running through Seoul.

There is no parallel to this Chinese restaurant in our town.

22 eradicate [irǽdəkèit]
v. 제거하다, 근절하다

to destroy something completely
n eradication 근절, 박멸 a eradicative 근절시키는
syn remove, eliminate, erase, obliterate

The government tried to eradicate smoking in public places.

23 incense [ínsens]
v. 매우 화나게 하다, 격노하다

to make someone angry
n incensement 몹시 화나게 함, 격분시킴
syn anger, infuriate, inflame ant soothe, pacify, placate

He was so incensed with her attitude that he went out without words.

24 meditate [médətèit]
v. 명상하다, 숙고하다, 생각하다

to think about something very deeply
n meditation 명상, 숙고 a meditative 명상적인
syn ponder, contemplate

She always meditates for an hour before breakfast.

25 divulge [divʌ́ldʒ]
v. 폭로하다, 누설하다

to make something that should be secret known
n divulger 누설하는 사람 divulgence 누설, 폭로
syn reveal, expose ant conceal, hide

His duty is to get the spies to divulge secrets about nuclear weapons.

---

19 모든 학생들이 선생님의 질문에 대한 그의 무례한 대답에 넌더리를 친다. 20 로마 유적지를 방문하면 얼마나 로마인들이 사치스러웠는지 알게 될 것이다. 21 올림픽 도로는 서울을 관통하여 흐르는 강과 나란히 놓여있다. 우리 마을에 이 중국 음식점과 필적 할 만한 음식점은 없다. 22 정부는 공공장소에서 흡연을 근절 하려고 노력했다. 23 그는 그녀의 태도에 화가 나서 말없이 나가버렸다. 24 그녀는 아침 식사 전에 한 시간씩 명상을 한다. 25 그의 임무는 스파이들이 핵무기 에 대한 비밀을 말하도록 하는 것이다.

Exercise

Word Check 각 단어의 뜻으로 알맞은 것을 찾아 연결하시오.

01 exquisite
02 subsidy
03 meditate
04 parallel
05 infirm

(a) to spend time in deep religious or spiritual thought
(b) the same distance apart at every point
(c) a sum of money given
(d) weak or ill especially from old age
(e) extremely beautiful or skillfully produced

Syn & Ant Check 주어진 단어의 동의어, 반의어를 골라 쓰시오.

| introvert | reveal | stubborn | modest | depressed |
| trick | unhealthful | simple | temporary | infuriate |

06 incense =
07 guile   =
08 obstinate =
09 transient =
10 divulge =

11 exuberant ↔
12 insolent ↔
13 intricate ↔
14 extrovert ↔
15 sanitary ↔

Sentence Practice 문장을 읽고 빈칸에 알맞은 단어를 고르시오.

16 The anniversary celebration will be modeled on the colorful floats and _____ costumes of Rio's Mardi Gras festival.

ⓐ extravagant   ⓑ insolent   ⓒ obstinate   ⓓ infirm

17 Luckily our _____ dog has inherited the most appealing and distinctive features of both its parents.

ⓐ hybrid   ⓑ posture   ⓒ maneuver   ⓓ subsidy

18 Penguins remind me of gentlemen clad in the formal attire of _____ white shirts and gleaming tuxedos.

ⓐ hectic   ⓑ immaculate   ⓒ imminent   ⓓ exquisite

19 It is impossible for us to _____ disease without doing exercise.

ⓐ eradicate   ⓑ incense   ⓒ divulge   ⓓ meditate

20 The governor evaded inconvenient questions from the press about the scandal with his _____ answers.

ⓐ parallel   ⓑ latent   ⓒ equivocal   ⓓ sanitary

suffix

형용사 suffix

can

-able : reason ⇨ **reason**able, rely ⇨ **reli**able

If the demand is reasonable, it is easily accepted in the annual conference.

만약 그 주장이 합리적이라면 연례회의에서 쉽게 받아들여질 것 이다.

-ible : sense ⇨ **sens**ible, flex ⇨ **flex**ible

Normally many Koreans confuse the English word "sensible" with "sensitive".

보통 많은 한국인들이 영어 단어 sensible과 sensitive를 혼동한다.

do

-ant : attend ⇨ **attend**ant, assist ⇨ **assist**ant

When we plan the urban development, we consider attendant circumstances.

우리가 도시개발을 기획할 때 부수적 상황을 고려해야 한다.

-ent : appear ⇨ **appar**ent, reside ⇨ **resid**ent

For no apparent reason, the cloned cows ended in miscarriages.

아무런 이유 없이 복제된 소들이 결국 유산되었다.

-en : choose ⇨ **chos**en, earth ⇨ **earth**en

To be chosen as a representative is the highest honor for anyone.

대표로 선출된다는 것은 모두에게 대단한 영예이다.

-(t)ive : create ⇨ **crea**tive, abuse ⇨ **abus**ive

The job on naming products needs some creative imagination.

상품에 이름을 짓는 직업은 독창적인 상상력을 필요로 한다.

possess

-al : practice ⇨ **practic**al, center ⇨ **centr**al

He was very hurt by a practical joke.

그는 심한 장난에 상처를 많이 받았다.

-ical : biology ⇨ **biolog**ical, economy ⇨ **econom**ical

The researchers examined all possibilities of biological side effects on human bodies.

연구원들은 인간의 몸에 미치는 생물학적 부작용의 모든 가능성을 검사했다.

-ary : moment ⇨ **moment**ary, legend ⇨ **legend**ary

After a momentary decrease, the customers hesitated over the selling shares.

잠시 주가 하락이 있은 후 고객들은 주식을 파는 것을 머뭇거렸다.

A 영어 풀이에 알맞은 단어를 보기에서 찾아 쓰시오.

| incriminate | encroach | deride | constrain | extrovert |

01 to involve in an accusation _____

02 to produce in a forced manner _____

03 to laugh at or make fun of someone _____

04 a person concerned with the outside world and social relationship _____

05 to trespass upon the property _____

B 문장을 읽고 빈칸에 알맞은 표현을 고르시오. (둘 중에 하나 고르기)

06 Participants at the competition (allege/allocate) that the judges were partial to some of the contenders.

07 The gathering expected his speech to be inspiring rather than (mundane/monetary).

08 It's wonderful to sit back and relax after the (ingenious/hectic) schedule of last week.

09 The main speaker decided to (curtail/covet) his talk upon seeing the audience get highly impatient.

C 표시된 부분과 뜻이 가장 가까운 것을 고르시오.

10 Scientists working on the project were under strict orders not to divulge any of its details.

ⓐ expose   ⓑ coagulate   ⓒ denote   ⓓ meditate

11 Mosquitoes that cause dengue and malaria breed rapidly in stagnant pools of water.

ⓐ mortal   ⓑ motionless   ⓒ enigmatic   ⓓ prevalent

12 The progressively debilitating illness ultimately confined Susan to her home.

ⓐ allure   ⓑ restricted   ⓒ detached   ⓓ censured

13 Hypocrisy is a trait that I absolutely abhor because of the harm it does to others and its dishonesty.

ⓐ constrain   ⓑ defer   ⓒ abominate   ⓓ encroach

D 표시된 부분의 반대말로 가장 알맞은 것을 고르시오.

14 The manager was careful not to rebuke his assistants with harsh words in the presence of their colleagues.

    ⓐ enervate   ⓑ compliment   ⓒ subside   ⓓ comply

15 My parents deferred making a decision on their trip.

    ⓐ hastened   ⓑ incensed   ⓒ conscripted   ⓓ disregarded

16 Some philosophers believe that death is not a cessation of life but an onward journey.

    ⓐ misgiving   ⓑ dignity   ⓒ hybrid   ⓓ commencement

17 He didn't let success or fame change him because he knew they were transient.

    ⓐ systematic   ⓑ parallel   ⓒ latent   ⓓ permanent

E 주어진 단어를 알맞은 형태로 바꿔 빈칸에 쓰시오.

18 According to law, the heirs can declare the _____ of succession to the Court within two months. (renounce)

19 The newly unearthed inscriptions make an _____ to important rituals and traditions in the tribe's ancient past. (allude)

20 We need an engineer who is responsible for _____ these parts. (fabricate)

21 Everyone was surprised that Alice denied the fact _____. (obstinate)

F 빈 칸에 알맞은 단어를 보기에서 찾아 쓰시오. (필요한 경우 형태를 바꾸시오.)

| expose | defer | comply | retaliate | latent | avalanche | allure | parallel |

22 All roads leading to the town were blocked in the wake of the sudden rock _____.

23 The _____ of poetry lies in its ability to communicate differently to different people.

24 Automobiles are being made to _____ with more stringent safety and emission standards.

25 My uncle believed that to _____ against someone's insult was to admit that it affected you.

Accumulative test Day 1 ~ Day 15

영어를 우리말로 옮기시오.

01 esteem

02 jargon

03 curtail

04 commence

05 stagnant

06 intricate

07 procure

08 allege

09 morbid

10 equivocal

11 allocate

12 reiterate

13 allude

14 meditate

15 encroach

16 alleviate

17 embody

18 deceptive

19 forsake

20 extravagant

21 philanthropist

22 enunciate

23 abstain

24 perplex

25 disregard

26 ebullient

27 incorporate

28 eradicate

29 manifest

30 divulge

31 rebuke

32 constrain

33 prevalent

34 innumerable

35 contempt

36 entreat

37 subsidy

38 mortal

39 censure

40 intent

41 incense

42 enervate

43 renounce

44 maneuver

45 enigmatic

46 qualm

47 confine

48 ameliorate

49 remnant

50 abhor

51 infirm

52 prosecute

53 avid

54 immaculate

55 depreciate

56 legitimate

57 camouflage

58 precarious

59 hectic

60 gratify

우리말을 영어로 옮기시오.

61	매혹하다, 꾀다		91	긴박한, 급박한
62	미루다		92	불 붙이다
63	비웃다		93	수많은, 무수한
64	의미하다		94	완고한, 고집 센
65	숙련된, 정통한		95	도약, 돌파구
66	행운의, 길조의		96	징집하다
67	꾸물거리다		97	합동, 연합
68	엄한, 단호한		98	떼어놓다
69	불안, 걱정		99	잠재(잠복)의
70	조심성 있는		100	최면(술)의
71	예비의, 준비의		101	몹시 바쁜
72	탐내다		102	숭배하다
73	눈사태		103	평범한, 일상적인
74	제멋대로의		104	성운, 성좌
75	죄를 씌우다		105	위생의, 청결한
76	득이 되는		106	환호하다
77	야만적인		107	검열하다
78	외면하다		108	평행의
79	응하다, 따르다		109	영리한
80	잘 속는		110	중단, 정지
81	과묵한		111	교활, 책략
82	확신(설득)하다		112	제작하다
83	구성되다		113	일화
84	적합하지 않은		114	응고하다
85	이해(파악)하다		115	존엄, 위엄
86	일시적인		116	무례한, 오만한
87	복수(보복)하다		117	금전상의
88	잡종		118	마취제
89	외향적인 사람		119	외부의
90	아름다운		120	믿지 않는

Part 4

🎧 **01 deterrent** [ditə́:rənt]
n. 방해물, 억제력

stopping someone from doing something

ⓝ deterrer 방해자, 단념하게 할 수 있는 사람

syn preventive, impediment   ant incentive, catalyst, inducement

Many countries want to develop nuclear weapons to use them as a war deterrent.

Concertina wire was slung over top of the fence as a deterrent for would be thieves.

02 commotion [kəmóuʃən]
n. 동요, 소동, 폭동

noisy activity

ⓐ commotional 격동[동란]의 commove 동요하다, 선동하다

syn tumult, uproar, clamor, upheaval   ant calm, peace

He was awakened from a sleep due to a commotion in the back yard.

03 connoisseur [kànəsə́:r]
n. 감정가, 감식가, 전문가

a specialist who knows a lot about something

ⓝ connoisseurship 감식안, 감정업

syn specialist, aficionado, expert   ant amateur, novice, beginner

Even if John is not a connoisseur, he knows a good wine.

04 detour [dí:tuər]
n. 우회, 우회길
v. 우회하다, 돌아가다

a secondary route

syn bypass, diversion, deviation

To avoid the congestion the road crews set up a detour quickly around the accident site.

The police told us to detour round the construction site.

05 adversary [ǽdvərsèri]
n. (시합의) 적, 상대자
a. 적의, 반대하는

someone who is competing with you

ⓝ adversaryism 적대주의   ⓐ adversarial 두 사람의 당사자가 적대 관계에 있는

syn opponent, combatant, foe   ant ally, friend, supporter

Jane had a cordial relationship with him, but it was clear that they were adversaries in the game.

The adversarial relationship between the two countries has been worse since the soccer game.

---

01 많은 국가들이 전쟁 억제수단으로 사용하기 위해 핵무기를 개발하기를 원한다. 도둑의 침입에 대한 방해물로 담 위에 가시철조망을 설치했다. 02 뒷마당에서 벌어진 소동 때문에 그는 잠에서 깼다. 03 비록 John이 전문가는 아니지만 좋은 와인을 볼 줄 안다. 04 교통체증을 막기위해 도로 직원들이 사고 주위에 우회 길을 재빨리 만들었다. 경찰은 공사현장을 우회하라고 우리에게 얘기했다. 05 Jane은 그와 절친한 사이이나 경기에서는 확실한 적수였다. 두 나라의 적대적인 관계는 축구경기이후 더욱 악화되었다.

06 detrimental [dètrəméntl]
a. 해로운, 불리한

bad for something
[ad] detrimentally 손해를 입히게, 해롭게
[syn] harmful, destructive, injurious [ant] helpful, beneficial

The educational policy that the new government announced yesterday is detrimental to our business.

07 comprehensive [kàmprihénsiv]
a. 포괄적인, 넓은, 이해가 빠른

including a lot or wide scope
[ad] comprehensively 포괄적으로, 광범위하게
[syn] extensive, inclusive [ant] limited

We need comprehensive cooperation from you to finish this project ahead of schedule.

08 archaic [áːrkéiik]
a. 구식의, 고대의, 원시의

old or relating to ancient times
[ad] archaically 고풍으로, 옛 말투로
[syn] old, ancient, obsolete, primitive [ant] new, current, young

In the past, terrorists were limited to archaic weapons that did little damage to government forces.

09 dexterous [dékstərəs]
a. 손재주가 있는, 영리한, 민첩한

using hands skillfully
[ad] dexterously 솜씨 좋게, 교묘하게
[syn] proficient, adept, able, quick [ant] clumsy, inept, slow

My brother is very dexterous at playing computer games.

10 aquatic [əkwátik]
a. 물의, 물속의

living in the water or relating to water
[ad] aquatically 물 속에서, 물 속에 살면서
[syn] maritime, marine [ant] land, terrestrial

Many aquatic creatures are able to draw air from water.

11 discreet [diskríːt]
a. 분별있는, 사려 깊은, 신중한

careful or sensible
[ad] discreetly 분별 있게, 사려 깊게 [n] discreetness 분별 있음, 사려깊음
[syn] tactful, prudent, diplomatic, cautious

It wasn't very discreet of him to do such a thing.

12 dubious [djúːbiəs]
a. 의심스러운, 모호한

feeling uncertain
[ad] dubiously 수상하게, 의심스럽게 [n] dubiousness 수상함, 의심스러움
[syn] vague, unclear, indefinite [ant] decided, settled, unambiguous

We couldn't make any decisions at the annual meeting due to his dubious attitude toward our sales strategy.

---

06 어제 새 정부가 발표한 교육정책은 우리 사업에 불리하다. 07 계획에 앞서 이 프로젝트를 끝내려면 당신의 포괄적인 협력이 필요하다. 08 과거에 테러리스트들은 정부군에 피해를 주지 못하는 구식 무기만 사용했다. 09 내 남동생은 컴퓨터 게임에 매우 소질이 있다. 10 많은 수중 동물들이 물속에서 공기를 빨아들인다. 11 그가 그러한 일을 했다는 것은 신중하지 못했다. 12 판매 전략에 대한 그의 모호한 태도 때문에 우리는 연례 회의에서 어떠한 결정도 내리지 못했다.

13 deteriorate [ditíəriərèit]
v. 악화시키다, (질을) 저하시키다

to become worse

ⓐ deteriorative 악화되는, 타락적인 ⓝ deterioration 악화, 타락

syn breakdown, decay, degrade ant improve, ameliorate

Trucks loaded with heavy things were the main reason for deteriorating the condition of the road.

14 concede [kənsí:d]
v. 인정하다, 승인하다, 양보하다

to make concession, to admit to be true

ⓝ concession 양보 ⓐ concessive 양보의

syn admit, capitulate, accept, yield ant refute, reject, deny

After nearly two hours of grueling competition, one player finally conceded a defeat.

15 appease [əpí:z]
v. (사람을)달래다, 진정시키다

to attempt to placate someone

ⓝ appeasement 진정, 타협

syn placate, satisfy, allay, mollify ant exacerbate, irritate, provoke

France's efforts to appease the Germans during World War II did little to satisfy their ambitions.

16 conjecture [kəndʒéktʃər]
v. 추측하다, 짐작하다
n. 짐작, 추측

to guess

ⓝ conjecturer 짐작하는 사람

syn surmise, guess

The press conjectured that North Korea would agree to stop a nuclear weapon test.

Her conjecture that we would win the game turned out to be wrong.

17 console [kənsóul]
v. 위로하다, 위문하다

to make someone feel comfortable in a time of grief

ⓐ consolable 위안할 수 있는

syn comfort, solace

He consoled himself by playing computer games all day long when he lost his dog.

18 augment [ɔːgmént]
v. 증가하다, 증가시키다

to increase or to make something larger

ⓝ augmentation 증가, 증가율 ⓐ augmented 증가된

syn increase, enhance, add ant decrease, reduce, degrade

The farmers want to export strawberries to Japan to augment their income.

---

13 무거운 물건을 실은 트럭들이 도로상태를 악화시키는 주요 원인이었다. 14 거의 두 시간의 치열한 경기 후에 결국 한 선수가 패배를 인정했다. 15 2차 대전 동안 독일인들을 달래려는 프랑스인들의 노력이 독일인들의 야망을 만족시키지는 못했다. 16 언론은 북한이 핵무기 테스트를 중단하는데 합의할 거라고 추측했다. 경기에서 우리가 승리할 거라는 그녀의 예상은 틀렸다. 17 개를 잃어 버렸을 때 온종일 그는 컴퓨터 게임을 하면서 마음을 달랬다. 18 농부들은 수입을 증가시키기 위해 딸기를 일본으로 수출하기를 원했다.

19 devastate [dévəstèit]
v. 파괴하다, 황폐시키다

to destroy something totally
ⓐ devastative 유린하는, 황폐시키는 ⓝ devastation 파괴, 황폐
ⓢⓨⓝ destroy, wreck, ruin ⓐⓝⓣ build, construct, produce
Hurricane Katrina devastated the City of New Orleans.

20 detract [ditrǽkt]
v. 가치를 떨어뜨리다,
  (주의를) 다른 데로 돌리다

to reduce the value of something
ⓝ detraction 욕설, 비난 ⓐ detractive 욕을 하는, 비난하는
ⓢⓨⓝ lessen, reduce, cheapen ⓐⓝⓣ enhance, intensify
The singer's poor style of dress detracted from her performance.

21 dwindle [dwíndl]
v. 작아지다, 감소되다

to get smaller or less
ⓝ dwindler 발육이 나쁜 사람
ⓢⓨⓝ ebb, fade, wane ⓐⓝⓣ grow, increase, enlarge
The population of the rural area has been dwindling for the last decade.

22 breach [briːtʃ]
v. (법, 약속을) 위반하다, ~을 깨뜨리다,
n. 위반, 불이행, 파손, 돌파구

to act contrary to a law
ⓢⓨⓝ break, gap, fissure, opening ⓐⓝⓣ bridge, connection, link
If the tourists stay in Korea over 90 days, they will breach the law.
It's a breach of the rule not to wear a uniform while you are on duty.

23 emancipate [imǽnsəpèit]
v. 해방하다, 자유롭게 하다

to set free from political or legal restrictions
ⓐ emancipated 해방된, 자주적인 ⓝ emancipation 해방, 자유, 이탈
ⓢⓨⓝ free, loosen, release ⓐⓝⓣ imprison, incarcerate, indenture
Many African countries have been emancipated from European colonialist rule for several decades.

24 appall [əpɔ́ːl]
v. 섬뜩하게 하다, 질리게 하다

to horrify someone
ⓐ appalling 소름끼치는, 무서운 ⓐⓓ appallingly 소름끼치도록, 형편없이
ⓢⓨⓝ horrify, shock, terrify ⓐⓝⓣ comfort, reassure
The child's behavior in the supermarket appalled his mom and many of the shoppers.

25 deviate [díːvièit]
v. 벗어나다, 빗나가다

to turn away from the expected path
ⓝ deviation 벗어남, 탈선
ⓢⓨⓝ sway, diverge, turn, digress ⓐⓝⓣ conform
The director's latest film deviated from his previous releases.

---

19 허리케인 카트리나가 뉴올리언즈시를 파괴했다. 20 가수의 촌스러운 의상이 그녀의 공연 수준을 떨어뜨렸다. 21 지난 10년 동안 농촌의 인구가 감소하였다. 22 만약에 그 여행객들이 90일 이상 한국에 체류하면 법을 위반하게 된다. 근무 중에 유니폼을 입지 않으면 규칙위반이다. 23 지난 수십 년 동안 많은 아프리카 국가들이 유럽의 식민지 지배에서 해방되었다. 24 슈퍼마켓에서 그 어린이의 행동은 엄마뿐 아니라 많은 고객들을 놀라게 했다. 25 그 감독의 최근영화는 그의 이전 작품에서 벗어나 있다.

Exercise

Word Check 각 단어의 뜻으로 알맞은 것을 찾아 연결하시오.

01 breach
02 comprehensive
03 discreet
04 appease
05 detour

(a) covering or including a large area or scope
(b) breaking of a law or promise
(c) to calm by making some kind of concession.
(d) careful to prevent suspicion or embarrassment
(e) a route away from the direct route

Syn & Ant Check 주어진 단어의 동의어, 반의어를 골라 쓰시오.

terrestrial	enlarge	surmise	improve	impediment
release	current	destroy	beneficial	opponent

06 adversary =
07 emancipate =
08 deterrent =
09 devastate =
10 conjecture =

11 deteriorate ↔
12 aquatic ↔
13 archaic ↔
14 dwindle ↔
15 detrimental ↔

Sentence Practice 문장을 읽고 빈칸에 알맞은 단어를 고르시오.

16 We were curious to know what the _____ in the street was all about.
ⓐ adversary　　ⓑ connoisseur　　ⓒ aquatic　　ⓓ commotion

17 Some surgeons learn to play the violin to keep their fingers _____ and sensitive.
ⓐ adversary　　ⓑ discreet　　ⓒ detrimental　　ⓓ dexterous

18 It was impossible to _____ the little girl over the loss of her favorite doll.
ⓐ console　　ⓑ conjecture　　ⓒ appall　　ⓓ breach

19 The police suspect that he has amassed wealth through _____ means.
ⓐ aquatic　　ⓑ archaic　　ⓒ dubious　　ⓓ comprehensive

20 The game turned ugly when one of the teams refused to _____ defeat and alleged foul play.
ⓐ concede　　ⓑ detract　　ⓒ appease　　ⓓ augment

01 patron [péitrən]
n. 후원자, 보호자, 고객

a person who supports artists
ⓥ patronize 후원하다, 보호하다 ⓝ patronization 후원, 지원
syn supporter, financier, guide

He is very interested in paintings, and his wife is well known as a patron of poor artists.

02 nuance [njú:a:ns]
n. 미묘한 차이, 함축성

a small difference in meaning
syn hint, subtlety, refinement

We learned that the nuance in his speech was due to his learning English in New Zealand.

03 foliage [fóuliidʒ]
n. 잎, 잎 무늬

leaves of a tree
ⓐ foliaged 잎이 있는
syn leaves, herbage

His home fell into disrepair and was partially covered with dense foliage.

04 volition [voulíʃən]
n. 결단, 의지력

the act of willing
ⓐ volitional 의지의, 의지에 관한 ad volitionally 의지로, 의욕적으로
syn will, desire, choice, preference

Tim left his position as vice president of his own volition despite rumors that he had had little choice in the matter.

05 pedagogue [pédəgàg]
n. 교사, 학자

a teacher, especially a strict one
ⓝ pedagogy 교육학, 교육
syn educator, professor, instructor

He is a credible pedagogue, and he has spoken on a number of topics pertaining to international relations.

06 mediocre [mì:dióukər]
a. 보통의, 평범한

not exceptional or special
ⓝ mediocrity 평범, 보통 ⓥ mediocritize 평범하게 하다
syn ordinary, average, common ant extraordinary, exceptional, superior

His parents were disappointed with his mediocre score on the test.

01 그는 그림에 많은 관심이 있으며 그의 부인은 가난한 화가를 후원하는 것으로 잘 알려져 있다. 02 우리는 그의 말에서 미묘한 차이가 있는 것은 그가 영어를 뉴질랜드에서 배웠기 때문이라는 것을 알았다. 03 그의 집은 폐허가 되었고 일부분이 나뭇잎으로 덮여있었다. 04 선택의 여지가 없었다는 소문도 있었지만 Tim은 부 사장직을 스스로 결단에 의해 물러났다. 05 그는 믿을 만한 학자로 국제 관계에 대한 주제로 많은 연설을 해왔다. 06 그의 부모는 그의 평범한 시험성적에 실망했다.

07 **menace** [ménəs]
n. 협박, 위협, 공갈
v. 협박하다, 위협하다

expression of a threat
[ad] menacingly 위협(협박)적으로
[syn] threat, warning, intimidation

Wolves, once a menace to farm livestock, were hunted nearly into extinction.

War, drought, and AIDS menaced the country for twenty years.

08 **noxious** [nákʃəs]
a. 해로운, 유해한, 불건전한

very harmful
[n] noxiousness 유해
[syn] foul, toxic, poisonous, putrid   [ant] pleasant, fresh, innocuous

The gas emanating from the storage tank is very noxious.

09 **emaciated** [iméiʃièitid]
a. 야윈, 쇠약한, (땅이) 메마른

very thin
[v] emaciate 쇠약하게 하다, (토지)를 메마르게 하다
[syn] skinny, thin   [ant] corpulent, fat, rotund

Those who are living in the refugee camp are haggard and emaciated.

10 **impromptu** [imprámptʃu:]
a. 즉흥적인, 즉석의

made or done without preparation
[syn] spontaneous, improvised, unrehearsed   [ant] planned, rehearsed

The impromptu speech the actor gave was hardly understood.

11 **improvised** [ímprəvàizd]
a. 즉흥의, 즉석의

to make or provide something quickly
[v] improvise 즉석에서 하다
[syn] impromptu   [ant] planned, prepared

We served them an improvised meal because they visited us too late at night.

12 **grotesque** [groutésk]
a. 기괴한, 이상한

something deformed
[n] grotesquery 기괴한 성질[것]   [ad] grotesquely 기괴하게, 우스꽝스럽게
[syn] ugly, abnormal, bizarre   [ant] beautiful, lovely, normal

Lights placed at odd angles gave the actor a grotesque appearance.

13 **pecuniary** [pikjú:nièri]
a. 재정상의, 금전상의

relating to money
[ad] pecuniarily 금전상으로, 재정상으로
[syn] financial, fiscal

Some African nations have chronic pecuniary difficulties.

---

07 한 때 농장 가축에 위협이 되었던 늑대가 거의 멸종위기에 처했다. 전쟁, 가뭄, AIDS가 그 나라를 20년간 위협했다. 08 저장 창고에서 분출되는 가스는 매우 유해하다. 09 난민 캠프에 사는 사람들은 수척하고 야위었다. 10 그 배우가 한 즉흥 연설은 거의 이해할 수 없었다. 11 그들이 늦게 방문했기 때문에 우리는 그들에게 즉석 요리를 제공했다. 12 이상한 각도로 놓여진 조명 때문에 배우의 모습이 이상하게 보였다. 13 일부 아프리카 국가들은 만성적인 재정상 어려움을 겪고 있다.

14 volatile [válətil]
a. 휘발성의, 증발하기 쉬운

changing quickly from a solid or liquid into a vapour
ⓥ volatilize 휘발[증발]하다
syn flammable, inflammable, explosive, unstable ant stable, steady

Dynamite is composed of nitroglycerine, a volatile compound that provides its explosiveness.

15 gregarious [grigέəriəs]
a. 사교적인

liking the company of others
ad gregariously 떼지어, 군거하여 ⓝ gregariousness 군거성, 군생
syn outgoing, sociable ant reserved, unsociable, introverted

Gregarious individuals are well suited for fields that put them in contact with people.

16 voluminous [vəlú:mənəs]
a. 권수가 많은, 부피가 큰

writing a large volume
ad voluminously 권수가 많아, 저서가 많아
syn extensive, abundant, massive, expansive ant small, diminutive, tiny

His voluminous notes were instrumental in detailing the structure of tropical plants found on the island.

17 lethargic [liθá:rdʒik]
a. 혼수상태의, 졸리는, 둔한

lacking in energy or vitality
ad lethargically 혼수 상태로, 둔감하게 ⓥ lethargize 혼수 상태에 빠지게 하다
syn lazy, passive, sluggish, slow ant lively, fit, energetic

Their frequent lethargic behavior does not mean that they cannot move quickly.

18 flounder [fláundər]
v. 허우적거리다, 허둥대다

to struggle helplessly or make mistakes
ad flounderingly 허둥대며, 실수를 저지르며
syn blunder, stumble ant flourish, succeed

He floundered primarily during his freshman year in college.

19 patronize [péitrənàiz]
v. ～와 거래하다, ～를 후원하다

to behave in an offensively condescending manner
ⓝ patron 후원자, 고객 ⓐ patronizing 후원하는, 은인인 체하는
syn sponsor, assist, fund

Some people like to patronize businesses that sell products produced in their own country.

---

14 다이나마이트는 폭발성을 제공하는 휘발성 물질 니트로 글리세린으로 구성되어 있다. 15 사교적인 사람들은 사람들과 접촉하는 일이 그들에게 적합하다. 16 그의 많은 기록들이 섬에서 발견된 열대 식물의 체계를 자세히 설명하는데 도움이 되었다. 17 그들의 잦은 무기력한 행동이 빠르게 움직이지 못한다는 것을 의미하는 것은 아니다. 18 그는 대학 일년 동안 실수를 많이 했다. 19 일부 사람들은 그들 국가에서 생산되는 제품을 판매하는 업체를 후원했다.

20 bewilder [biwíldər]
v. 당황하다, 어리둥절하다

to perplex or confuse

ⁿ bewilderment 당황, 당혹 ᵃ bewildering 당혹케 하는

ˢʸⁿ confuse, daze, fluster, addle ᵃⁿᵗ explain, clarify

The travelers looked bewildered when the train stopped suddenly.

---

21 inaugurate [inɔ́:gjərèit]
v. 취임하다

to start with an official ceremony

ⁿ inauguration 개시, 취임 ᵃ inaugural 취임(식)의, 개회의

ˢʸⁿ install, begin, commence ᵃⁿᵗ end, close, complete

The President of the United States is inaugurated on January 20th of every fourth year.

---

22 elucidate [ilú:sədèit]
v. 자세히 설명하다

to make something clearer

ⁿ elucidator 설명자, 해설자 ᵃ elucidative 설명적인, 해명적인

ˢʸⁿ clarify, explain, illustrate ᵃⁿᵗ obscure, muddy, confuse

They didn't elucidate the reason why his brother was killed in action.

---

23 admonish [ædmániʃ]
v. 충고하다, 훈계하다

to scold or reprove in a mild manner

ⁿ admonishment 충고, 훈계 ᵃᵈ admonishingly 충고하는 투로, 훈계조로

ˢʸⁿ scold, chide, warn, berate ᵃⁿᵗ praise, flatter, compliment

The teacher admonished the naughty boy for his mischievous behavior.

---

24 cede [si:d]
v. (권리를) 양도하다, 양보하다

to give something to another

ˢʸⁿ grant, transfer, surrender ᵃⁿᵗ retain, gain, withhold, win

Congressman Lewis ceded the remaining portion of his speaking time to the current speaker.

---

25 dehydrate [di:háidreit]
v. 탈수 하다, 건조시키다

to remove water from

ⁿ dehydration 탈수, 건조 dehydrator 탈수기

ˢʸⁿ dry, evaporate, parch ᵃⁿᵗ soak, hydrate, moisten

Adventure travelers have to know how to dehydrate their foods.

---

20 기차가 갑자기 멈추었을 때 여행객들은 당황스러워 보였다. 21 미국 대통령은 매 4년마다 1월 20일에 취임한다. 22 그들은 그의 동생이 작전 중 사망한 이유를 설명하지 않았다. 23 선생님은 개구쟁이 소년에게 그의 잘못된 행동을 꾸짖었다. 24 국회의원인 Lewis는 그의 남아있는 연설시간을 현재 연설자에게 양보했다. 25 탐험가들은 그들의 식량을 건조시키는 방법을 알아야 한다.

Exercise

Word Check 각 단어의 뜻으로 알맞은 것을 찾아 연결하시오.

01 nuance   (a) a subtle variation in color or meaning

02 volition   (b) producing great quantities of writing

03 noxious   (c) harmful or poisonous

04 patronize   (d) to treat someone in an condescending manner

05 voluminous   (e) the act of willing or choosing

Syn & Ant Check 주어진 단어의 동의어, 반의어를 골라 쓰시오.

supporter	financial	leaves	planned	stable
unsociable	educator	soak	skinny	compliment

06 patron = _____

07 pecuniary = _____

08 pedagogue = _____

09 emaciated = _____

10 foliage = _____

11 improvised ↔ _____

12 admonish ↔ _____

13 dehydrate ↔ _____

14 gregarious ↔ _____

15 volatile ↔ _____

Sentence Practice 문장을 읽고 빈칸에 알맞은 단어를 고르시오.

16 Most readers were _____ by the nearly incomprehensible twists and turns in the plot of the novel.

ⓐ dehydrated   ⓑ bewildered   ⓒ ceded   ⓓ elucidated

17 A side effect of globalization is that _____ from AIDS to computer viruses spread very rapidly.

ⓐ menaces   ⓑ patrons   ⓒ volition   ⓓ nuances

18 This school is known for its commitment to helping _____ learners upgrade themselves through academic rigor.

ⓐ noxious   ⓑ pecuniary   ⓒ volatile   ⓓ mediocre

19 The animal rescue squad labored for hours to get the _____ horse out of the deep muddy ditch.

ⓐ admonishing   ⓑ patronizing   ⓒ floundering   ⓓ inaugurating

20 Tim was not known to be _____ except when he was with his roommate.

ⓐ impromptu   ⓑ emaciated   ⓒ gregarious   ⓓ voluminous

01 melancholy [mélənkɑ̀li]
n. 우울함, 의기소침

sad state of mind
[a] melancholic 우울한, 침울한 [ad] melancholically 우울하게, 침울하게
[syn] depressed, sad, glum, somber [ant] happy, cheerful, positive

The graduates were melancholy, knowing that this would be the last time they would all be together at their school.

02 peril [pérəl]
n. 위험, 모험

exposure to danger
[a] perilous 위험한, 모험적인 [ad] perilously 위험하게, 모험적으로
[syn] trouble, danger, risk, uncertainty [ant] safety, security

The cave's owner reminded the group that they were entering the cave at their own peril.

03 verdict [və́:rdikt]
n. 판결, 심판

a decision made by a jury in a court
[syn] judgment, decision, outcome, finding [ant] charge, accusation

The verdict was not what his legal team had hoped for.

04 tenacious [tinéiʃəs]
a. 단단히 잡고 있는, 집요한, 완강한

holding or sticking firmly
[ad] tenaciously 집요하게, 끈질기게 [n] tenaciousness 집요함, 끈질김
[syn] strong, determined, stout [ant] surrendering, weak, yielding

The ants are tenacious defenders, using both painful bites and acid sprays to fend off attackers.

05 blunt [blʌnt]
a. 무딘, 퉁명스러운

having a dull edge, slow in understanding
[ad] bluntly 무디게, 무뚝뚝하게 [n] bluntness 무딤, 뭉툭함, 무뚝뚝함
[syn] straightforward, dull [ant] tactful, sharp

His utterances are blunt and brief, so he sometimes makes the audience disappointed.

06 celestial [siléstʃəl]
a. 하늘의, 천국의

belonging or relating to the sky
[syn] supernatural, transcendental, heavenly [ant] mundane, secular

Many astronomers seek to find the celestial body that has heretofore been undiscovered.

---

01 졸업생들은 이번이 그들이 학교에 함께 있는 마지막 시간이라는 것을 알자 우울해했다. 02 동굴 소유자는 그 단체에게 그들이 위험을 감수하고 동굴에 들어간다는 것을 상기시켰다. 03 그 판결은 그의 법률팀이 희망한 것은 아니었다. 04 개미들은 완강한 방어자로 적들의 공격에 저항하기 위해 상대방을 물거나 산성이 강한 액체를 뿌린다. 05 그의 연설은 퉁명스럽고 짧아서 때때로 청중들을 실망시킨다. 06 많은 천문학자들은 지금까지 발견하지 못한 천체를 찾는다.

07 dejected [didʒéktid]
a. 낙담한, 기가 죽은

feeling depressed

ad dejectedly 기가 죽어, 낙담하여   n dejectedness 기가 죽음, 낙담

syn sad, miserable

Students who are not accepted at the college might be dejected.

08 therapeutic [θèrəpjú:tik]
a. 치료의, 치료법의

relating to the healing and curing of disease

ad therapeutically 치료상으로, 치료법으로   n therapeutics 치료학, 치료법

syn healing, curative, beneficial   ant damaging, harmful

There are a number of therapeutic methods that can be used to improve one's mental health.

09 terrestrial [təréstriəl]
a. 지구상의, 육지의

relating to the earth

ad terrestrially 지구(상)에, 육지로

syn earthly, temporal, worldly   ant cosmic, heavenly, celestial

Though some scientists had looked toward the heavens, he had a more terrestrial focus.

10 tepid [tépid]
a. 미지근한, 미온의

slightly warm

n tepidness 미지근함   ad tepidly 미지근하게

syn lukewarm, cool, apathetic   ant enthusiastic, excited

His tepid response to the salary increase confused his supervisor.

11 inadvertent [ìnədvə́:rtənt]
a. 부주의 한, 우연한

not done deliberately

ad inadvertently 부주의하게, 무심코   n inadvertence 부주의, 실수

syn accidental, unintentional, chance   ant intentional, deliberate

His inadvertent observation was to lead to Penicillin.

12 vulgar [vʌ́lgər]
a. 상스러운, 천한

marked by a lack of politeness

ad vulgarly 상스럽게, 천하게   n vulgarity 속됨, 상스러움

syn rude, crass, offensive, obscene   ant polite, refined, decent

Many teachers have thought using vulgar language is harmful to young students.

13 sedate [sidéit]
a. 조용한, 침착한, 냉정한

not showing hurry, calm

ad sedately 조용히, 침착하게   a sedative 진정시키는, 누그러뜨리는

syn calm, placid, quiet, tranquil   ant unruly, wild, uncontrollable

Its sedate atmosphere helped him to gather his thoughts and relax.

---

07 대학 입학허가를 받지 못한 학생들은 매우 실망할 것이다. 08 정신 건강을 향상시킬 수 있는 많은 치료 방법들이 있다. 09 일부 과학자들은 천체에 관심이 있었지만 그는 지질에 관심이 더 많았다. 10 급여인상에 대한 그의 미온적인 태도가 상관을 혼란스럽게 했다. 11 그의 우연한 관찰이 페니실린을 발견하게 되었다. 12 많은 선생님들은 상스러운 말을 사용하는 것이 어린 학생들에게 해롭다고 생각한다. 13 그곳의 조용한 분위기는 그가 생각을 하거나 쉬는데 도움을 준다.

14 pedantic [pidǽntik]
a. 현학적인, 박식한 체하는

overly concerned with small details

[ad] pedantically 현학적으로, 박식한 체하여 [n] pedanticalness 현학적임

[syn] academic, erudite, pompous, scholarly [ant] ignorant, untaught

The Dean was privately criticized for his pedantic speeches, which tended to be long-winded and devoid of interest for the listener.

15 penitent [pénətənt]
a. 뉘우치는, 후회하는

feeling sorry for wrong one has done

[a] penitentiary 후회의, 참회의

[syn] sorry, regretful, ashamed, apologetic [ant] unrepentant, unashamed

He hardly appeared penitent for his assassination of Robert F. Kennedy.

16 sedentary [sédəntèri]
a. 앉아 있는, 앉아서 일하는

involving much sitting

[ad] sedentarily 앉아 있으면서, 앉아 일하며

[syn] idle, inactive, motionless, sitting [ant] active, mobile, energetic

Senior citizens incur significant health risks if they are constantly sedentary.

17 timid [tímid]
a. 겁많은, 소심한

easily frightened

[n] timidity 겁, 소심, 내성적임 [ad] timidly 겁많게, 소극적으로

[syn] shy, meek, reserved, hesitant [ant] bold, fearless, brave

A timid person usually avoids confronting things that managers must deal with effectively in order to be successful.

18 belligerent [bəlídʒərənt]
a. 용감한, 호전적인

aggressive and unfriendly, ready to argue

[n] belligerence 호전성, 전쟁을 좋아함 [ad] belligerently 호전적으로, 용감하게

The defendant grew belligerent on the witness stand and it caused the judge to ask him to calm down.

19 delegate [déligət]
v. ~을 대표로 임명하다,
권한을 위임하다

to give part of one's power or work to someone else for a certain time

[n] delegation 대표로 임명하기

[syn] select, name, appoint, assign [ant] revoke, reject, refuse

The government will delegate Jimmy to the conference that will be held in Paris next month.

The manager delegated many of the office's responsibilities to his staff during his vacation.

---

14 학장은 그의 현학적인 연설이 길고 청중들에게 흥미를 주지 못한다고 비난을 받았다. 15 그는 로버트 케네디를 암살한 것에 대해 해 뉘우치지 않는 것 같다. 16 노인들은 계속해서 앉아 있으면 심각한 건강상 위험이 있을 수 있다. 17 소심한 사람들은 관리자들이 성공을 위해 효과적으로 다루어야 할 문제들을 일반적으로 피한다. 18 피고가 증인석에서 공격적이 되어 판사가 그를 진정시켰다. 19 정부는 Jimmy를 다음 달 파리에서 열리는 회의에 대표자로 참석하도록 할 것이다. 그 관리자는 휴가 동안 사무실의 많은 일들을 직원에게 위임했다.

20 vacillate [væsəléit]
v. 흔들리다, 비틀거리다

to change opinions frequently

n vacillation 흔들림, 동요

syn waver, hesitate, change, hedge ant remain, stay

A president must not appear to vacillate on key issues in the public eye.

21 recur [rikə́:r]
v. 다시 일어나다, 재발하다

to happen again

a recurrent 빈발하는, 재발하는

syn repeat, return

The theme of emancipation of slaves recurred throughout his writing.

The mistake she made at a job interview recurs to her mind.

22 elude [ilú:d]
v. ~를 교묘히 피하다, ~를 벗어나다

to avoid something by quickness

n elusion 회피, 도피

syn evade, dodge, avoid, escape ant encounter, face, meet

Cocoons are designed to elude the sight of their enemies.

23 reconcile [rékənsàil]
v. ~를 중재하다, 만족시키다

to bring into harmony

n reconciliation 조정, 화해 a reconciliatory 화해의, 조화의

syn settle, resolve, adjust ant argue, quarrel, fight

The politicians will occasionally reconcile their differences for a common cause.

24 verify [vérəfài]
v. …을 검증하다, 입증하다

to check the truth of something

a verifiable 확인할 수 있는 n verifiability 실증할 수 있음

syn confirm, validate, substantiate, prove ant invalidate, disprove

A currency expert was brought in to verify the authenticity of the items.

25 adulterate [ədʌ́ltərèit]
v. ~를 떨어 뜨리다, 절하하다

to debase something or make it impure by adding inferior elements

a adulterated (섞음질해서) 품질을 떨어뜨린 n adulteration 섞음질, 불량품

syn abase, degrade, taint, pollute ant purify

His father did not allow him to put steak sauce on his steak, arguing that it adulterated the meat.

---

20 대통령은 대중 앞에서 중요한 일에 대해 흔들리면 안된다. 21 노예해방에 대한 주제가 그의 책 전반에 걸쳐 되풀이되어 나타나 있다. 그녀가 면접시험 때 저지른 실수가 머리에 떠오른다. 22 누에고치는 적의 눈을 교묘히 피할 수 있다. 23 정치인들은 공동의 목적을 위해 그들의 이견을 조정할 것이다. 24 지폐의 진위를 감정하기 위해 지폐 전문가를 불렀다. 25 고기 맛을 떨어뜨리기 때문에 그의 아버지는 그가 스테이크에 스테이크 소스를 치는 것을 허락하지 않았다.

Exercise

Score [/ 20]

Word Check 각 단어의 뜻으로 알맞은 것을 찾아 연결하시오.

01 adulterate   (a) to put them on friendly terms again

02 tepid   (b) slightly or only just warm

03 blunt   (c) to debase something or render it impure

04 sedentary   (d) having no point or sharp edge.

05 reconcile   (e) work that involves much sitting

Syn & Ant Check 주어진 단어의 동의어, 반의어를 골라 쓰시오.

disprove	depressed	brave	healing	purify
judgment	safety	accidental	repeat	unashamed

06 melancholy = _____   11 adulterate ↔ _____

07 recur   = _____   12 verify   ↔ _____

08 inadvertent = _____   13 peril   ↔ _____

09 verdict   = _____   14 penitent ↔ _____

10 therapeutic = _____   15 timid   ↔ _____

Sentence Practice 문장을 읽고 빈칸에 알맞은 단어를 고르시오.

16 Everyone knows that Jack is a decisive character who can be depended upon not to _____ in an emergency.

   ⓐ reconcile   ⓑ recur   ⓒ vacillate   ⓓ adulterate

17 Clare's only failing is that she isn't _____ enough to take on challenges and wilts when confronted with them.

   ⓐ blunt   ⓑ dejected   ⓒ tenacious   ⓓ vulgar

18 The recent meteor showers were a delightful _____ phenomenon that we enjoyed observing through our telescopes.

   ⓐ terrestrial   ⓑ tepid   ⓒ sedentary   ⓓ celestial

19 Success has always _____ Susan despite her enterprising endeavors in the field of biomechanics.

   ⓐ verified   ⓑ eluded   ⓒ delegated   ⓓ reconciled

20 Carl wanted to show that he was _____ by agreeing to rebuild the garage he had wrecked.

   ⓐ penitent   ⓑ sedate   ⓒ belligerent   ⓓ pedantic

🎧 **01 blot** [blɑt]
n. 얼룩, 오점

a drop of liquid, a stain of someone's good reputation
syn flaw, stain, smudge, blemish, stigma

The man received a terrible blot on his reputation when he was accused of theft.

---

02 benediction [bènədíkʃən]
n. 축복, 기도

a prayer giving blessing
ⓐ benedictional 축복의, 감사 기도의
syn prayer, blessing, invocation ant curse, condemnation

The Catholic Church's benediction is an integral part of their religious ceremonies.

---

03 fidelity [fidéləti]
n. 충실, (약속)엄수

loyalty or devotion
syn allegiance, loyalty, faith, reliability ant unfaithful, disloyal, unreliable

Her fidelity to her country was unparalleled.

---

04 fervor [fə́:rvər]
n. 열정, 열렬

lively or passionate interest
ⓐ fervent 열렬한, 강렬한 ⓐ fervid 열렬한, 열정적인
syn excitement, enthusiasm, eagerness ant indifference, apathy

He spoke with a fervor that caused his voice to raise and crack.

---

05 hierarchy [háiərɑ̀:rki]
n. 계층, 서열

a system that classifies people in order of rank
ⓐ hierarchical 계급 제도의
syn ranking, position

The school's reorganization included restructuring of the administrative hierarchy.

---

06 faculty [fǽkəlti]
n. 능력, 교수단

the teachers in a school or college or the natural abilities of an organism
ⓐ facultative 권한을 주는
syn teachers, professors, aptitude ant pupils, incompetence

The North American jack rabbit has an excellent faculty of hearing.

The university president introduced the new faculty members to the students.

---

01 그가 도둑으로 고소당했을 때 그의 명성에 오점을 남겼다. 02 카톨릭 교회의 기도는 종교 예식에서 없어서는 안될 부분이다. 03 그녀의 조국애는 대단하다. 04 그는 열정적으로 연설하여 목소리가 높아지고 갈라졌다. 05 학교의 조직 개편은 행정적 서열을 재개편하는 것도 포함되었다. 06 북미산 산토끼는 청력이 매우 좋다. 대학 총장은 새로운 교수진을 학생들에게 소개했다.

07 lavish [lǽviʃ]
a. 풍부한, 사치스러운

spending or giving generously

n lavishness 낭비, 헤픔　ad lavishly 아낌없이, 낭비적으로

syn excessive, extravagant, luxurious　ant humble, scant, paltry

The lavish home decorations and designer clothing put them in arrears with the rent for 2 months.

The hotel where we are going to stay provides lavish accommodation.

---

08 capricious [kəpríʃəs]
a. 변덕스런, 불안정한

changing often without reason

n caprice 변덕, 일시적 기분　ad capriciously 변덕스럽게, 불규칙적으로

syn flighty, erratic, fanciful　ant steady, dependable, predictable

The troupe grew tired of his capricious behavior during rehearsal and called him into a meeting to discuss the problem.

---

09 ignoble [ignóubəl]
a. 품위가 없는, 천한

dishonorable or mean

n ignobleness 품위가 없음, 비열함

syn abject, baseborn, coarse　ant noble

Such ignoble pursuits as drinking and gambling are seen by members of the clergy as lowly habits.

---

10 paramount [pǽrəmàunt]
a. 최고의, 최고 권력을 쥔

higher than others in rank

n paramountcy 최고권, 탁월

syn foremost, predominant, premier　ant ancillary, lesser, secondary

It is of paramount importance that we understand the safety-first policy before starting working.

---

11 scrupulous [skrú:pjuləs]
a. 견실한, 양심적인, 정확한

taking care to do nothing morally wrong

ad scrupulously 양심적으로, 용의주도하게　n scrupulousness 양심적임, 용의주도함

syn careful, conscientious, correct　ant careless, unscrupulous

Nancy was elected treasurer based on her reputation as a scrupulous money manager.

---

12 immutable [immjú:təbəl]
a. 바꿀 수 없는, 불변의

not subject to change

n immutability 불변　ad immutably 불변하게

syn permanent, inflexible, unchangeable　ant changeable, variable

Supreme Court decisions are considered immutable as the Court is the highest in the U.S.

---

07 사치스러운 집안 장식과 값비싼 옷을 구매하여 그들은 2개월 동안 집세를 내지 못했다. 우리가 체류하게 될 호텔은 숙박시설이 잘 갖추어져 있다. 08 곡예단은 연습 동안 그의 불안한 행동에 지쳐서 그 문제에 대해 토론하기 위해 그를 회의에 불렀다. 09 많은 성직자들은 음주나 도박과 같은 행위를 비천한 습관으로 간주하고 있다. 10 일 하기 전에 안전 제일 정책을 이해하는 것이 무엇보다 중요하다. 11 Nancy는 양심적으로 돈을 관리한다는 평판 때문에 회계원으로 선출되었다. 12 대법원은 미국 최고의 법원이기 때문에 대법원 결정은 바꿀 수 없다.

13 astute [əstʃúːt]
a. 빈틈없는, 기민한

having ability to behave intelligently

ad astutely 날카로운 통찰력으로, 빈틈없이 n astuteness 빈틈없음

syn shrewd, clever, keen ant dumb, stupid, unintelligent

The astute judge made a wise decision during the trial.

14 versatile [və́ːrsətl]
a. 다재 다능한, 만능의

having many different skills

n versatility 융통성, 다재다능

syn pliable, adaptable, adjustable, flexible ant inflexible, inadaptable

He is a versatile actor who has experience in many different ways.

15 deficient [difíʃənt]
a. 부족한, 불충분한

not good enough

n deficiency 부족, 결핍 n deficit 부족액, 부족

syn inadequate, insufficient, scant ant adequate, ample, sufficient

The college terminated their contract with the company, citing a continuously deficient effort in lawn maintenance.

16 impeccable [impékəbəl]
a. 흠이 없는, 죄를 저지르지 않은

free from fault, perfect in every way

a impeccant 죄가 없는, 결백한 ad impeccably 결점이 없게

syn flawless, perfect, immaculate ant flawed, blemished, unkempt

James was said to have impeccable speech in front of people gathering at the park.

17 inept [inépt]
a. 부적당한, 서투른

having no skill

ad ineptly 서투르게, 적합치 않게 n ineptness 서투름, 적합치 않음

syn clumsy, awkward, inefficient, improper ant competent

The inept reporter quoted the official incorrectly many times in the newspaper.

18 captivate [kǽptəvèit]
v. 매혹하다, 사로잡다

to delight, charm or fascinate

n captivation 매혹, 매료 a captivating 매혹적인

syn mesmerize, intrigue, dazzle, interest ant turn off, offend, revolt

The boy who wants to be a singer captivated a large audience in the gym last night.

19 nullify [nʌ́ləfài]
v. 무효로하다, 취소하다

to make of no effect

n nullification 무효(화), 파기, 취소

syn invalidate, annul, cancel ant confirm, ratify, validate

The two nations will nullify the old treaty and sign a new one.

---

13 그 빈틈없는 판사는 재판 동안 현명한 결정을 했다. 14 그는 여러 분야에 경험이 있는 다재다능한 배우다. 15 그 대학은 잔디 관리 노력이 부족하다는 이유를 들면서 그 회사와의 계약을 종결지었다. 16 James는 공원에 모인 사람들 앞에서 완벽한 연설을 했다고 한다. 17 그 서투른 기자는 신문에 여러 차례 그 공무원을 부정확하게 인용했다. 18 가수를 꿈꾸는 소년은 어제 밤 체육관의 청중들을 사로잡았다. 19 두 국가는 구 조약을 무효로 하고 새로운 조약을 체결할 것이다.

20 veto [víːtou]

v. 거부권을 행사하다

n. 거부권

to refuse to allow to do something

ⓐ veto-proof 거부권에 대항하는

ⓢⓨⓝ stop, negate, refuse, block ⓐⓝⓣ permit, allow, approve

The President will veto the Immigration Bill that has already passed by Congress.

They put a veto on identifying information about themselves.

---

21 glisten [glísn]

v. 반짝 빛나다. 번쩍거리다

to shine or sparkle

ⓐⓓ glisteningly 반짝반짝

ⓢⓨⓝ sparkle, gleam, glitter, shine

When they entered the museum, his son's eyes glistened with curiosity.

---

22 vex [veks]

v. 괴롭히다, 성나게하다

to irritate someone, to displease someone

ⓝ vexation 짜증내기, 괴롭히기 ⓐ vexed 속타는, 짜증나는

ⓢⓨⓝ aggravate, harass, irritate, upset ⓐⓝⓣ soothe, assist, help

Scientists were vexed by the lack of consistent DNA between the mother and her child.

---

23 tantalize [tǽntəlàiz]

v. 남을 애태우다, 감질나게 하다

to excite someone by keeping something he wants just out of reach

ⓐ tantalizing 남의 기대를 부추기는, 감질나는

ⓢⓨⓝ tease, tempt, entice, captivate ⓐⓝⓣ disgust, repel, revolt

The rival firm tantalized her with promises of a salary increase and profit sharing.

---

24 manipulate [mənípjulèit]

v. 잘 다루다, 조정하다

to handle something in a skillful way

ⓐ manipulative 손으로 다루는, 솜씨 있게 다루는

ⓢⓨⓝ shape, direct, maneuver, guide

Parents are advised to be firm with their young children so as to avoid being manipulated.

---

25 antagonize [æntǽgənàiz]

v. 대항하다, 적대하다

to make someone feel angry

ⓝ antagonist 적대자, 경쟁자 ⓐ antagonistic 적대하는, 대립하는

ⓢⓨⓝ irritate, provoke, offend, anger ⓐⓝⓣ befriend

He continued to antagonize his sister despite his parents' admonitions.

---

20 의회에서 이미 통과된 이민법에 대통령이 거부권을 행사할 것이다. 그들은 자신들의 신원을 밝히는 것을 거부했다. 21 그들이 박물관에 들어서자 그의 아들의 눈이 호기심으로 빛났다. 22 과학자들은 어머니와 그녀 자식 사이에 DNA가 일치하지 않아 난처했다. 23 경쟁회사는 급여 인상과 이익 분배를 약속하며 그녀를 애태우게 했다. 24 부모들은 자녀에게 조정되지 않도록 엄격하라고 충고를 듣는다. 25 그는 부모님의 충고에도 불구하고 누나에게 계속해서 대항했다.

Exercise

Word Check 각 단어의 뜻으로 알맞은 것을 찾아 연결하시오.

01 hierarchy   (a) the right to formally reject a proposal

02 impeccable   (b) a graded organization classifying people or things

03 veto   (c) free from fault or error

04 versatile   (d) of supreme importance

05 paramount   (e) adapting easily to different tasks

Syn & Ant Check 주어진 단어의 동의어, 반의어를 골라 쓰시오.

noble	changeable	blessing	sparkle	competent
flaw	enthusiasm	sufficient	charm	scant

06 captivate = _____

07 fervor = _____

08 benediction = _____

09 glisten = _____

10 blot = _____

11 immutable ↔ _____

12 ignoble ↔ _____

13 lavish ↔ _____

14 inept ↔ _____

15 deficient ↔ _____

Sentence Practice 문장을 읽고 빈칸에 알맞은 단어를 고르시오.

16 The judge may _____ the election due to widespread implications of fraud and voter intimidation.

   ⓐ nullify   ⓑ tantalize   ⓒ veto   ⓓ vex

17 Adultery is socially and legally unacceptable because it violates the pledge of _____ a married couple makes.

   ⓐ fervor   ⓑ fidelity   ⓒ hierarchy   ⓓ faculty

18 I chose to drop the megaphone and remain silent rather than speak up and _____ the seething crowd.

   ⓐ glisten   ⓑ manipulate   ⓒ antagonize   ⓓ captivate

19 The _____ banquet at the coronation was discussed for weeks by the media, ordinary citizens and of course the fortunate attendees.

   ⓐ impeccable   ⓑ inept   ⓒ lavish   ⓓ astute

20 The famous racehorse Seabiscuit had a _____ temperament and could only be ridden by a handful of extremely skilled jockeys.

   ⓐ paramount   ⓑ versatile   ⓒ capricious   ⓓ scrupulous

🎧 01 **hygiene** [háidʒiːn]
n. 위생, 위생학

the science of maintaining health through cleanliness

ⓝ hygienic 위생적인, 청결한 hygienist 위생 학자

syn cleanliness, sanitation

Public hygiene is very important to a person's health.

---

02 **snare** [snɛər]
n. 덫, 올가미

a trap for catching animals

syn trap, allurement, lure, decoy

The wolf caught its leg in a snare that had been set by a hunter.

---

03 **sprout** [spraut]
n. 새싹, (식물의)눈
v. 싹트다, 발생하다

a new growth on a plant

ⓝ sproutling 작은 싹, 새싹

syn germinate, spring, bud, burgeon

I was so excited when I saw new sprouts in my garden.

Water them twice a day until they start to sprout.

---

04 **deluge** [déljuːdʒ]
n. 대홍수, 범람
v. 범람시키다

a large flood

syn flood, inundation   ant drought, lack

The deluge of student's questions kept the professor at the meeting for two hours.

The city was deluged with rain for about a week last year.

---

05 **siege** [siːdʒ]
n. 포위, 포위공격

a persistent attempt to gain control by surrounding an enemy

ⓐ siegeable 포위(공격)할 수 있는

syn offense, assault, attack

The enemy army laid siege to the city for a year.

---

06 **latency** [léitənsi]
n. 숨어있음, 잠복

something that is hidden and not active

ⓐ latent 숨은, 잠재한

syn inactivity, dormancy   ant activity, openness

The researchers discovered the unique latency of the virus.

---

01 공중위생은 우리 건강에 매우 중요하다. 02 늑대의 다리가 사냥꾼이 설치한 덫에 걸렸다. 03 나는 정원에서 새싹을 보고 매우 흥분했었다. 그들이 싹이 트기 시작할 때까지 하루에 두 번씩 물을 주어라. 04 학생들의 많은 질문 때문에 교수는 두 시간 동안 회의 장소에 있었다. 도시는 지난 해 약 일주일 동안 범람했다. 05 적군은 일년 동안 그 도시를 포위하고 있었다. 06 연구원들은 그 바이러스의 독특한 잠복기를 발견했다.

07 **tremor** [trémər]
n. 떨림, 전율

a shaking movement

ⓐ tremorous 떨리는, 진동하는

ⓢⓨⓝ shiver, shudder, quiver, oscillation　ⓐⓝⓣ stillness

The scientists studied the data from the earthquake's tremor for many months.

08 **sphere** [sfiər]
n. 구, 구체, 지구의

something in the shape of a ball

ⓐ spherical 구형의, 구면의

ⓢⓨⓝ ball, globe, orbit, scope

Do you know how to calculate the surface area of a sphere?

09 **chubby** [tʃʌ́bi]
a. 토실토실한, 살찐

round and plump

ⓝ chubbiness 오동통함

ⓢⓨⓝ plump, round, pudgy, fat, stout　ⓐⓝⓣ lean, skinny, thin, slim

The chubby young girl stared at an exercise program on the bulletin.

10 **adroit** [ədrɔ́it]
a. 손재주가 있는, 재치가 있는

skillful and clever

ⓐⓓ adroitly 능숙하게, 영리하게　ⓝ adroitness 솜씨있음, 영리함

ⓢⓨⓝ skillful, adept, expert, proficient　ⓐⓝⓣ clumsy, unskilled, inept

The man who has been making watches at the company for 20 years is a very adroit worker.

11 **sullen** [sʌ́lən]
a. 묵뚝뚝한, 시무룩한

gloomy or silently showing anger

ⓝ sullenness 시무룩함, 뚱함　ⓐⓓ sullenly 시무룩하게, 뚱하게

ⓢⓨⓝ glum, sulky, sour, grumpy　ⓐⓝⓣ cheerful

The man with the sullen expression is my uncle from France.

12 **corpulent** [kɔ́ːrpjulənt]
a. 뚱뚱한, 비만의

very fat

ⓐⓓ corpulently 뚱뚱하게, 비대하게　ⓝ corpulence 비만, 비대

ⓢⓨⓝ stout, fat, bulky　ⓐⓝⓣ bony, skinny, slender

The corpulent guard could not chase the thief any longer.

13 **dismal** [dízməl]
a. 음산한, 침울한

causing gloom and misery

ⓐⓓ dismally 음울하게, 쓸쓸하게　ⓝ dismalness 음울, 쓸쓸함

ⓢⓨⓝ gloomy, melancholy, murky, bleak　ⓐⓝⓣ joyful, cheerful, pleasant

The slumping American economy is making the global economic outlook dismal.

---

07 과학자들은 수개월 동안 지진의 진동 자료를 연구했다. 08 구면의 면적을 어떻게 계산하는지 알고 있니? 09 살이 좀 찐 어린아이가 게시판 위의 운동 프로그램을 쳐다보았다. 10 그 회사에서 시계를 20년 동안 제작해온 저 사람은 매우 손재주가 있는 직원이다. 11 무뚝뚝한 표정을 짓고 있는 사람은 프랑스에서 온 나의 삼촌이다. 12 뚱뚱한 경비는 도둑을 더 이상 쫓아가지 못했다. 13 미국의 침체된 경제로 인해 세계 경제 전망이 침울하다.

14 **downcast** [dáunkæ̀st]
a. 의기소침한, 풀이죽은

feeling sad

[ad] downcastly 의기소침하게, 풀이 죽어 [n] downcastness 의기소침함

[syn] discouraged, desolate [ant] cheerful, elated, joyous, vivacious

He saw the world through downcast eyes because of his misfortune.

---

15 **static** [stǽtik]
a. 정적인, 고정된
n. 소음

tending to not to move

[ad] statically 정적으로

[syn] still [ant] dynamic, kinetic

The consumer prices that have been static for almost a year begin to rise due to increase of oil price.

The loud static from the storm interrupted my radio program this evening.

---

16 **prolific** [prou̯lífik]
a. 다산의, 비옥한

producing a lot of something

[n] prolificity 다산성, 다산력 prolificacy 다산, 다작

[syn] teeming, abundant, fruitful [ant] unproductive barren

Kyle is a prolific writer who completes at least 7 books and 12 magazine articles every year.

---

17 **despotic** [dispátik]
a. 독재의, 절대군주의

tyrannical or cruel and unfair

[ad] despotically 독재적으로, 절대 군주로 [n] despoticalness 독재적임, 절대 군주임

[syn] autocratic, tyrannical, oppressive [ant] democratic

Jack was a despotic employer whom people didn't want to work for.

---

18 **sluggish** [slʌ́giʃ]
a. 느린, 둔한, 기능이 활발하지 못한

moving, working, or reacting more slowly than normal

[ad] sluggishly 게으르게, 나태하게 [n] sluggishness 게으름, 나태

[syn] inactive, indolent, torpid, lethargic, slack [ant] active, brisk

Economists say that our economy remains more sluggish than they predicted.

The high summer heat is making everyone in the office sluggish and unwilling to work hard.

---

19 **loathsome** [lóuðsəm]
a. 싫은, 기분 나쁜

very unpleasant

[v] loath 싫어서, 질색하여

[syn] disgusting, detestable, abhorrent, abominable [ant] attractive, lovable

Who do you think is the most loathsome politician in the country?

---

14 그는 불행 때문에 의기소침한 눈으로 세상을 보았다. 15 오일 가격의 상승으로 거의 일년 동안 정지해 있던 소비자 물가가 오르기 시작했다. 태풍으로 인한 소음 때문에 오늘 저녁 나의 라디오 프로그램이 방해를 받았다. 16 Kyle은 다작하는 작가로 매년 7권의 책과 12개의 잡지기사를 쓴다. 17 Jack은 사람들이 같이 일하길 원치 않는 횡포가 심한 고용주였다. 18 경제학자들은 우리 경제가 그들이 예상한 것보다 더욱 좋지 않다고 말한다. 여름의 높은 기온으로 사무실의 모든 사람이 나태해졌고 열심히 일할 욕구를 떨어뜨리고 있다. 19 우리나라에서 가장 기분 나쁜 정치인은 누구라고 생각하니?

20 copious [kóupiəs]
a. 많은, 대량의, 풍부한

a large amount

ad copiously 풍부[풍성]하게 n copiousness 풍부함, 풍성함

syn ample, plentiful, profuse ant scanty, scarce

The farm produced a copious number of crops this year.

---

21 congruous [káŋgruəs]
a. 일치하는, 조화하는

appropriate and harmonious

n congruity 적합, 조화

syn harmonious, consistent ant disagreeing, incongruous

The new by-law is congruous with the constitution of our organization.

---

22 coax [kouks]
v. 달래어 ~시키다

to urge gently

n coaxing 감언으로 꾀기, 달래기

syn persuade, cajole, allure ant compel, dissuade, force

His mother coaxed him to take care of his brother while she was washing dishes.

---

23 mortify [mɔ́ːrtəfài]
v. 분하게 하다, 굴욕을 느끼다

to feel humiliated

n mortification 굴욕, 치욕

syn humble, abase, disgrace ant exalt, dignify

Sam will be mortified when he finds out that he has been demoted from his present position.

---

24 reckon [rékən]
v. 계산하다, 생각하다, 기대하다

to count or estimate

n reckoning 계산, 셈 a reckonable 계산할 수 있는, 짐작할 수 있는

syn enumerate, account, calculate, compute

The students were surprised very much when the professor reckoned the cost of Iraq war.

The company reckoned on supplying parts to five factories next year.

---

25 propagate [prápəgèit]
v. 보급하다, 선전하다, 번식시키다

to reproduce oneself or spread

n propagation 번식, 증식 a propagational 번식의, 증식의

syn reproduce, breed, multiply, spread

The writer propagated his dream of traveling to other planets.

Dandelions propagate wildly in almost any kind of terrain and choke off other forms of plant life.

---

20 그 농장에서 올해 많은 곡식을 생산했다. 21 새로운 내규는 우리 조직의 정관과 조화를 이룬다. 22 그의 어머니는 설거지를 하는 동안 그가 동생을 돌보도록 설득했다. 23 Sam이 현재 자신의 지위에서 강등되었다는 것을 알면 굴욕감을 느낄 것이다. 24 교수가 이라크의 전쟁 비용을 계산했을 때 학생들은 매우 놀랐다. 그 회사는 내년에 다섯 개의 공장에 부품 납품할 생각을 했다. 25 그 작가는 다른 행성으로 여행하고픈 그의 꿈을 전파했다. 민들레는 거의 모든 토양에서 번식하며 다른 식물들을 잠식해 간다.

Exercise

Word Check 각 단어의 뜻으로 알맞은 것을 찾아 연결하시오.

01 dismal   (a) exhibiting harmony of parts

02 latency   (b) the state living or developing in a host without producing

03 congruous   (c) not cheerful to cause or suggest sadness

04 prolific   (d) producing plentiful fruit or offspring

05 siege   (e) the act or process of surrounding a fort or town

Syn & Ant Check 주어진 단어의 동의어, 반의어를 골라 쓰시오.

skillful	plentiful	tyrannical	stillness	active
drought	ball	skinny	trap	cheerful

06 snare = _____

07 adroit = _____

08 sphere = _____

09 despotic = _____

10 copious = _____

11 downcast ↔ _____

12 tremor ↔ _____

13 deluge ↔ _____

14 sluggish ↔ _____

15 corpulent ↔ _____

Sentence Practice 문장을 읽고 빈칸에 알맞은 단어를 고르시오.

16 Maintaining high levels of personal _____ is an important part of staying healthy.

   ⓐ latency   ⓑ deluges   ⓒ siege   ⓓ hygiene

17 My little nephew is delighted to see leaves _____ on the seedling he planted a month ago.

   ⓐ reckon   ⓑ sprout   ⓒ coax   ⓓ mortify

18 Some hyacinths _____ swiftly and choke small water bodies with their profusion.

   ⓐ propagate   ⓑ coax   ⓒ reckon   ⓓ mortify

19 Continual overeating has made Martin go from slightly _____ to morbidly obese.

   ⓐ dismal   ⓑ corpulent   ⓒ adroit   ⓓ chubby

20 Alicia adopted a _____ outlook toward life after her fiance abandoned her without giving any explanation.

   ⓐ static   ⓑ sluggish   ⓒ sullen   ⓓ loathsome

suffix

동사형 suffix

-ize : sympathy ⇨ **sympathize, industrial ⇨ industrialize, familiar ⇨ familiarize**
Though society sympathizes with the women's movement, normally people hate extreme feminists.
비록 사회가 여성운동에 공감하지만 극단적 여성운동가는 싫어한다.

-en : fright ⇨ **frighten, deep ⇨ deepen, wide ⇨ widen**
The agenda was how to frighten illegal aliens to reduce the crime rates.
논제는 범죄율을 낮추기 위해 불법체류자들을 어떻게 겁을 주느냐였다.

-ify : simple ⇨ **simplify, just ⇨ justify, terror ⇨ terrify**
Simplify the safety instructions for children to understand clearly.
아이들이 분명하게 이해할 수 있도록 안전 지시문을 간단하게 써라.

-ish : ban ⇨ **banish, pub ⇨ publish, pun ⇨ punish**
The Chinese government banished Dalai Lama for Tibetan independence movement.
중국정부는 티베트 독립운동을 지지했다는 이유로 달라이라마를 추방했다.

-e : breath ⇨ **breathe, wreath ⇨ wreathe, bath ⇨ bathe**
Whales come up for air when they breathe and navigate the ocean.
고래는 숨 쉬고 바다를 항해하면서 물 위로 올라온다.

-ate : assassin ⇨ **assassinate, carbon ⇨ carbonate, compassion ⇨ compassionate**
One of the secret agents was apparently sent to try to assassinate the Princess.
비밀요원 중 한 명이 그 왕비를 암살하려고 파견된 것이 분명하다.

의미별 suffix

-ism(학설) : **criticism, nihilism**
When you give some advice to someone, constructive criticism is always welcome.
누군가에게 조언을 해줄 때, 건설적인 조언이면 언제나 환영을 받는다.

-oloby(study) : **uranology**
Uranology is a branch of physics studying the universe and celestial bodies.
천문학은 우주와 천체를 연구하는 물리학의 한 분야이다.

-some(like) : **cumbersome, awesome**
The new president said that he would improve the cumbersome administrative procedures.
새 대통령은 업무에 방해되는 행정 절차를 개선하겠다고 말했다.

Review test Day 16 ~ Day 20

A 영어 풀이에 알맞은 단어를 보기에서 찾아 쓰시오.

connoisseur	bewilder	verdict	vex	propagate

01 the answer of a jury given to the court _____

02 to confuse or puzzle completely _____

03 a person who is knowledgeable about a particular subject such as arts _____

04 to annoy or irritate someone _____

05 to multiply by any process of natural reproduction _____

B 문장을 읽고 문맥에 적절한 단어를 고르시오.

06 The recent instance of spectator unruliness in the stadium during the semifinals will remain a (deterrent/blot) upon the history of American Football.

07 (Aquatic/Archaic) animals have special marine adaptations that help them survive in water.

08 The young man put his own life in (peril/verdict) by rushing into the building engulfed in flames to save the little child.

09 Heavy rains caused the lake to finally burst the dam and (cede/deluge) the entire town with over 25 feet of water.

C [   ] 표시된 부분과 뜻이 가장 가까운 것을 고르시오.

10 Her astute analysis of cost production factors saved the company several million dollars.

ⓐ shrewd ⓑ mediocre ⓒ capricious ⓓ comprehensive

11 It wouldn't be wrong to say that we were a congruous group despite our personal differences.

ⓐ lavish ⓑ sullen ⓒ consistent ⓓ celestial

12 She was so engrossed in her work that she didn't notice her tea had gone tepid from sitting out for over an hour.

ⓐ inept ⓑ prolific ⓒ volatile ⓓ lukewarm

13 Mexico ceded its northwestern states to the U.S. after its defeat in the Mexican-American War.

ⓐ inaugurated ⓑ surrendered ⓒ recurred ⓓ propagated

D 표시된 부분의 반대말로 가장 알맞은 것을 고르시오.

14 We will have to make your cat sedate with a powerful tranquilizer before we can operate on her.

 ⓐ uncontrollable   ⓑ dexterous   ⓒ captivate   ⓓ penitent

15 Gary cannot be called a prolific writer since he publishes just one book every two years.

 ⓐ dexterous   ⓑ unproductive   ⓒ pedantic   ⓓ dismal

16 The faculty was expanded in size when 3 more professors were induced to join from a renowned university.

 ⓐ verdict   ⓑ hierarchy   ⓒ pupils   ⓓ connoisseur

17 The company decided to augment its taskforce by recruiting workers locally.

 ⓐ patronize   ⓑ reduce   ⓒ reckon   ⓓ appall

E 주어진 단어를 알맞은 형태로 바꿔 빈칸에 쓰시오.

18 The _____ in the dam was noticed before it could do any harm to life. (breach)

19 The new president obviously enjoyed his _____ . (inaugurate)

20 Please make sure you should check all _____ facts on the import contract before you affix your signature. (verify)

21 It is glorious to wake up in the morning and see the flowers _____ with dew. (glisten)

F 빈 칸에 알맞은 단어를 보기에서 찾아 쓰시오. (필요한 경우 형태를 바꾸시오.)

vex	verdict	dwindle	versatile	sullen	impromptu	recur	belligerent

22 We found that Sean was a highly _____ musician who could play four instruments with ease.

23 Sheila was prompted by the urgings of the guests to put on a(n) _____ performance of Frank Sinatra's hit *My Way*.

24 The doctor had to use a sedative to calm the increasingly _____ patient.

25 The desert dwellers migrate to nearby towns during the dry summer months when water _____ .

➤ 영어를 우리말로 옮기시오.

01	inadvertent		31	sedate
02	immutable		32	hybrid
03	antagonize		33	patronize
04	commotion		34	impeccable
05	inept		35	bewilder
06	deficient		36	noxious
07	mediocre		37	therapeutic
08	detract		38	concede
09	elucidate		39	timid
10	celestial		40	detrimental
11	benediction		41	pedagogue
12	downcast		42	tenacious
13	connoisseur		43	deteriorate
14	dismal		44	captivate
15	loathsome		45	comprehensive
16	melancholy		46	translucent
17	dwindle		47	delegate
18	tantalize		48	faculty
19	discreet		49	glisten
20	adulterate		50	volition
21	foliage		51	dubious
22	congruous		52	ignoble
23	vacillate		53	gregarious
24	breach		54	differentiate
25	reckon		55	pecuniary
26	verify		56	emancipate
27	tremor		57	corpulent
28	grotesque		58	reconcile
29	propagate		59	static
30	hamper		60	flounder

우리말을 영어로 옮기시오.

61	야윈, 쇠약한		91	방해물, 억제력	
62	판결, 심판		92	새싹	
63	뉘우치는		93	구식의, 고대의	
64	무딘, 뭉툭한		94	많은, 대량의	
65	적, 상대자		95	게걸스레 먹는	
66	잘 다루다		96	후원자, 보호자	
67	재치가 있는		97	다재다능한	
68	낙담한, 기가 죽은		98	계층, 서열	
69	다산의, 비옥한		99	즉흥적인	
70	충고[훈계]하다		100	즉흥[즉석]의	
71	(사람을) 달래다		101	영리한, 민첩한	
72	견실한, 양심적인		102	숨어있음, 잠복	
73	절대군주의		103	대홍수, 범람	
74	지구상의		104	협박, 위협	
75	추측[짐작]하다		105	물의, 물속의	
76	양도[양보]하다		106	우회하다	
77	토실토실한		107	무효로 하다	
78	무뚝뚝한		108	남아도는	
79	미지근한		109	혼수상태의	
80	교묘히 피하다		110	빈틈없는	
81	탈수하다		111	열정, 열렬	
82	위로[위문]하다		112	충실	
83	용감한, 호전적인		113	휘발성의	
84	느린, 둔한		114	황폐시키다	
85	분개하다		115	취임하다	
86	상스러운, 천한		116	괴롭히다	
87	증가시키다		117	변덕스런	
88	벗어나다		118	섬뜩하게 하다	
89	최고권력을 쥔		119	보충물	
90	다시 일어나다		120	위험, 모험	

Part 5

Day 21

01 punctuality [pʌ̀ŋktʃuǽləti]
n. 시간엄수

arrival at the right time
ⓐ punctual 시간을 지키는　ⓐ𝖽 punctually 시간을 엄수하여, 정확하게
ⓢ𝗒𝗇 meticulousness, exactness　ⓐ𝗇𝗍 late

The other workers admired his continued punctuality even though his leg was broken.

02 abode [əbóud]
n. 주소, 주거

a dwelling or home
ⓢ𝗒𝗇 residence, dwelling, habitation

His humble abode was a small apartment in the city.

03 hindrance [híndrəns]
n. 방해, 장애

an obstacle that prevents progress
ⓥ hinder 방해하다, 훼방놓다
ⓢ𝗒𝗇 obstacle, intervention, interference, obstruction　ⓐ𝗇𝗍 advantage, aid

His long coat was a hindrance to his ability to work, so he removed it.

04 lineage [líniidʒ]
n. 혈통, 계통

the series of families of a particular ancestor
ⓢ𝗒𝗇 pedigree, genealogy, heredity, line

My father wants me to marry a man of good lineage.

05 fortitude [fɔ́ːrtətjùːd]
n. 인내, 강건함

courage during a time of pain or trouble
ⓐ fortitudinous 불굴의 정신이 있는
ⓢ𝗒𝗇 firmness, courage, resolution, persistence　ⓐ𝗇𝗍 weakness

The hiker demonstrated great fortitude during the difficult walk to save his injured friend.

06 forfeit [fɔ́ːrfit]
n. 벌금, 위약금
v. 상실하다, 몰수당하다

to give up something or have it taken away
ⓝ forfeiture 몰수, 벌금, 과료　ⓝ forfeiter 권리(재산)의 상실자
ⓢ𝗒𝗇 relinquish, lose, renounce　ⓐ𝗇𝗍 retain

A forfeit was the decision of the court after a lengthy trial.

The football team forfeited the game due to the new rule.

---

01 다리를 다쳤음에도 불구하고 그가 계속해서 시간을 엄수하자 다른 동료들이 감탄했다. 02 도시의 조그만 아파트가 그의 소박한 거주지이다. 03 그의 긴 코트가 일하는데 방해가 되어서 코트를 벗었다. 04 나의 아버지는 내가 좋은 가문의 남자와 결혼하기를 원한다. 05 그 도보 여행자는 부상당한 친구를 구하기 위해 어려운 여행기간 동안 강인함을 보여주었다. 06 오랜 재판 후 법원은 벌금 판결을 내렸다. 새로운 규칙 때문에 그 축구팀은 게임을 몰수당했다.

07 elastic [ilǽstik]
a. 탄력의, 탄력 있는

able to stretch and return to its original shape
ⓥ elasticate (옷감·옷 따위)에 신축성을 지니게 하다 ⓝ elasticity 탄력, 신축성
syn resilient, flexible ant rigid, inflexible, inelastic

My mother sewed a new elastic waistband into my skirt which she bought me last year.

08 arduous [á:rdʒuəs]
a. 고된, 힘든

needing a lot of hard and continuous effort
ad arduously 힘들게, 정열적으로 ⓝ arduousness 불요불굴, 끈기
syn severe, laborious, burdensome ant easy, painless, simple, facile

The explorers faced an arduous journey through the jungle.

09 titanic [taitǽnik]
a. 거대한, 강력한

a big, strong, or important person or thing
ad titanically 거대하게
syn gigantic, enormous, massive, immense

The titanic problem will not be easy to solve without your help.

10 tactile [tǽktil]
a. 촉각의

tangible or touchable
ⓝ tactility 감촉성
syn tangible, touchable, physical

The man discovered a change in the tactile sensation in his hand after the car accident.

11 meager [mí:gər]
a. 메마른, 빈약한

not enough in quantity or quality
ad meagerly 빈약하게 결핍되어 ⓝ meagerness 빈약함, 결핍됨
syn scanty, skinny, bare, deficient, insufficient ant abundant, large, fat

The farmer had a meager harvest from his fields this year.

12 haughty [hɔ́:ti]
a. 건방진, 도도한

very arrogant
ad haughtily 건방지게, 오만하게 ⓝ haughtiness 건방짐, 오만
syn arrogant, disdainful, conceited ant humble, unpretentious, modest

The man in charge of customer service spoke with a haughty tone in his voice.

13 perfunctory [pəːrfʌ́ŋktəri]
a. 형식적인, 마지못한

done without genuine care
ad perfunctorily 형식적으로
syn unconcerned, indifferent, apathetic, superficial ant careful, thorough

The security guard made a perfunctory check of the doors and quickly walked back to his office.

---

07 어머니는 작년에 내게 사준 치마에 신축성 있는 새로운 허리 밴드를 꿰매주셨다. 08 탐험가들은 정글을 통과하는 힘든 여행에 직면했다. 09 이 중요한 문제를 당신 도움 없이는 쉽게 해결할 수 없을 것이다. 10 그 남자는 자동차 사고 후 손의 촉감에 변화가 있음을 발견했다. 11 그 농부는 올해 수확이 좋지 않았다. 12 고객서비스를 담당하는 그 남자는 도도한 목소리로 얘기했다. 13 안전요원은 형식적으로 문을 점검하고 서둘러 사무실로 돌아갔다.

14 manifold [mǽnəfòuld]
a. 다양한, 다수의

many different kinds
[ad] manifoldly 다양하게, 복합적으로 [n] manifoldness 다양함, 복합적임
[syn] various, diverse, multiple, numerous [ant] simple, single

My new job is to collect manifold data about climate change in North America.

15 obliterate [əblítəréit]
v. 지우다, 제거하다

to destroy something
[n] obliteration 말소, 제거
[syn] expunge, delete, eradicate, efface [ant] create

The fire which broke out last month obliterated many buildings in the downtown area.

16 efface [iféis]
v. 지우다, 제거하다

to remove something
[n] effacement 지움, 삭제 [a] effaceable 지울 수 있는
[syn] erase, delete, destroy, eliminate, expunge, obliterate

The child who had survived the crash finally effaced the unhappy memories that he kept in his mind.

17 sprinkle [spríŋkəl]
v. ~을 뿌리다, 끼얹다

to scatter drops or particles
[n] sprinkler 물뿌리개, 살수차 [n] sprinkling 흩뿌림
[syn] spray, scatter, strew

Smith sprinkled water on his friends playing basketball at the back yard.

My little sister sprinkled some sugar on the cookies.

18 reprehend [rèprihénd]
v. 비난하다, 꾸짖다

to criticize
[a] reprehendable 책망할 수 있는
[syn] rebuke, blame, criticize, reproach, admonish

The boy's mother reprehended him for his bad behavior.

19 exterminate [ikstə́ːrmənèit]
v. 박멸하다, 몰살하다

to destroy something completely
[n] extermination 멸종, 전멸 [a] exterminatory 근절[박멸]적인
[syn] destroy, eradicate, abolish, eliminate [ant] create, generate

My grandparents called a pest company to exterminate the insects in their basement.

Some scientists say that all humankind will be exterminated by a virus.

---

14 나의 새 임무는 북 아메리카의 기후변화에 대한 다양한 자료를 수집하는 것이다. 15 지난달 발생한 화재로 시내의 많은 건물들이 파괴되었다. 16 충돌사고 때 살아남은 그 어린이는 결국 마음속에서 불행한 기억들을 지웠다. 17 Smith는 뒤뜰에서 농구를 하고 있는 친구들에게 물을 뿌렸다. 나의 여동생은 과자 위에 약간의 설탕을 뿌렸다. 18 소년의 어머니는 소년의 잘못된 행동을 꾸짖었다. 19 나의 조부모님은 지하실에 있는 벌레를 제거하기 위해 해충 박멸회사에 전화했다. 일부 과학자들은 모든 인류가 바이러스에 의해 멸종될 것이라고 말한다.

20 wane [wein]

v. 작아지다, 쇠약해지다

to lessen gradually

[a] waney 쇠퇴해 가는, 감소한

[syn] decline, diminish, weaken [ant] grow, increase, rise, wax

As the soccer team failed to enter the World Cup tournament, the popularity of soccer began to wane.

---

21 cleave [kliːv]

v. 쪼개다, 틈을 내다

to divide or cut

[n] cleavage 분열, 갈라진 틈

[syn] halve, rend, cut, dissect [ant] attach, join, meld, unite

The scientist picked up a branch and cleaved it with a sharp knife.

---

22 feign [fein]

v. ~인체하다, 가장하다

to pretend

[ad] feigningly 가장하여, 꾸며내어 [a] feigned 가장한, 겉치레의

[syn] simulate, pretend, dissemble

The student feigned illness to get out of taking the math test.

---

23 revoke [rivóuk]

v. (약속, 면허 등을) 취소하다, 철회하다

to take back or with draw

[n] revocation 폐지, 축소

[syn] cancel, annul

Your license will be revoked if you are convicted of a crime.

---

24 disseminate [disémənèit]

v. (씨를) 뿌리다, 퍼트리다

to spread widely

[a] disseminative 살포하는, 보급하는 [n] dissemination 살포, 보급

[syn] distribute, spread, disperse, propagate [ant] contain

They will disseminate the flyers for the concert which will be held at the gym next week.

---

25 ascribe [əskráib]

v. ~의 탓으로 하다

to believe that something happens because of someone or something else

[a] ascribable ~에 돌릴 수 있는, ~ 탓인

[syn] attribute, credit, impute, refer

The governor ascribed the flooding to a break in the dam which was built 50 years ago.

---

20 축구팀의 월드컵 본선이 좌절되자 축구의 인기가 줄어들기 시작했다. 21 과학자는 나뭇가지를 주어서 날카로운 칼로 틈을 내었다. 22 그 학생은 수학시험을 보지 않기 위해 아픈체 했다. 23 범죄를 저지르면 당신의 면허는 취소될 것입니다. 24 그들은 다음주에 체육관에서 열리는 음악회 전단지를 뿌릴 것이다. 25 주지사는 홍수를 50년 전에 지어진 댐의 균열 탓으로 돌렸다.

Exercise

Word Check 각 단어의 뜻으로 알맞은 것을 찾아 연결하시오.

01 fortitude   (a) to believe that something happens because of others

02 cleave   (b) to cut or divide

03 perfunctory   (c) mental and emotional strength in facing difficulty

04 ascribe   (d) done merely as a duty or routine

05 punctuality   (e) the quality or habit of adhering to an appointed time

Syn & Ant Check 주어진 단어의 동의어, 반의어를 골라 쓰시오.

habitation	massive	fat	humble	pretend
create	erase	eradicate	single	inflexible

06 efface   = _____   11 elastic   ↔ _____

07 abode   = _____   12 meager   ↔ _____

08 titanic   = _____   13 manifold   ↔ _____

09 exterminate = _____   14 haughty   ↔ _____

10 feign   = _____   15 obliterate ↔ _____

Sentence Practice 문장을 읽고 빈칸에 알맞은 단어를 고르시오.

16 The new employee proved to be a _____ to our work as he needed constant supervision.

ⓐ hindrance   ⓑ lineage   ⓒ forfeit   ⓓ punctuality

17 Ben's enthusiasm for rugby _____ when the coach warned him of the long practice sessions required.

ⓐ waned   ⓑ cleaved   ⓒ effaced   ⓓ reprehended

18 The Internet is proving to be one of the most efficient ways to _____ both information and disinformation.

ⓐ sprinkle   ⓑ revoke   ⓒ ascribe   ⓓ disseminate

19 The view from the mountain peak is so stunning that most people don't mind the _____ climb to get there.

ⓐ arduous   ⓑ haughty   ⓒ perfunctory   ⓓ elastic

20 Infants receive _____ impressions of objects when they put them in their mouths.

ⓐ titanic   ⓑ meager   ⓒ tactile   ⓓ manifold

01 advent [ǽdvent]
n. 출현, 도래

arrival, coming into place
syn appearance, arrival   ant end, exit, departure

The advent of the steam engine was to signal the emergence of a new kind of warship.

02 antecedent [æntəsíːdənt]
n. 선조, 전례

something occurred or existed before the current one
ad antecedently 앞서, 선행하여   n antecedence 앞섬, 선행
syn precursor, forerunner   ant subsequence, following

He along with several other of his antecedents had purchased land in the Appalachian Mountains.

03 gleam [gliːm]
n. 미광, 희미한 빛
v. 어슴프레 빛나다

sparkle in the light
a gleamy 빛나는, 희미하게 빛나는   a gleaming 반짝반짝 빛나는
syn bright, sparkling, twinkle   ant dull, dim

There was a gleam coming from a crack on the roof.

Mercury needed the moon's reflection of the sun's rays in order to gleam brightest.

04 quest [kwest]
n. 탐구, 추구

a search to find something
n question 물음, 질문   a questing 탐색[탐구]하는
syn mission, journey, expedition, adventure

The United States' quest to reach space was prompted by the Soviet Union's successful launch of the satellite in 1957.

05 impetus [ímpətəs]
n. 힘, 자극, 충동

a force that moves something
syn incentive, stimulus, push, motivation

The economist suggests that tax cuts are needed to give impetus to the economy.

06 impulse [ímpʌls]
n. 추진력, 자극, 충동

an urge to do something
n impulsion 추진, 강제   a impulsive 충동적인, 추진적인
syn urge, inclination, desire

Grocery stores are arranged to appeal to impulse buyers.

---

01 증기기관의 도래는 새로운 종류의 군함이 출현한다는 신호가 되었다. 02 그는 몇몇 그의 선조들과 애팔래치아 산맥의 토지를 구입했다. 03 지붕의 갈라진 틈으로 빛이 들어왔다. 수성이 가장 밝게 빛나려면 태양빛을 반사하는 달빛이 필요하다. 04 1957년 소련의 성공적인 위성 발사로 인해 미국의 우주개발 탐구가 자극을 받았다. 05 그 경제학자는 경제를 살리기 위해서 세금감면이 필요하다고 제안했다. 06 소매점들은 충동 소비자들이 구매하도록 물건을 배열한다.

07 **custody** [kʌ́stədi]
n. 보호, 감금

care of someone, being kept in prison
n custodian 관리인, 보관자 ⓐ custodial 보관(보호)의
syn protection, keeping, imprisonment, detention

When the man was held in custody for tax evasion, he denied his wrongdoing.

08 **paranoia** [pæ̀rənɔ́ia]
n. 편집증, 망상증

a fear that people will hurt you
ⓐ paranoiac 편집광의
syn distrust, suspicion, fear

We thought that he had paranoia because he was suspicious of his neighbors and feared that they were spying on him through his windows.

09 **residue** [rézidʒùː]
n. 잔여, 나머지

a small amount after the whole of something is gone
ⓐ residual 나머지의, 찌꺼기의   ⓐ residuary 잔여의, 나머지의
syn debris, remainder, leftover, remnant

The police hoped that any residue from the gunpowder could be analyzed, and proffer clues as to the identity of the assailant.

10 **prestige** [prestíːdʒ]
n. 위신, 명성

high reputation someone or something has
ⓐ prestigious 명성이 있는, 유명한   ad prestigiously 유명하게, 일류로
syn fame, renown, celebrity

If the bribery scandal is revealed to the public, the politician will lose his prestige.

11 **requisite** [rékwəzit]
a. 필수의, 필요한

necessary for a special purpose
ad requisitely 필요하게, 필수적으로   n requisiteness 필수적임, 필요 불가결함
syn necessary, required, mandatory   ant optional, dispensable

When they ran out of requisite items such as corn, meal and salt, they asked for help to their neighbors.

12 **combustible** [kəmbʌ́stəbəl]
a. 타기 쉬운, 흥분하기 쉬운

burn easily, easily excited
n combustibility 연소성, 가연성
syn flammable, explosive, volatile   ant noncombustible, non-explosive

The damage caused by the fire was worse than we expected due to combustible material in our building.

---

07 탈세로 인해 구금되었을 때 그는 잘못을 부인했다. 08 그가 이웃을 의심하고 그들이 창문을 통해 자신을 감시한다고 두려워하기 때문에 우리는 그가 망상증에 걸렸다고 생각했다. 09 경찰은 화약의 잔여물이 분석되어 침입자의 신원을 밝히는데 실마리가 되기를 기대했다. 10 만약에 뇌물 스캔들이 대중에 밝혀지면 그 정치인은 명예를 잃을 것이다. 11 그들이 옥수수, 육류, 소금과 같은 필수 품목이 떨어지면 이웃에 도움을 청했다. 12 건물의 가연성 물질 때문에 화재로 인한 피해가 예상보다 심했다.

13 **inquisitive** [inkwízətiv]
a. 질문을 좋아하는, 탐구적인

showing curiosity, eager to find out things

ad inquisitively 연구를 좋아하여, 호기심이 많아　n inquisition 조사(탐구)하는 일

syn curious, inquiring　ant unconcerned, uninterested

The children are looking at the dinosaur in the book with inquisitive eyes.

14 **naive** [nɑːíːv]
a. 순진한, 천진난만한

having no experience

syn inexperienced, immature　ant mature, experienced

People from the country are less naive than many think.

15 **obscure** [əbskjúər]
a. 분명치 않은, 어두컴컴한

difficult to see

ad obscurely 애매하게, 희미하게

syn cloudy, blurred, murky　ant plain, clear

The journal was found in an obscure closet at the back of the house.

16 **colossal** [kəlásəl]
a. 거대한, 엄청난

immense in scale

ad colossally 거대하게

syn huge, immense, giant　ant tiny, miniscule, small

The "Big Room" is a colossal cave found in the Carlsbad Caverns in Southeastern New Mexico.

17 **vicious** [víʃəs]
a. 나쁜, 잔인한, 악의 있는

showing nature of vice

n viciousness 사악함, 심술궂음

syn fierce, terrible, malicious, ferocious　ant amiable, kind, nice

If communities offered any resistance to his armies, his retribution would be vicious.

18 **facilitate** [fəsílətèit]
v. 용이하게 하다, 쉽게 하다

to make something easy or less difficult

a facilitative 촉진하는　n facilitation 용이하게 하기, 촉진, 조장

syn help, assist, aid　ant block, impede

To facilitate the on-time arrival of buses at bus stops, lifts were added to aid those unable to climb stairs.

19 **glaze** [gleiz]
v. 판유리를 끼우다, 유약을 칠하다

to cover something

a glazed 유약을 바른, 유리를 끼운　n glazer 유약을 바르는 직공, 윤내는 기계

syn varnish, coat, cover　ant strip

Porcelain must be properly glazed if it is to retain its luster.

---

13 어린이들은 호기심 가득한 눈빛으로 책에 있는 공룡을 바라보고 있다. 14 시골에서 온 사람들이 많은 사람이 생각하는 것보다 덜 순진하다. 15 그 잡지는 집 뒤쪽의 어두컴컴한 벽장에서 발견되었다. 16 "Big Room"은 뉴 멕시코 남동부 Carlsbad Canverns에서 발견된 거대한 동굴이다. 17 어떤 집단이 그의 군대에 저항하면 그는 잔인하게 보복할 것이다. 18 버스가 정류장에 정시에 도착하도록 계단을 이용할 수 없는 사람들을 위해 버스에 리프트가 설치되었다. 19 도자기의 광택을 유지하려면 적절하게 유약을 칠해야 한다.

20 invigorate [invígərèit]
v. 기운나게 하다, 고무하다

to give someone energy

ⓐ invigorative 기운을 북돋우는, 격려하는 ⓐⓓ invigoratingly 기운나게 하여, 격려하여

ⓢⓨⓝ energize, renew, revitalize ⓐⓝⓣ discourage

Invigorated by the headmaster's speech, the freshmen exited the grand hall with a renewed sense of purpose.

21 interrogate [intérəgèit]
v. 심문하다, 질문 하다

to ask questions

ⓐ interrogative 의문의, 묻고 싶은 듯한 ⓝ interrogation 질문, 심문

ⓢⓨⓝ ask, question, inquire

His argument was that he had been improperly interrogated by the police for nearly 9 hours without a lawyer present.

22 inflame [infléim]
v. 불태우다, 흥분시키다, 노하게 하다

to set something on fire, to make someone angry

ⓐⓓ inflamingly 불을 붙여, 불태워 ⓐ inflammable 가연성의

ⓢⓨⓝ provoke, stimulate, enrage ⓐⓝⓣ calm, dampen, cool, compose

The speaker's comments inflamed the crowd who were already excited by his appearance.

23 overstate [òuvərstéit]
v. 과장하다

to state something to make it more important than it really is

ⓝ overstatement 과장한 말, 허풍

ⓢⓨⓝ exaggerate, magnify ⓐⓝⓣ minimize, understate

The company overstated the merits of its products which it produced last month.

24 retreat [ri:trí:t]
v. 물러나다, 후퇴하다, 은퇴하다

to go back

ⓢⓨⓝ withdraw, leave ⓐⓝⓣ advance

The general said that he had no plan to retreat the soldiers deployed at the border.

25 discharge [distʃá:rdʒ]
v. 짐을 내리다, (총을) 발사하다

to unload from a vehicle, to shoot

ⓝ discharger 짐 부리는 사람

ⓢⓨⓝ release, fire, clear

The ship which was suspected of smuggling was not allowed to discharge its cargo.

The gun discharged accidentally when it dropped to the floor.

---

20 교장선생님의 연설에 고무되어 신입생들이 새로운 목표의식을 가지고 대강당을 나갔다. 21 그는 변호사 참석없이 거의 9시간 동안 경찰에 의해 부당하게 조사받았다고 주장하고 있다. 22 그의 연설은 이미 그의 출현으로 격앙된 군중들을 흥분시켰다. 23 그 회사는 지난달에 생산한 상품들의 장점을 과장했다. 24 장군은 국경에 배치된 군대를 철수할 계획이 없다고 말했다. 25 밀수선으로 의심되는 배는 하적 허가를 받지 못했다. 총이 바닥에 떨어지면서 뜻하지 않게 발사되었다.

Exercise

Word Check 각 단어의 뜻으로 알맞은 것을 찾아 연결하시오.

01 facilitate   (a) to allow someone to leave
02 custody   (b) to make something easier to do
03 impulse   (c) a sudden force forwards
04 gleam   (d) protective care especially the guardianship of a child
05 discharge   (e) a flash or beam of light

Syn & Ant Check 주어진 단어의 동의어, 반의어를 골라 쓰시오.

tiny	amiable	coat	dispensable	advance
leftover	flammable	curious	discourage	exaggerate

06 combustible =   11 colossal   ↔
07 residue   =   12 requisite ↔
08 glaze   =   13 vicious   ↔
09 overstate   =   14 invigorate ↔
10 inquisitive =   15 retreat   ↔

Sentence Practice 문장을 읽고 빈칸에 알맞은 단어를 고르시오.

16 A sense of expectation seemed to prevail at the _____ of a new government committed to economic liberalization.
　　ⓐ antecedent   ⓑ advent   ⓒ paranoia   ⓓ prestige

17 Our team maintained its scoring _____ after the first goal and finally won the heatedly contested match 3-0.
　　ⓐ quest   ⓑ impetus   ⓒ gleam   ⓓ residue

18 He was too _____ to understand that his colleagues were taking advantage of him.
　　ⓐ vicious   ⓑ inquisitive   ⓒ obscure   ⓓ naive

19 Philosophy seems _____ to people who don't know how to relate Lao Tzu, Kierkegaard or Socrates to daily life.
　　ⓐ obscure   ⓑ colossal   ⓒ requisite   ⓓ combustible

20 The monkey _____ to the treetop to escape from the predator lurking below.
　　ⓐ discharged   ⓑ inflamed   ⓒ retreated   ⓓ interrogated

01 gratitude [grǽtətjùːd]
n. 감사

giving thanks
ⓥ gratify ~에게 고맙게 하다   ⓐ gratifying 만족을 주는
ⓢⓨⓝ thanks, appreciation   ⓐⓝⓣ ingratitude

We'd like to express our gratitude for the kindness you showed to us during our visit.

02 hypothesis [haipáθəsis]
n. 가설, 전제

a possible statement for a particular condition
ⓐ hypothetical 가설의
ⓢⓨⓝ theory, premise , proposition

The research team is looking into much evidence supporting the hypothesis.

03 imposter [impástər]
n. 협잡꾼, 사기꾼

a person who pretends to be someone else in order to deceive others
ⓢⓨⓝ swindler, charlatan

A number of imposters have claimed to be the heir of the millionaire.

04 mutiny [mjúːtəni]
n. 반항, 폭동
v. 반란을 일으키다

an act of rebellion against established authority
ⓐ mutinous 반항적인   ⓝ mutineer 모반자
ⓢⓨⓝ revolution, overthrow, coup

Many students staged a mutiny against the dictatorship.

05 affinity [əfínəti]
n. 애호, 호감

a strong natural liking for something
ⓐ affinitive 혈연의
ⓢⓨⓝ affection, attraction   ⓐⓝⓣ dislike, hatred, hostility

He had an affinity for golf and spent his free time practicing it.

06 euphemism [júːfəmìzəm]
n. 완곡어법

a mild term used in place of one considered offensive
ⓐ euphemistic, euphemistical 완곡한   ⓐⓓ euphemistically 완곡하게
ⓢⓨⓝ delicacy, purism   ⓐⓝⓣ dysphemism

Because of strong taboos about the death in our culture, countless euphemisms for dying have evolved over the years.

---

01 우리가 머무는 동안 베풀어주신 친절에 감사드립니다. 02 그 연구팀은 가설을 뒷받침하기 위해 많은 증거를 조사하고 있다. 03 많은 사기꾼들이 백만장자의 상속인이라고 주장하고 있다. 04 많은 학생들이 독재에 대항하여 반란을 계획했다. 05 그는 골프를 좋아해서 여가시간에는 골프 연습을 한다. 06 우리 문화에 죽음에 대한 강한 금기로 인해 그것에 대한 완곡한 표현들이 발달되어 있다.

07 forage [fɔ́:ridʒ]
n. 사료, 식량 수집

food for horses or cattle
ⓝ forager 징발자, 약탈자   ⓝ foraging 채집, 수렵
syn food, pasturage, fodder

They decided to euthanize the cows that ate contaminated forage.

08 reign [rein]
n. 치세, 통치기간

the period of time for which a king or queen rules
ⓐ reigning 군림하는, 정권을 잡고 있는
syn administration, control, dominion

During his 5-year reign, the president's regal powers were enough to control the Legislature, Judicial system, and the Administration.

09 innocuous [inákju:əs]
a. 해가 없는, 악의가 없는

not likely to upset or harm anyone
syn harmless, inoffensive   ant harmful, offensive
ad innocuously 무해하여, 지루하여

The plastic bags seem innocuous, but they are harmful to our environment.

10 notorious [noutɔ́:riəs]
a. 유명한, 악명 높은

famous, usually for something bad
syn infamous, disreputable   ant famous
ad notoriously 유명하게

The politicians are notorious for adding properties by dodging a tax.

11 prodigious [prədídʒəs]
a. 거대한, 놀랄만한

very large and impressive
ad prodigiously 터무니 없이, 경이적으로
syn enormous, vast. extraordinary   ant small, unexceptional

Michael Jordan had a prodigious amount of basketball skill and could easily overcome even two players at once.

12 apathetic [æ̀pəθétik]
a. 무감동한, 냉담한

feeling or showing little or no emotion
ad apathetically 냉담하게
syn unfeeling, unmoved, stolid   ant caring, concerned, interested

Many students have an apathetic attitude toward the education reform.

13 verbose [vəːrbóus]
a. 장황한, 용장한

using or containing too many words
ⓝ verbosity 장황함   ad verbosely 장황하게
syn tedious, flowery, inflated, turgid   ant concise, laconic

The previous president was well known for being a verbose speaker.

---

07 그들은 오염된 사료를 먹은 소들을 안락사시키기로 했다. 08 대통령은 재임 5년 동안 입법부,사법부,행정부를 통제할 수 있는 제왕적 권한을 가졌다. 09 비닐봉투는 해가 없을것 같지만 환경에 매우 해롭다. 10 정치가들은 탈세로 재산을 증식한 것으로 악명이 높다. 11 마이클 조단은 농구 실력이 매우 뛰어나서 동시에 2명의 선수도 쉽게 상대할 수 있었다. 12 많은 학생들이 교육개혁에 대해 무관심하다. 13 전 대통령은 말이 많은 연설가로 잘 알려졌다.

14 **luminous** [lúːmənəs]
a. 빛나는, 밝은

emitting or giving out light

n luminary 발광체, 인공 조명

syn lucid, radiant, bright   ant dark, obscure

When you work on the street at night, don't forget to wear luminous clothes.

---

15 **condone** [kəndóun]
v. 용서하다

to accept behavior that is wrong

n condonation 용서, 묵과

syn overlook, forgive   ant condemn

They will not condone the employee who was arrested on charge of embezzlement.

---

16 **gasp** [gæsp]
v. 헐떡거리다, 숨이 막히다

to breathe noisily

ad gaspingly 헐떡거리며

syn wheeze, heave, pant, puff

He gasped as he crossed the finish line and looked for something to drink.

I saw her gasp with surprise when she opened her birthday gift.

---

17 **connive** [kənáiv]
v. 묵인하다, 음모를 꾸미다

to cooperate secretly

n conniver 묵인자   n connivery 묵인

syn conspire, intrigue, contrive

The teacher watched the students carefully, concerned that they were conniving to do something bad.

---

18 **dilapidate** [dilǽpədèit]
v. 파손시키다

to bring into a state of partial ruin

a dilapidated 황폐한, 파손된

syn ruin, consume, annihilate, crack   ant build, construct

U.N. Security Council announced they needed the time to rebuild the buildings dilapidated during the war.

---

19 **equivocate** [ikwívəkèit]
v. 말끝을 흐리다, 얼버무리다

to speak in a way that is intentionally unclear

n equivocation 애매한 말씨   a equivocal 미적지근한, 불안정한

syn deceive, elude   ant confront, encounter, face

The former prime minister equivocated to hide her mistakes that she had made during her tenure.

---

14 밤에 거리에서 일할 때는 야광 옷을 입어야 한다. 15 그들은 횡령혐의로 체포된 직원을 용서하지 않을 것이다. 16 그가 결승점을 지날 때 숨을 헐떡거렸고, 뭔가 마실걸 찾았다. 나는 그녀가 생일 선물을 열었을 때 놀라 말문이 막히는 것을 보았다. 17 선생님은 학생들이 뭔가 나쁜 것을 꾸미지 않을까 걱정하면서 그들을 주의 깊게 지켜보았다. 18 UN 안보리는 전쟁 중에 파괴된 건물들을 수리하는데 시간이 필요하다고 발표했다. 19 전 수상이 재임기간에 저지른 잘못을 숨기려고 말끝을 흐렸다.

20 **exalt** [igzɔ́:lt]

v. 승진시키다, 칭찬하다

to praise someone highly

ⓐ exalted 고귀한　ⓐd exaltedly 의기 양양하게, 과장되게

syn acclaim, advance, applaud　ant condemn, criticize, degrade

His grandfather exalted him as a pillar of his family because he was the only grandson.

---

21 **deplete** [diplí:t]

v. 감소시키다, 다 써버리다

to reduce greatly in number or quantity

ⓝ depletion 감소, 고갈

syn bankrupt, decrease, diminish　ant add, expand, increase

Stocks of natural gas and oil will have been seriously depleted and it also means the necessity of developing alternative sources.

---

22 **perjure** [pə́:rdʒər]

v. ~에게 위증시키다

to make a false statement under oath

ⓐ perjured 위증한, 위증죄를 범한　ⓝ perjury 위증죄

syn deceive, delude, equivocate

The witness perjured himself in court and was sentenced to three years in prison.

---

23 **reproach** [ripróutʃ]

v. 비난하다

n. 질책, 수치

to express disapproval, an act of reproaching

ⓐ reproachful 나무라는, 책망하는

syn abuse, admonition, blame　ant command, praise

All day long my mom reproached me for being idle.

---

24 **tarnish** [tá:rniʃ]

v. 흐리게 하다, 녹슬게 하다

to make dirty or become dull and discolored

ⓐ tarnishable 흐려지기 쉬운

syn taint, blemish, soil　ant brighten, clean

Canned food is safe in a vacuum but tarnishes when it is exposed to the air.

---

25 **impede** [impí:d]

v. 방해하다, 지연시키다

to retard or obstruct the progress

ⓝ impediment 방해, 훼방

syn delay, block, thwart　ant advance, encourage

England's efforts to impede the German invasion seemed fruitless.

---

20 그의 할아버지는 그가 유일한 손자였기 때문에 집안의 기둥으로 여겼다. 21 천연가스와 원유의 재고량이 심각하게 줄어들 것이고 그것은 곧 대체 에너지의 개발 필요성을 의미한다. 22 목격자는 법정에서 위증을 해서 3년형을 선고받았다. 23 온종일 엄마는 나의 나태함을 꾸짖었다. 24 통조림 음식은 진공상태에서는 안전하지만 공기에 노출되면 변한다. 25 독일의 침공을 저지해보려는 영국의 노력은 헛되어 보였다.

Exercise

Word Check 각 단어의 뜻으로 알맞은 것을 찾아 연결하시오.

01 forage   (a) to make or become dull and discoloured

02 euphemism   (b) a mild term used instead of one considered offensive

03 condone   (c) a crop grown for consumption by livestock

04 tarnish   (d) to pardon or forgive an offense

05 dilapidate   (e) to fall into a state of disrepair

Syn & Ant Check 단어의 동의어, 반의어를 골라 쓰시오.

appreciation	dislike	infamous	degrade	laconic
dominion	small	blame	unfeeling	obscure

06 notorious = _____   11 affinity ⟷ _____

07 gratitude = _____   12 exalt ⟷ _____

08 reproach = _____   13 luminous ⟷ _____

09 reign = _____   14 prodigious ⟷ _____

10 apathetic = _____   15 verbose ⟷ _____

Sentence Practice 문장을 읽고 빈칸에 알맞은 단어를 고르시오.

16 He heard the thieves _____ with the guard to break into the James' mansion late at night.

   ⓐ dilapidate   ⓑ perjure   ⓒ deplete   ⓓ connive

17 Every _____ suggested by scientists today is likely to be challenged by detractors tomorrow.

   ⓐ reign   ⓑ euphemism   ⓒ hypothesis   ⓓ gratitude

18 _____ creatures like the earthworm actually play a large part in revitalizing soil.

   ⓐ Notorious   ⓑ Innocuous   ⓒ Prodigious   ⓓ Verbose

19 Sailors rose in _____ against their officers during the Spanish Civil War and killed most of them in vicious gunfights.

   ⓐ mutiny   ⓑ affinity   ⓒ forage   ⓓ imposter

20 Nolan is hugely successful because he never allows his physical disability to _____ his performance.

   ⓐ impede   ⓑ tarnish   ⓒ equivocate   ⓓ gasp

01 proponent [prəpóunənt]
n. 제안자, 지지자

a supporter or advocate of something

v propone 제안하다, 제의하다

syn supporter, backer ant critic, detractor

The president is an avid proponent of equal rights for both genders.

02 anguish [ǽŋgwiʃ]
n. 고통
v. 괴로워하다, 괴롭히다

severe mental distress or torture

syn affliction, distress, torment ant euphoria, comfort

My daughter has been in anguish since we arrived at the hospital.

The nation anguished over the loss of their beloved president.

03 enmity [énməti]
n. 적의, 반목

feeling of hatred

syn acrimony, alienation, animosity ant adoration, affection, amity

The two families had been warring for generations, and their enmity toward one another ran deep.

04 upheaval [ʌphíːvəl]
n. 대변동, 격변

strong or violent change

v upheave 밀어 올리다

syn disturbance, catastrophe, disruption

It might cause a tremendous upheaval if you chose a different computer program.

05 longevity [lɑndʒévəti]
n. 장수, 장기근속

great length of life

a longevous 장수의

syn durability, endurance, lastingness ant discontinuance

In terms of longevity, women tend to have the advantage over men.

06 overt [óuvərt]
a. 명백한, 공개적인

not hidden or secret

n overture 제안, 예비교섭

syn apparent, definite, manifest ant covert, hidden

His overt references to the Italian restaurant made it clear that he wanted to eat lunch there.

---

01 그 대통령은 남녀평등을 열렬히 지지하는 사람이다. 02 나의 딸은 병원에 도착한 이후 고통에 시달리고 있다. 그 나라는 사랑하는 대통령을 잃어서 괴로워했다. 03 두 가문은 수 대에 걸쳐 앙숙이었으며, 서로에 대한 적대감은 깊었다. 04 만약 다른 컴퓨터 프로그램을 선택하면 엄청난 변화가 일어날 수 있을 것이다. 05 장수에 관련해서 여성이 남성보다 유리한 것 같다. 06 그가 이태리 식당을 공공연히 언급한 것은 그 곳에서 점심을 먹었으면 하는 것이다.

07 liable [láiəbl]
a. 책임을 져야 할, 의무가 있는

legally bound or responsible
ⓝ liability 책무, 의무
syn accountable   ant exempt

Offenders are liable for the illegal act and the tax fine is up to 10 million won.

08 intrinsic [intrínsik]
a. 본질적인, 내재된

belonging to something or someone by its very nature
ad intrinsically 본질적으로
syn congenital, essential, inherent   ant extrinsic, acquired, learned

The extrinsic value of the coin is 10 won, but its intrinsic value is much larger because it isn't printed any longer.

09 intrepid [intrépid]
a. 용기 있는, 대담한

showing no fear
ⓝ intrepidity 용맹, 대담
syn audacious, courageous   ant cowardly, fearful, timid

The intrepid fire fighter ran into the building to save a boy even if he knew the building would collapse at any moment.

10 devoid [divɔ́id]
a. 빠진, 없는

no possessing, free from something
syn bare, lacking, bereft   ant replete, supplied

The spring session was devoid of the core courses I needed to graduate.

11 intact [intǽkt]
a. 완전한, 손대지 않은

not changed or diminished
ad intactly 원래대로
syn complete, perfect   ant broken, damaged

All packages remained intact despite rough handling.

The mummy found by the anthropologist in the ancient tomb was intact.

12 serene [sərí:n]
a. 조용한, 화창한

calm and peaceful
ad serenely 잔잔하게
syn comfortable, dispassionate, content   ant agitated, anxious

After weeks of late evenings at work, they longed for a serene place for rest.

Travelers around the world visit the island to enjoy its beautiful beach and serene weather.

---

07 위반자는 불법 행위에 대한 책임을 지고 천만 원까지 벌금이 부과될 수 있다. 08 외관적 가치는 10원이지만 더 이상 제작되지 않기 때문에 내재적인 가치는 훨씬 크다. 09 그 용감한 소방관은 건물이 어느 순간 붕괴될 수 있다는 것을 알았지만 소년을 구하기 위해 건물로 뛰어 들어갔다. 10 봄학기에는 내가 졸업하기 위해 수강 해야 할 핵심 강의가 없었다. 11 모든 짐들이 험하게 다뤄졌음에도 완전했다. 고대 무덤에서 인류학자에 의해 발견된 그 미이라는 손상되지 않고 완전했다. 12 몇 주 동안 야근을 한 후에 그들은 휴식을 위해 조용한 장소를 찾았다. 전세계에서 온 여행객들이 아름다운 해변과 맑은 날씨를 즐기기 위해 그 섬을 방문한다.

13 equivalent [ikwívələnt]
a. 동등한
n. 동의어

equal in value, power or meaning

n equivalence 같음

syn analogous, commensurate ant differing, dissimilar

He made sure that an equivalent amount of treasure was obtained by each member of his crew.

14 compound [kámpaund]
a. 혼합의, 복합의

composed of two or more elements

syn complex, multiple ant simple

He diagnosed her with a compound fracture in her waist.

15 reprove [riprúːv]
v. 비난하다, 잔소리하다

to blame or condemn someone for a fault

n reproof 책망, 꾸지람

syn admonish, berate, chide ant compliment, praise

If the children are not consistently reproved, they will not learn the difference between right and wrong.

16 precipitate [prisípətèit]
v. ~를 촉진하다

to make something happen sooner

a precipitative 촉진시키는 ad precipitately 거꾸로, 다급하게

syn accelerate, dispatch, expedite

The media's story precipitated the company's demise.

17 constrict [kənstríkt]
v. 압축하다, (발육)을 저해하다

to squeeze or compress

a constrictive 단단히 죄는

syn astringe, choke, concentrate ant expand, widen

Consult a doctor because this drug causes the blood vessels to constrict.

18 disdain [disdéin]
v. 멸시하다
n. 경멸, 오만한 태도

to treat someone with contempt

a disdainful 오만한

syn abhor, despise ant admire, praise

Never disdain those who have less than you or who are disadvantaged in some way.

19 dissolve [dizálv]
v. 용해시키다, 녹이다

to break up and merge with a liquid

a dissolvent 용해력이 있는

syn deliquesce, diffuse, flux ant coagulate, congeal

Dissolve the tablet in the warm water first and mix lemon.

---

13 그는 그의 선원들이 동일한 양의 보물을 얻게될 것이라고 확신시켰다. 14 그는 복합골절이 그녀의 허리에 발생했다고 진단했다. 15 만약에 아이들을 계속해서 야단을 치지 않으면 그들은 옳고 그릇됨을 구별하지 못할 것이다. 16 언론이 그 회사의 부도를 몰아 부쳤다. 17 그 약은 혈관이 수축될 수 있으니 의사와 상의하세요. 18 당신보다 덜 가졌거나 약점이 있는 사람을 절대 무시하지 마라. 19 알약을 먼저 따뜻한 물에 녹이고 레몬을 섞어라.

20 exhilarate [igzílərèit]
v. 기운을 북돋우다, 고무시키다

to fill someone with a lively cheerfulness

ⓐ exhilarative 명랑한 ⓝ exhilaration 활기 불어 넣기

syn boost, commove, elate ant deject, depress, dispirit

The people usually find hobbies that exhilarate themselves and enjoy them with relish.

21 contrive [kəntráiv]
v. 발명하다, 연구하다

to make something in spite of difficulty

ⓝ contrivance 발명품

syn concoct, devise, fabricate ant demolish, wreck

Members of both air and ground reconnaissance met to contrive a method for assaulting the fortress.

22 despise [dispáiz]
v. 경멸하다, 몹시 싫어하다

to look down on someone

ⓐ despicable 경멸할 수 있는

syn abhor, abominate, disdain ant admire, appreciate, cherish

Don't despise a person just because he is poorly dressed.

23 evict [ivíkt]
v. 쫓아내다, ~를 되찾다

to force a person to leave the place

ⓝ eviction 축출

syn expel, chase

My teacher threatened to evict us if we were late for class three more times.

24 adhere [ædhíər]
v. 부착하다

to stick or remain fixed to something

ⓐ adherent 접착성의, 부착력이 있는

syn attach, cohere, unite ant loosen, repel

The students in the dormitory must adhere to the rules.

25 disassemble [dìsəsémbəl]
v. 분해하다, 해체하다

to take apart

ⓝ disassembly 분해된 상태

syn detach, splinter ant combine

He disassembled his bike so that he could put the forgotten part back on the bike.

---

20 사람들은 보통 자신들을 유쾌하게 해주는 취미들을 찾고 기꺼이 즐긴다. 21 요새 공격 방안을 연구하기 위해 항공과 지상 정찰대가 만났다. 22 옷을 남루하게 입었다고 사람을 경멸하지 말라. 23 선생님은 만약 우리가 세 번 이상 수업에 지각할 경우 쫓겨날 것이라고 위협하셨다. 24 기숙사의 학생들은 규칙을 잘 지켜야 한다. 25 그는 깜박 잊어버렸던 부품을 다시 집어넣기 위해 자전거를 분해했다.

Exercise

Score ___ / 20

Word Check 각 단어의 뜻으로 알맞은 것을 찾아 연결하시오.

01	anguish	(a) to manage or succeed by a plan
02	overt	(b) to take something apart
03	intact	(c) not broken or damaged
04	contrive	(d) not hidden or secret
05	disassemble	(e) severe mental distress or torture

Syn & Ant Check 주어진 단어의 동의어, 반의어를 골라 쓰시오.

cowardly	admonish	dissimilar	adoration	accountable
replete	attach	elate	admire	essential

06 exhilarate = _____

07 liable = _____

08 adhere = _____

09 reprove = _____

10 intrinsic = _____

11 intrepid ↔ _____

12 despise ↔ _____

13 devoid ↔ _____

14 equivalent ↔ _____

15 enmity ↔ _____

Sentence Practice 문장을 읽고 빈칸에 알맞은 단어를 고르시오.

16 The squatters protest so aggressively because they will have nowhere to go if they are _____ from their shacks.

ⓐ contrived　　ⓑ evicted　　ⓒ reproved　　ⓓ dissolved

17 The Everyday Heroes TV program features the _____ acts of ordinary people who overcame real-life dangers.

ⓐ intrepid　　ⓑ intrinsic　　ⓒ intact　　ⓓ compound

18 It is important to _____ to the instructions on the food pack if you wish to get the best cooking results.

ⓐ disassemble　　ⓑ adhere　　ⓒ disdain　　ⓓ precipitate

19 Gregor Mendel is widely recognized as both the founder of modern genetics and the _____ of the Theory of Inheritance.

ⓐ proponent　　ⓑ enmity　　ⓒ anguish　　ⓓ longevity

20 Sarah has the enviable ability to stay _____ in even the most difficult situations and provide crucial and cool leadership.

ⓐ liable　　ⓑ devoid　　ⓒ serene　　ⓓ overt

Day 25

01 discrepancy [diskrépənsi]
n. 불일치, 모순

a failure to correspond

ⓐ discrepant 일치하지 않는   ⓐⓓ discrepantly 모순되게

ⓢⓨⓝ disparity, difference   ⓐⓝⓣ agreement, concordance

They could not reach an agreement due to the many discrepancies in opinions.

02 discretion [diskréʃən]
n. 분별, 신중, 결정권

the ability to make wise judgement

ⓐ discretionary 자유재량의

ⓢⓨⓝ acumen, calculation, canniness   ⓐⓝⓣ indiscretion, rashness

The staff that organized the event showed great tact and discretion.

03 descent [disént]
n. 하강, 하산

the act or process of coming or going down

ⓐ descendent 내려가는   ⓝ descendant 자손, 후예

ⓢⓨⓝ declination, declivity   ⓐⓝⓣ ascent, elevation

The captain announced the final information about the arrival and the plane began descent.

04 predicament [pridíkəmənt]
n. 곤경, 궁지

a difficult situation

ⓢⓨⓝ hardship, dilemma, distress

They may be in a predicament when travelers lose passports and airline tickets.

05 coherent [kouhíərənt]
a. 응집성의, 일치한

reasonably connected to something

ⓝ coherence 일관성

ⓢⓨⓝ articular, consistent, identified   ⓐⓝⓣ confusing, incoherent

He was barely coherent during the presentation, irritating the audience with his mumbling and slurring.

06 erratic [irǽtik]
a. 별난, 이상한

having no fixed pattern or course

ⓐ erratical 괴상한

ⓢⓨⓝ unpredictable, aberrant, abnormal   ⓐⓝⓣ certain, consistent

Few students predict his tests because his behavior is very erratic.

---

01 그들은 많은 견해 차이로 합의하지 못했다. 02 그 행사를 주관했던 직원들은 상당한 재치와 신중함을 보여줬다. 03 기장이 마지막 도착 안내 방송을 한 후 비행기는 하강하기 시작했다. 04 여행객이 여권과 항공권을 잃어 버렸을 때 어려움에 처할 수 있다. 05 그는 발표하는 동안 일관성 없이 중얼거리거나 말을 분명히 하지 못해 청중들을 짜증 나게 했다. 06 그의 행동은 아주 특이해서 그의 시험문제를 예견하는 학생은 거의 없다.

07 tenable [ténəbəl]
a. 주장할 수 있는, 조리 있는

able to be believed
syn acceptable, admissible, defensible ant unjustifiable, inexcusable
His explanation for his late arrival was hardly tenable.

08 desolate [désəlit]
a. 황폐한

deserted, barren and lonely
n desolation 무인상태
syn abandoned, bare, bleak ant inhibited, mobbed
The new town where he lives used to be a desolate area.

09 engrossed [ingróust]
a. 열중하는

taking up someone's attention completely
n engrossment 열중, 정서 ad engrossingly 열중하게 하도록
syn absorbed, attentive ant disinterested
The boy was completely engrossed in making a model plane.

10 incompatible [ìnkəmpǽtəbl]
a. 양립하지 않는, 모순된

unable to live, work or get on together in harmony
n incompatibility 양립불가
syn adverse, antipathetic, conflicting ant compatible, complementary
The designer asked for changing the color of the curtain because the color was totally incompatible with that of the wall.

11 valiant [vǽljənt]
a. 용감한, 씩씩한

very brave
ad valiantly 용감하게
syn brave, assertive, audacious ant afraid, cowardly
The woman made a valiant attempt to prevent the hijacking and finally saved her daughter.

12 tangible [tǽndʒəbəl]
a. 유형의, 실체가 있는

capable of being felt by touch
n tangibility 명확함, 확실 ad tangibly 명백히
syn actual, concrete, corporeal ant abstract, conceptual
Meteorologists look for tangible evidence of tornado activity before warning the public.

13 callow [kǽlou]
a. 미숙한, 경험이 없는

young and inexperienced
n callowness 미숙함
syn inexperienced, jejune, puerile ant mature, sophisticated
When we first met the physic's professor, he looked like a callow youth.

07 지각에 대한 그의 설명은 신빙성이 없다. 08 그가 살고 있는 신도시는 황폐한 지역이었다. 09 소년은 모형 비행기의 조립에 완전히 몰입해 있었다. 10 디자이너는 커튼 색이 벽 색깔과 어울리지 않기 때문에 바꿀 것을 건의했다. 11 그녀는 납치를 막기 위해 용감한 시도를 했고 결국 딸을 구했다. 12 기상학자들은 주민에게 경고하기 전에 토네이도의 움직임에 대한 확실한 증거를 찾는다. 13 우리가 처음 물리학 교수를 만났을 때 그는 풋내기 청년 같아 보였다.

14 aggravate [ǽgrəvèit]

v. ~를 악화 시키다

to make worse

syn bother, exasperate, worsen ant appease, clam

n aggravation 중대화

Some economists say the increase of the oil price will aggravate our economic situation.

15 diffuse [difjúːz]

v. 발산하다, 보급하다

to spread or send out

n diffuser 보급자

syn bestow, broadcast, distribute ant receive, take

The internet is a powerful means of diffusing world news or gathering new ideas.

16 contend [kənténd]

v. 주장하다

to assert or maintain earnestly

n contention 말다툼, 논쟁

syn argue, maintain, allege

She contended that we have to begin a FTA negotiation with Japan.

17 repudiate [ripjúːdièit]

v. 거절하다, ~을 부인하다

to deny or reject something

n repudiation 거부

syn reject, abjure ant confirm, acknowledge

The department of consumer service has to make efforts not to repudiate the customers' claim.

18 plunge [plʌndʒ]

v. 담그다, 밀어 넣다

to bring suddenly or forcibly into some condition

syn submerge, descend, dive

The Korean economic crisis made stock markets plunge and the currencies lose value.

19 sojourn [sóudʒəːrn]

v. 묵다, 체류하다

n. 체류

to stay for a short while

n sojourner 일시 체류자

syn stay, abide ant depart, leave

We sojourned at the hotel near Oxford for two months during the summer vacation.

Our children returned yesterday from a week sojourn in London.

---

14 일부 경제학자들은 오일가격 상승이 우리 경제를 악화시킬 것이라고 말한다. 15 인터넷은 세계의 새로운 소식을 보급하고 새로운 아이디어를 수집하는 좋은 수단이다. 16 그녀는 우리가 일본과 FTA 협상을 시작해야 한다고 주장했다. 17 고객 관리부서는 고객들의 주장을 무시하지 않기 위해 최선의 노력을 해야 한다. 18 한국의 경제위기가 주식 시장을 폭락하게 하고 화폐 가치를 떨어뜨렸다. 19 우리는 여름 방학 동안 Oxford 근처의 호텔에서 머물렀다. 우리 아이들이 런던 에서 일주일간 체류한 후 어제 돌아왔다.

20 annihilate [ənáiəlèit]
v. 몰살시키다

to destroy something completely

n annihilation 멸종

syn abolish, abrogate ant preserve, save

The project which they proposed may threaten to annihilate the remaining green-belt area.

21 crumble [krʌmbl]
v. 부수다

to break into crumbs or powdery fragments

n crumbling 부스러기

syn collapse, crumb, decompose ant build, expand

The national treasure standing in the center of the city crumbled due to the arson by a mentally deranged person.

22 renovate [rénəvèit]
v. 혁신하다

to renew or make new again

n renovation 개혁 n renovator 혁신자

syn modernize, restore, reconstitute ant maintain, retain

They launched a fund raising campaign to renovate the school that was built about 80 years ago.

23 preside [prizáid]
v. 사회를 보다, 통솔하다

to take the lead at

a presiding 통솔하는 n presidium 이사회

syn officiate, chair, moderate

James will preside over the board meeting that will be held tomorrow.

He had to preside over the whole estate that was inherited by his father.

24 deter [ditə́:r]
v. 주저하게 하다

to discourage or prevent someone

n determent 방해물

syn discourage, intimidate, dissuade ant encourage, facilitate

The stricter disarmament has to be proposed to deter horrible wars.

25 dilute [dilú:t]
v. 희석시키다

to reduce the strength

n dilution 희석

syn adulterate, attenuate, decrease ant condense, enrich, thicken

He diluted the cleaner with water as the directions indicated.

---

20 그들이 제안한 도시 계획안은 남아 있는 녹지대를 파괴할 수도 있다. 21 도시 중심부에 있던 그 국보는 정신병자의 방화로 무너졌다. 22 그들은 80년 전에 지어진 학교를 다시 수리하기 위해 기금 모금 운동을 실시했다. 23 James가 내일 열릴 임원회의 사회를 볼 것이다. 그는 아버지에게 상속 받은 모든 재산을 총괄해야 했다. 24 끔찍한 전쟁을 막기 위해 더 강력한 군비축소가 제안되어야 한다. 25 안내서에 쓰여 있는 대로 그는 물로 세제를 희석시켰다.

Exercise

Word Check 각 단어의 뜻으로 알맞은 것을 찾아 연결하시오.

01 preside   (a) unable to exist together in harmony
02 coherent   (b) the quality of behaving in a discreet way
03 discretion   (c) logically and clearly developed
04 deter   (d) to occupy the place of authority
05 incompatible   (e) to discourage someone from doing something

Syn & Ant Check 주어진 단어의 동의어, 반의어를 골라 쓰시오.

aberrant	cowardly	disinterested	maintain	depart
condense	inexperienced	reject	abandoned	ascent

06 repudiate = _____   11 engrossed ↔ _____
07 desolate = _____   12 sojourn   ↔ _____
08 callow   = _____   13 dilute   ↔ _____
09 contend   = _____   14 valiant   ↔ _____
10 erratic   = _____   15 descent   ↔ _____

Sentence Practice 문장을 읽고 빈칸에 알맞은 단어를 고르시오.

16 The callous approach of the mediator only served to _____ what was already a precarious situation.

ⓐ renovate   ⓑ invigorate   ⓒ deter   ⓓ aggravate

17 Lily was _____ in an adventure story to that point that she hardly noticed it when her mother came in to wish her good night.

ⓐ erratic   ⓑ engrossed   ⓒ incompatible   ⓓ callow

18 Any _____ in the data must be reported to the supervisor immediately.

ⓐ descent   ⓑ predicament   ⓒ discretion   ⓓ discrepancy

19 _____ assets such as buildings or factories are sometimes not worth as much as intellectual properties like trademarks or brands.

ⓐ Tangible   ⓑ Coherent   ⓒ Tenable   ⓓ valiant

20 Admiral Yi Sun-shin _____ a Japanese invading fleet through the ingenious use of his self-designed "turtle ships."

ⓐ diffused   ⓑ annihilated   ⓒ crumbled   ⓓ presided

suffix

부사 suffix

-ly : sudden ⇨ suddenly, frank ⇨ frankly, usual ⇨ usually

A glacial lake in Chile suddenly disappeared and the scientists investigated the reason.

칠레의 한 빙하호수가 갑자기 사라져서 과학자들이 이유를 조사했다.

-ward(s) : back ⇨ backward, for ⇨ forwards, on ⇨ onwards

The analyst described the phenomenon that the river seems to be running backward.

분석가는 강이 거꾸로 흐르는 것처럼 보이는 현상을 설명했다.

-wise : clock ⇨ clockwise, side ⇨ sidewise, end ⇨ endwise

The doctor says the inner ear senses changes in the body as the position is down or sideways.

의사는 몸의 위치가 아래나 옆쪽으로 바뀜에 따라 내이가 변화를 느낀다고 했다.

-ways : length ⇨ lengthways, side ⇨ sideways

If you cut the paper lengthways, the texture will be changed, which makes the printing hard.

만약 종이를 세로로 자른다면 결이 달라져서 인쇄를 힘들게 한다.

기타

┌─────────────────────────────┐
│ 반의어를 나타내는 형용사형 suffix │
└─────────────────────────────┘

-ful ↔ -less : hopeful ↔ hopeless, careful ↔ careless, useful ↔ useless

┌──────────────────────────────────┐
│ 명사 +ly = 형용사/ 형용사, 동사 +ly = 부사 │
└──────────────────────────────────┘

형용사형 suffix -ly : cost ⇨ costly, friend ⇨ friendly

Drivers avoid driving behind the luxurious cars on the street because it would be too costly to repair when they have a car accident.

운전자들은 사고가 났을 때 수리비가 너무 비쌀 것 같아서 값비싼 차 뒤에서 운전하는 것을 꺼린다.

부사형 suffix -ly : order ⇨ orderly, serious ⇨ seriously

Beijing is becoming a clean and orderly city in preparation for the 2008 Olympics.

북경은 2008년 올림픽을 준비하여 깨끗하고 정돈된 도시가 되고 있다.

※ 접미사가 -ate인 경우는 동사와 형용사가 될 수 있다. 동사인 경우는 주로 강세가 있어서 [-eit]로 발음되고 형용사인 경우는 [-it]로 발음된다.

Review test Day 21 ~ Day 25

A 영어 풀이에 알맞은 단어를 보기에서 찾아 쓰시오.

| wane | paranoia | overstate | reign | intrepid |

01 a mental disorder characterized by strong and irrational feeling _____

02 to decline in power _____

03 bold and fearless _____

04 to state something too strongly _____

05 the period when a king or queen rules _____

B 문장을 읽고 문맥에 적절한 단어를 고르시오.

06 The atomic attack on Hiroshima (obliterated/invigorated) the city and killed thousands of civilians in a fraction of a second.

07 The newly (crumbled/renovated) store has several novel features.

08 We expect the leader of the banned organization to be taken into police (custody/fortitude) immediately.

09 The emergence of the European Union put an end to the (lineage/enmity) between the great Continental powers of Germany and France.

C ▒▒▒▒ 표시된 부분과 뜻이 가장 가까운 것을 고르시오.

10 Tennis players showing excessive argumentativeness on the court will forfeit their games.

ⓐ wane   ⓑ disdain   ⓒ renounce   ⓓ preside

11 Twin children tend to have an inexplicably strong mental and emotional affinity to each other.

ⓐ gratitude   ⓑ impulse   ⓒ abode   ⓓ affection

12 High silicate residue levels in the drinking water samples led to fears of severe contamination.

ⓐ remainder   ⓑ prestige   ⓒ quest   ⓓ hindrance

13 We watched in horror as the huge building crumbled to dust under the earthquake's impact.

ⓐ inflamed   ⓑ discharged   ⓒ exalted   ⓓ collapsed

D 표시된 부분의 반대말로 가장 알맞은 것을 고르시오.

14 I deserve to be reproached for deserting my friend in his time of need.

    ⓐ sprinkled   ⓑ praised   ⓒ interrogated   ⓓ despised

15 No one can repudiate the findings of this survey since they are backed by solid empirical evidence.

    ⓐ sojourn   ⓑ annihilate   ⓒ deter   ⓓ acknowledge

16 Jane has always displayed the most admirable fortitude in the face of hardship.

    ⓐ weakness   ⓑ reign   ⓒ imposter   ⓓ impetus

17 She was filled with anguish at the news that her childhood home had been demolished.

    ⓐ forage   ⓑ euphoria   ⓒ forfeit   ⓓ paranoia

E 주어진 단어를 알맞은 형태로 바꿔 빈칸에 쓰시오.

18 You have the right to have a lawyer present during _____ by authorities. (interrogate)

19 Scientists plan to revive traditional farming methods to prevent our agricultural resources from being _____ . (deplete)

20 Some animals lie and even _____ death to fool predators into leaving them alone. (feign)

21 You have to overcome a speech _____ when you study abroad. (impede)

F 빈 칸에 알맞은 단어를 보기에서 찾아 쓰시오. (필요한 경우 형태를 바꾸시오.)

wane	equivocate	impulse	diffused	reprehend	quest	disdain	inflame

22 Visitors at the spa receive treatment in rooms _____ with the fragrance of lavender.

23 Honest individuals with nothing to hide never _____ over inconvenient questions.

24 Our teacher would _____ us when she felt we were not performing to our potential.

25 The haughty emperor looked in _____ at his lowly subjects scrambling for the coins he had thrown to them.

Accumulative test Day 1 ~ Day 25

A	B	C	D
120~101	100~81	80~61	60 이하

➤ 영어를 우리말로 옮기시오.

01 lineage _____

02 gratitude _____

03 impede _____

04 descent _____

05 retreat _____

06 combustible _____

07 exalt _____

08 predicament _____

09 inquisitive _____

10 forsake _____

11 intrepid _____

12 connive _____

13 advent _____

14 reproach _____

15 facilitate _____

16 sphere _____

17 reprehend _____

18 sojourn _____

19 evict _____

20 impulse _____

21 efface _____

22 manifold _____

23 deter _____

24 overt _____

25 invigorate _____

26 adhere _____

27 tangible _____

28 perfunctory _____

29 aggravate _____

30 diffuse _____

31 disdain _____

32 repudiate _____

33 euphemism _____

34 residue _____

35 intact _____

36 plunge _____

37 deplete _____

38 fortitude _____

39 exhilarate _____

40 inflame _____

41 subside _____

42 forage _____

43 impetus _____

44 arduous _____

45 intrinsic _____

46 obscure _____

47 perjure _____

48 obliterate _____

49 coherent _____

50 contrive _____

51 tactile _____

52 wane _____

53 tenable _____

54 anguish _____

55 prodigious _____

56 despise _____

57 apathetic _____

58 engrossed _____

59 disassemble _____

60 candor _____

61 말끝을 흐리다

62 동등한

63 잔잔한, 조용한

64 장황한

65 시간 엄수

66 용서하다

67 보호, 감금

68 거대한, 엄청난

69 제안자, 지지자

70 방해, 장애

71 가설, 전제

72 쪼개다

73 위신, 명성

74 파손시키다

75 선조, 선례

76 짐을 내리다

77 메마른, 빈약한

78 빠진, 없는

79 나쁜, 잔인한

80 건방진, 도도한

81 편집증, 망상증

82 비난(잔소리)하다

83 녹슬게 하다

84 순진한

85 위생, 위생학

86 황폐한, 외로운

87 거부권을 행사하다

88 별난, 이상한

89 과장하다

90 양립하지 않는

91 ~을 끼었다

92 용감한, 씩씩한

93 중간의, 매개의

94 반항, 폭동

95 빛나는, 밝은

96 애호, 호감

97 주소, 주거

98 박멸하다

99 탄력의

100 헐떡거리다

101 탐구, 추구

102 벌금, 위약금

103 적의, 반목

104 미숙한

105 몰살시키다

106 ~인 체하다

107 사회를 보다

108 해가 없는

109 장수

110 책임을 져야 할

111 압축하다

112 (씨를) 뿌리다

113 미묘한 차이

114 필수의

115 용해시키다

116 희석시키다

117 악명 높은

118 불일치, 모순

119 분별, 신중

120 달래어 ~시키다

Appendices 부록

INDEX

ANSWERS

Day 1 | Exercise   p.16

Word check
01 ⓒ   04 ⓓ
02 ⓑ   05 ⓐ
03 ⓔ

Syn & Ant Check
06 scale   11 assist
07 noticeable   12 talkative
08 live   13 aggravate
09 old-fashioned 14 absorb
10 disaster   15 thoughtless

Sentence Practice
16 ⓐ   19 ⓒ
17 ⓓ   20 ⓐ
18 ⓑ

Day 2 | Exercise   p.21

Word check
01 ⓑ   04 ⓓ
02 ⓐ   05 ⓔ
03 ⓒ

Syn & Ant Check
06 remains   11 normal
07 donate   12 disapprove
08 join   13 sentence
09 isolate   14 rejoice
10 skill   15 sensible

Sentence Practice
16 ⓑ   19 ⓑ
17 ⓓ   20 ⓓ
18 ⓐ

Day 3 | Exercise   p.26

Word check
01 ⓒ   04 ⓑ
02 ⓔ   05 ⓐ
03 ⓓ

Syn & Ant Check
06 story   11 unknown
07 religious   12 respect
08 balance   13 adore
09 abandon   14 reasonable
10 calm   15 stingy

Sentence Practice
16 ⓓ   19 ⓓ
17 ⓐ   20 ⓑ
18 ⓐ

Day 4 | Exercise   p.31

Word check
01 ⓑ   04 ⓐ
02 ⓒ   05 ⓔ
03 ⓓ

Syn & Ant Check
06 permanent   11 nice
07 sufficient   12 expert
08 appropriate   13 plain
09 formless   14 malevolent
10 misunderstanding 15 hopeful

Sentence Practice
16 ⓑ   19 ⓐ
17 ⓒ   20 ⓓ
18 ⓐ

Day 5 | Exercise　　　p.36

Word check

01 ⓒ　　　　04 ⓑ
02 ⓓ　　　　05 ⓔ
03 ⓐ

Syn & Ant Check

06 appeal　　　　11 weaken
07 scold　　　　12 mumbled
08 extinguish　　　13 compliment
09 pretender　　　14 shrink
10 fatal　　　　15 exciting

Sentence Practice

16 ⓐ　　　　19 ⓓ
17 ⓒ　　　　20 ⓐ
18 ⓓ

Review Test　Day 1 ~ Day 5　　　p.38

A

01 saturate　　　04 benevolent
02 endow　　　　05 vivacious
03 salient

B

06 pacify　　　　08 ornate
07 debris　　　　09 anarchist

C

10 ⓑ　　　　12 ⓐ
11 ⓒ　　　　13 ⓒ

D

14 ⓓ　　　　16 ⓒ
15 ⓐ　　　　17 ⓑ

E

18 atrocious　　　20 imploring
19 ventilate　　　21 perpetuated

F

22 smuggle　　　24 ominous
23 tactful　　　25 indulge

Accumulative Test　Day 1 ~ Day 5　　　p.40

01 존경하다　　　　61 knack
02 끊임 없는　　　　62 tactful
03 파편　　　　　63 symmetry
04 거품이 일다　　　64 misconception
05 비틀거리다, 비틀거림　65 inanimate
06 활발한, 생기 있는　66 lethal
07 영향 받기 쉬운　67 radiate
08 인정 많은, 너그러운　68 elicit
09 진지한, 진심의　69 indict
10 몹시 싫어하다　70 buffer
11 격리된　　　　71 spawn
12 자비로운, 관용적인　72 remorse
13 격려하다, 격리, 차단　73 slander
14 약하게 하다　74 metaphor
15 숨 막히게 하다　75 obdurate
16 열정적인, 격렬한　76 ornate
17 널리 퍼져 있는　77 ludicrous
18 포기하다, 그만두다　78 entail
19 자비로운　　　79 standpoint
20 해로운, 불리한　80 indulge
21 호되게 꾸짖다　81 amorphous
22 유연한, 유순한　82 replenish
23 간청[애원]하다　83 ominous
24 포기하다, 버리다　84 hallucinate
25 강화하다　　　85 ambivalent
26 충분한, 풍부한　86 implement
27 늘이다, 늘어나다　87 flinch

28	기부[기증]하다	88	capitulate
29	유명한, 저명한	89	smuggle
30	인정[시인]하다	90	coalesce
31	환기하다	91	nocturnal
32	방해하다, 막다	92	parable
33	올라가다, 상승하다	93	mock
34	두드러진, 눈에 띄는	94	edifice
35	흥분하다, 흥분	95	taboo
36	나머지, 잔여	96	ratify
37	호혜적인, 상호간의	97	squander
38	파괴, 방해	98	hypocrite
39	적절한, 관련된	99	plumage
40	유명한, 뛰어난	100	magnitude
41	흠뻑 적시다	101	symbiosis
42	비난[비방]하다	102	beleaguer
43	사려 깊은	103	calamity
44	극악한, 지독한	104	taciturn
45	조용한, 고요한	105	haphazard
46	때때로 일어나는	106	abide
47	원상복구하다	107	barter
48	분명한, 명료한	108	novice
49	슬퍼하다, 한탄하다	109	stammer
50	보상[보답]하다	110	enact
51	겸손하게 행동하다	111	wary
52	면제[사면]하다	112	mandatory
53	몹시 나쁜	113	coarse
54	지루한, 따분한	114	quaint
55	진정시키다	115	exorbitant
56	조용한, 차분한	116	ignite
57	노력하다, 노력	117	aesthetic
58	위압하다	118	sly
59	끊임없는, 가차없는	119	eccentric
60	슬퍼하다, 한탄하다	120	ingest

Day 6 | Exercise   p.48

Word check
01 ⓓ   04 ⓑ
02 ⓔ   05 ⓐ
03 ⓒ

Syn & Ant Check
06 noticeable   11 migrant
07 monarch   12 separate
08 annoyed   13 disparate
09 anxious   14 safe
10 leak   15 careless

Sentence Practice
16 ⓒ   19 ⓓ
17 ⓒ   20 ⓐ
18 ⓑ

Day 7 | Exercise   p.53

Word check
01 ⓔ   04 ⓐ
02 ⓓ   05 ⓑ
03 ⓒ

Syn & Ant Check
06 combine   11 congregate
07 nimble   12 fertile
08 mandatory   13 advantage
09 debasement   14 lengthen
10 obvious   15 unsatisfied

Sentence Practice
16 ⓓ   19 ⓐ
17 ⓑ   20 ⓓ
18 ⓐ

Day 8 | Exercise   p.58

Word check
01 ⓑ   04 ⓔ
02 ⓒ   05 ⓓ
03 ⓐ

Syn & Ant Check
06 conceal   11 genuine
07 flexible   12 inattentive
08 consider   13 encouraged
09 association   14 substandard
10 plan   15 important

Sentence Practice
16 ⓒ   19 ⓐ
17 ⓒ   20 ⓓ
18 ⓑ

Day 9 | Exercise   p.63

Word check
01 ⓓ   04 ⓑ
02 ⓒ   05 ⓔ
03 ⓐ

Syn & Ant Check
06 invade   11 dispensable
07 illusion   12 uncertain
08 strengthen   13 increase
09 discard   14 stiff
10 abundant   15 favorable

Sentence Practice
16 ⓐ   19 ⓑ
17 ⓐ   20 ⓓ
18 ⓒ

Day 10 | Exercise   p.68

Word check
01 ⓑ   04 ⓔ
02 ⓒ   05 ⓐ
03 ⓓ

Syn & Ant Check
06 disassemble   11 massive
07 fire   12 sympathy
08 backward   13 previous
09 sink   14 superior
10 deception   15 survive

Sentence Practice
16 ⓑ   19 ⓓ
17 ⓑ   20 ⓓ
18 ⓐ

Review Test Day 6 ~ Day 10   p.70

A
01 counterfeit   04 distort
02 trespass   05 submerge
03 integral

B
06 obsolete   08 vigilant
07 condolences   09 trite

C
10 ⓓ   12 ⓓ
11 ⓒ   13 ⓐ

D
14 ⓐ   16 ⓐ
15 ⓑ   17 ⓓ

E

18 delusion
19 conventional

20 treacherous
21 voracious

F.

22 incessant
23 resilient

24 languid
25 mimic

Accumulative Test Day 1 ~ Day 10 p.72

01 연합, 동맹
02 정복하다, 억제하다
03 낭비하는, 방탕자
04 매우 작은, 하찮은
05 처리[처분]하다
06 다시 젊어지게 하다
07 일치하는, 조화된
08 넘어지다, 비틀거리다
09 술 취하지 않은
10 잡아당기다
11 권위적인, 거만한
12 세계적인, 국제적인
13 그만두게 하다
14 병적인, 병리상의
15 건강에 좋은, 유익한
16 흉내내다, 모방하다
17 숨기다, 가장하다
18 다르다, 갈라지다
19 잠기다, 가라앉다
20 공기가 빠진
21 눈에 띄는, 뚜렷한
22 절대 필요한
23 분해하다, 떼어내다
24 나른한, 기운 없는
25 숙고[생각]하다
26 유발[야기]하다
27 정신이 혼란한, 산만한

61 decadence
62 denunciation
63 limber
64 compress
65 mishap
66 persevere
67 vigilant
68 trespass
69 placebo
70 perjury
71 conspire
72 frivolous
73 condolence
74 castigate
75 counterfeit
76 embed
77 condense
78 fracture
79 regressive
80 frugal
81 incessant
82 somber
83 tumult
84 agonize
85 ordeal
86 subsequent
87 complacent

28 약한, 깨지기 쉬운
29 새다, 누출되다
30 그림같이 아름다운
31 줄이다
32 세심한, 신중한
33 모방하다, 필적하다
34 헤아리다, 간파하다
35 중요한, 중대한
36 화난, 분개한
37 전통적인, 틀에 박힌
38 강화하다
39 명백한
40 주요 산물, 주요품
41 풍부한, 호사스러운
42 위험한, 믿을 수 없는
43 쓰다, 노력하다
44 의무[강제]적인
45 박해하다, 괴롭히다
46 필수적인, 긴요한
47 거친, 휘몰아치는
48 왜곡하다, 비틀다
49 종교적인, 신앙심 깊은
50 회복하는, 되돌아가는
51 해소하다
52 허가하다, 제재
53 유연한, 유연성 있는
54 중요하지 않는
55 흩뜨리다, 분산시키다
56 막다, 쫓아버리다
57 결점, 단점
58 포함하다, 둘러싸다
59 모범적인, 훌륭한
60 걱정하는, 염려하는

88 grudge
89 futile
90 agile
91 monopoly
92 zenith
93 gist
94 congregate
95 configuration
96 adverse
97 obsolete
98 loiter
99 adjacent
100 congestion
101 monotone
102 nutrition
103 malicious
104 anarchist
105 consolidate
106 figurative
107 indomitable
108 sovereign
109 sterile
110 delusion
111 erode
112 trite
113 premeditate
114 incontrovertible
115 indigenous
116 dismiss
117 antipathy
118 perish
119 lucid
120 subordinate

Day 11 | Exercise p.80

Word check
01 ⓔ 04 ⓑ
02 ⓓ 05 ⓐ
03 ⓒ

Syn & Ant Check
06 doubting 11 worsen
07 mean 12 reckless
08 congeal 13 keep
09 relieve 14 separate
10 countless 15 strengthen

Sentence Practice
16 ⓑ 19 ⓓ
17 ⓑ 20 ⓓ
18 ⓐ

Day 12 | Exercise p.85

Word check
01 ⓑ 04 ⓔ
02 ⓐ 05 ⓒ
03 ⓓ

Syn & Ant Check
06 baffle 11 appropriate
07 mysterious 12 increase
08 delay 13 compliment
09 invade 14 disobey
10 fairness 15 extraordinary

Sentence Practice
16 ⓐ 19 ⓒ
17 ⓓ 20 ⓑ
18 ⓐ

Day 13 | Exercise p.90

Word check
01 ⓓ 04 ⓒ
02 ⓑ 05 ⓔ
03 ⓐ

Syn & Ant Check
06 skillful 11 spiritless
07 hate 12 rare
08 disguise 13 civilized
09 reprimand 14 unfortunate
10 plead 15 terminate

Sentence Practice
16 ⓐ 19 ⓒ
17 ⓓ 20 ⓒ
18 ⓐ

Day 14 | Exercise p.95

Word check
01 ⓐ 04 ⓓ
02 ⓒ 05 ⓔ
03 ⓑ

Syn & Ant Check
06 ignore 11 dissatisfy
07 rightful 12 few
08 compel 13 misunderstand
09 revenge 14 respect
10 supplement 15 integrate

Sentence Practice
16 ⓑ 19 ⓐ
17 ⓓ 20 ⓒ
18 ⓑ

Day 15 | Exercise   p. 100

Word check

01 ⓔ   04 ⓑ
02 ⓒ   05 ⓓ
03 ⓐ

Syn & Ant Check

06 infuriate   11 depressed
07 trick   12 modest
08 stubborn   13 simple
09 temporary   14 introvert
10 reveal   15 unhealthful

Sentence Practice

16 ⓐ   19 ⓐ
17 ⓐ   20 ⓒ
18 ⓑ

Review Test Day 11 ~ Day 15   p. 102

A

01 incriminate   04 extrovert
02 constrain   05 encroach
03 deride

B

06 allege   08 hectic
07 mundane   09 curtail

C

10 ⓐ   12 ⓑ
11 ⓑ   13 ⓒ

D

14 ⓑ   16 ⓓ
15 ⓐ   17 ⓓ

E

18 renouncement   20 fabricating
19 allusion   21 obstinately

F

22 avalanche   24 comply
23 allure   25 retaliate

Accumulative Test Day 1 ~ Day 15 p. 104

01 존경[존중]하다   61 allure
02 특수용어, 전문어   62 defer
03 줄이다, 생략하다   63 deride
04 시작하다. 착수하다   64 denote
05 고여있는, 발전 없는   65 adept
06 복잡한, 난해한, 얽힌   66 auspicious
07 얻다, 획득하다   67 procrastinate
08 단언하다, 우기다   68 stern
09 병적인, 무시무시한   69 misgiving
10 불확실한, 모호한   70 circumspect
11 배분[할당]하다   71 preliminary
12 반복[되풀이]하다   72 covet
13 암시하다   73 avalanche
14 명상[숙고]하다   74 arbitrary
15 침해[침입]하다   75 incriminate
16 완화[경감]시키다   76 lucrative
17 나타내다   77 barbaric
18 속이는, 믿을 수 없는   78 avert
19 버리다   79 comply
20 낭비하는, 사치스러운   80 gullible
21 박애주의자   81 reticent
22 ~을 명확히 발음하다   82 convince
23 절제하다, 그만두다   83 comprise
24 당황하게 하다   84 inapt
25 무시하다, 경시하다   85 comprehend
26 (열정이) 넘치는   86 transient
27 법인으로 만들다   87 retaliate

28	제거[근절]하다	88	hybrid
29	명백한, 분명한	89	extrovert
30	폭로[누설]하다	90	exquisite
31	꾸짖다, 비난, 질책	91	imminent
32	강요하다	92	kindle
33	널리 퍼져있는	93	myriad
34	무수한, 수많은	94	obstinate
35	경멸, 모욕, 치욕	95	breakthrough
36	간청[탄원]하다	96	conscript
37	보조금, 장려금	97	coalition
38	죽음을 면할 수 없는	98	detach
39	비난하다, 비난, 책망	99	latent
40	의도, 의향	100	hypnotic
41	매우 화나게 하다	101	hectic
42	약하게 하다	102	idolize
43	버리다, 포기하다	103	mundane
44	책략, 기동 훈련	104	constellation
45	알 수 없는	105	sanitary
46	양심의 가책, 불안	106	hail
47	제한[한정]하다	107	censor
48	개선하다, 향상시키다	108	parallel
49	나머지, 잔여	109	ingenious
50	싫어하다, 혐오하다	110	cessation
51	약한, 우유부단한	111	guile
52	기소[고소]하다	112	fabricate
53	열망하는, 욕심 많은	113	anecdote
54	깨끗한, 순결한	114	coagulate
55	가치가 하락하다	115	dignity
56	합법적인, 정당한	116	insolent
57	위장하다, 위장	117	monetary
58	불안정한	118	anesthetic
59	몹시 바쁜, 광적인	119	extrinsic
60	만족시키다	120	incredulous

Day 16 | Exercise p.112

Word check

01	ⓑ	04	ⓒ
02	ⓐ	05	ⓔ
03	ⓓ		

Syn & Ant Check

06	opponent	11	improve
07	release	12	terrestrial
08	impediment	13	current
09	destroy	14	enlarge
10	surmise	15	beneficial

Sentence Practice

16	ⓓ	19	ⓒ
17	ⓓ	20	ⓐ
18	ⓐ		

Day 17 | Exercise p.117

Word check

01	ⓐ	04	ⓓ
02	ⓔ	05	ⓑ
03	ⓒ		

Syn & Ant Check

06	supporter	11	planned
07	financial	12	compliment
08	educator	13	soak
09	skinny	14	unsociable
10	leaves	15	stable

Sentence Practice

16	ⓑ	19	ⓒ
17	ⓐ	20	ⓒ
18	ⓓ		

Day 18 | Exercise
p. 122

Word check

01 ⓒ   04 ⓔ
02 ⓑ   05 ⓐ
03 ⓓ

Syn & Ant Check

06 depressed   11 purify
07 repeat   12 disprove
08 accidental   13 safety
09 judgment   14 unashamed
10 healing   15 brave

Sentence Practice

16 ⓒ   19 ⓑ
17 ⓒ   20 ⓐ
18 ⓓ

Day 19 | Exercise
p. 127

Word check

01 ⓑ   04 ⓔ
02 ⓒ   05 ⓓ
03 ⓐ

Syn & Ant Check

06 charm   11 changeable
07 enthusiasm   12 noble
08 blessing   13 scant
09 sparkle   14 competent
10 flaw   15 sufficient

Sentence Practice

16 ⓐ   19 ⓒ
17 ⓑ   20 ⓒ
18 ⓒ

Day 20 | Exercise
p. 132

Word check

01 ⓒ   04 ⓓ
02 ⓑ   05 ⓔ
03 ⓐ

Syn & Ant Check

06 trap   11 cheerful
07 skillful   12 stillness
08 ball   13 drought
09 tyrannical   14 active
10 plentiful   15 skinny

Sentence Practice

16 ⓓ   19 ⓓ
17 ⓑ   20 ⓒ
18 ⓐ

Review Test   Day 16 ~ Day 20
p. 134

A

01 verdict   04 vex
02 bewilder   05 propagate
03 connoisseur

B

06 blot   08 peril
07 Aquatic   09 deluge

C

10 ⓐ   12 ⓓ
11 ⓒ   13 ⓑ

D

14 ⓐ   16 ⓒ
15 ⓑ   17 ⓑ

E

18 breach 20 verifiable

19 inauguration 21 glistening

F

22 versatile 24 belligerent

23 impromptu 25 dwindles

Accumulative Test Day 1 ~ Day 20 p. 136

01 부주의한, 우연한
02 바꿀 수 없는, 불변의
03 대항하다, 적대하다
04 동요, 소동, 폭동
05 부적당한, 서투른
06 부족한, 불충분한
07 보통의, 평범한
08 가치를 떨어뜨리다
09 자세히 설명하다
10 하늘의, 천국의
11 축복, 기도
12 의기소침한, 풀이 죽은
13 감정가, 감식가
14 음산한, 쓸쓸한
15 싫은, 기분 나쁜
16 우울함, 의기소침
17 작아지다, 감소되다
18 남을 애 태우다
19 분별있는, 사려깊은
20 ~를 떨어뜨리다
21 잎, 잎무늬
22 일치하는, 조화하는
23 흔들리다, 비틀거리다
24 위반하다, 깨뜨리다
25 계산[생각]하다
26 검증[입증]하다
27 떨림, 전율

61 emaciated
62 verdict
63 penitent
64 blunt
65 adversary
66 manipulate
67 adroit
68 dejected
69 prolific
70 admonish
71 appease
72 scrupulous
73 despotic
74 terrestrial
75 conjecture
76 cede
77 chubby
78 sullen
79 tepid
80 elude
81 dehydrate
82 console
83 belligerent
84 sluggish
85 mortify
86 vulgar
87 augment

28 기괴한, 이상한
29 보급[선전]하다
30 방해하다, 막다
31 조용한, 침착한
32 잡종
33 거래[후원]하다
34 흠이 없는
35 당황하다
36 해로운, 유해한
37 치료, 치료법의
38 인정[승인]하다
39 겁많은, 소심한
40 해로운, 불리한
41 교사, 학자
42 단단히 잡고 있는
43 악화[저하]시키다
44 매혹하다, 사로잡다
45 포괄적인, 넓은
46 (반)투명한
47 ~을 대표로 임명하다
48 능력, 교수단
49 반짝 빛나다
50 결단, 의지력
51 의심스러운, 모호한
52 품위가 없는, 천한
53 사교적인
54 구별[차별]하다
55 재정상의, 금전상의
56 해방하다
57 뚱뚱한, 비만의
58 ~를 중재하다
59 소음, 정적인
60 허우적거리다

88 deviate
89 paramount
90 recur
91 deterrent
92 sprout
93 archaic
94 copious
95 voracious
96 patron
97 versatile
98 hierarchy
99 impromptu
100 improvised
101 dexterous
102 latency
103 deluge
104 menace
105 aquatic
106 detour
107 nullify
108 lavish
109 lethargic
110 astute
111 fervor
112 fidelity
113 volatile
114 devastate
115 inaugurate
116 vex
117 capricious
118 appall
119 complement
120 peril

Day 21 | Exercise p.144

Word check

01 © 04 ⓐ
02 ⓑ 05 ⓔ
03 ⓓ

Syn & Ant Check

06 erase 11 inflexible
07 habitation 12 fat
08 massive 13 single
09 eradicate 14 humble
10 pretend 15 create

Sentence Practice

16 ⓐ 19 ⓐ
17 ⓐ 20 ©
18 ⓓ

Day 22 | Exercise p.149

Word check

01 ⓑ 04 ⓔ
02 ⓓ 05 ⓐ
03 ©

Syn & Ant Check

06 flammable 11 tiny
07 leftover 12 dispensable
08 coat 13 amiable
09 exaggerate 14 discourage
10 curious 15 advance

Sentence Practice

16 ⓑ 19 ⓐ
17 ⓑ 20 ©
18 ⓓ

Day 23 | Exercise p.154

Word check

01 © 04 ⓐ
02 ⓑ 05 ⓔ
03 ⓓ

Syn & Ant Check

06 infamous 11 dislike
07 appreciation 12 degrade
08 blame 13 obscure
09 dominion 14 small
10 unfeeling 15 laconic

Sentence Practice

16 ⓓ 19 ⓐ
17 © 20 ⓐ
18 ⓑ

Day 24 | Exercise p.159

Word check

01 ⓔ 04 ⓐ
02 ⓓ 05 ⓑ
03 ©

Syn & Ant Check

06 elate 11 cowardly
07 accountable 12 admire
08 attach 13 replete
09 admonish 14 dissimilar
10 essential 15 adoration

Sentence Practice

16 ⓑ 19 ⓐ
17 ⓐ 20 ©
18 ⓑ

Day 25 | Exercise   p.164

Word check

01 ⓓ   04 ⓔ
02 ⓒ   05 ⓐ
03 ⓑ

Syn & Ant Check

06 reject   11 disinterested
07 abandoned   12 depart
08 inexperienced   13 condense
09 maintain   14 cowardly
10 aberrant   15 ascent

Sentence Practice

16 ⓓ   19 ⓐ
17 ⓑ   20 ⓑ
18 ⓓ

Review Test   Day 21 ~ Day 25   p.166

A

01 paranoia   04 overstate
02 wane   05 reign
03 intrepid

B

06 obliterated   08 custody
07 renovated   09 enmity

C

10 ⓒ   12 ⓐ
11 ⓓ   13 ⓓ

D

14 ⓑ   16 ⓐ
15 ⓓ   17 ⓑ

E

18 interrogation   20 feign
19 depleted   21 impediment

F

22 diffused   24 reprehend
23 equivocate   25 disdain

Accumulative Test Day 1 ~ Day 25 p.168

01 혈통, 계통   61 equivocate
02 감사   62 equivalent
03 방해하다, 지연시키다   63 serene
04 하강, 하산   64 verbose
05 물러나다, 후퇴하다   65 punctuality
06 타기 쉬운   66 condone
07 승진시키다, 높이다   67 custody
08 곤경, 궁지   68 colossal
09 질문을 좋아하는   69 proponent
10 ~을 저버리다   70 hindrance
11 용기 있는   71 hypothesis
12 음모를 꾸미다   72 cleave
13 출현, 도래   73 prestige
14 비난하다, 질책   74 dilapidate
15 용이하게 하다   75 antecedent
16 구, 구체   76 discharge
17 비난하다, 꾸짖다   77 meager
18 묵다, 체류하다   78 devoid
19 쫓아내다   79 vicious
20 추진력, 자극, 충동   80 haughty
21 지우다, 제거하다   81 paranoid
22 다양한, 다수의   82 reprove
23 주저하게 하다   83 tarnish
24 명백한, 공개적인   84 naive
25 기운나게 하다   85 hygiene
26 부착하다   86 desolate
27 유형의, 실체가 있는   87 veto

28	형식적인, 마지 못한	88	erratic
29	~를 악화시키다	89	overstate
30	발산[보급]하다	90	incompatible
31	멸시하다, 경멸	91	sprinkle
32	거절[부인]하다	92	valiant
33	완곡어법	93	medium
34	잔여, 나머지	94	mutiny
35	완전한, 손대지 않은	95	luminous
36	담그다, 밀어 넣다	96	affinity
37	감소시키다	97	abode
38	인내, 강건함	98	exterminate
39	기운을 북돋우다	99	elastic
40	불 태우다	100	gasp
41	가라앉다, 진정되다	101	quest
42	사료, 식량 수집	102	forfeit
43	힘, 자극, 충동	103	enmity
44	고된, 힘든	104	callow
45	본질적인, 내재된	105	annihilate
46	분명치 않은, 모호한	106	feign
47	~에게 위증시키다	107	preside
48	지우다, 제거하다	108	innocuous
49	응집성의, 일치한	109	longevity
50	발명[연구]하다	110	liable
51	촉각의	111	constrict
52	작아지다, 쇠약해지다	112	disseminate
53	견딜 수 있는	113	nuance
54	고통, 괴롭히다	114	requisite
55	거대한, 놀랄만한	115	dissolve
56	경멸하다	116	dilute
57	무감동한, 냉담한	117	notorious
58	열중하는	118	discrepancy
59	분해[해체]하다	119	discretion
60	솔직함, 정직	120	coax

□ **jargon**   n. 특수용어, 전문어

v. jargonize 뜻을 알 수 없는 말을 쓰다

□ **anecdote**   n. 일화

a. anecdotal 일화의, 일화적인

□ **anesthetic**   n. 마취제 a. 마취의, 무감각한

v. anesthetize 마취시키다, 마취하다   n. anesthetist 마취 전문의

□ **avalanche**   n. 눈사태

a. avalanchine 거대한, 눈사태와 같은

□ **ebullient**   a. (열정이) 넘치는, 열광적인

n. ebullience (감정 등의) 격발

□ **precarious**   a. 불안정한, 믿을 수 없는

□ **prevalent**   a. 널리 퍼져있는, 유행하는

v. prevail 널리 퍼지다   n. prevalence 널리 퍼짐, 유행

□ **medium**   a. 중간의

□ **avid**   a. 열망하는, 욕심 많은

n. avidity 욕망, 탐욕

□ **auspicious**   a. 행운의, 길조의

n. auspice 길조, 전조

□ **barbaric**   a. 야만적인, 야만인의

n. barbarian 미개인, 야만인   n. barbarism 미개

□ **adept**   a. 숙련된, 정통한

□ **abstain**   v. 절제하다, 그만두다

n. abstention 절제, 금주   a. abstentious 절제하는

□ **deride**   v. 비웃다, 조롱하다

n. derision 비웃음   a. derisive 조롱하는

□ **kindle**   v. 불 붙이다, 타오르다

n. kindler 불쏘시개

□ **entreat**   v. 간청하다, 탄원하다, 부탁하다

n. entreaty 간청, 탄원

□ **enunciate**   v. ～을 명확히 발음하다

n. enunciation 명확한 진술

□ **abhor**   v. 싫어하다, 혐오하다

n. abhorrence 증오, 혐오   a. abhorrent 질색인, 싫어하는

□ **idolize**   v. 숭배하다, 우상화 하다

n. idolism 우상화

□ **hail**   v. 환호하다, 소리치다

□ **avert**   v. 외면하다, 피하다

a. aversive 피하는, 혐오의

□ **camouflage**   v. 위장하다

□ **fabricate**   v. 꾸며대다, 제작하다

n. fabrication 제작, 제조   n. fabricant 제조업자

□ **censure**   v. 비난하다 n. 비난, 책망

a. censurable 비난할만한

□ **commence**   v. 시작하다, 착수하다

n. commencement 시작, 개시

contempt
n. 경멸, 모욕, 치욕
a. contemptible 경멸할 만한

jest
n. 농담, 익살
n. jester 농담하는 사람

dignity
n. 존엄, 위엄
v. dignify 위엄 있게 하다

complement
n. 보충물, 보어 v. 보충하다, 보완하다
a. complementary 보완적인

hypnotic
a. 최면의, 최면술의
v. hypnotize 최면을 걸다 n. hypnosis 최면

reticent
a. 과묵한, 말이 없는
n. reticence 과묵

myriad
a. 수많은, 무수한

stern
a. 엄한, 단호한

legitimate
a. 합법적인, 정당한
n. legitimacy 적법, 합법성

manifest
a. 명백한, 분명한 v. 분명하게 하다, 명백히 하다

gratify
v. 만족시키다, 기쁘게 하다
n. gratification 만족감, 희열

procure
v. 얻다, 획득하다
n. procuration 획득, 조달

preliminary
a. 예비의, 준비의

arbitrary
a. 제멋대로의, 임의의

embody
v. 나타내다, 구체화하다
n. embodiment 구체화

esteem
v. 존경하다, 존중하다 n. 존중, 존경

rebuke
v. 꾸짖다

censor
v. 검열하다 n. 검열관
a. censorable 검열에 걸릴만한

comply
v. 응하다, 따르다
n. compliance 응낙, 응함

renounce
v. 버리다, 포기하다
n. renunciation 포기, 폐기

perplex
v. 당황하게 하다
a. perplexed 당황한, 난처한 n. perplexity 당황, 곤혹

depreciate
v. 가치가 하락하다
n. depreciation 가치하락

encroach
v. 침해하다, 침입하다
n. encroachment 잠식, 침략

converge
v. 한 점에 집중하다, 모이다
a. convergent 점차 집합하는 n. convergence 한 점으로 모임

procrastinate
v. 꾸물거리다, 지연시키다
n. procrastination 지연, 연기

Day 12

☐ **intent**   n. 의도, 의향
n. intention 의향, 의도   a. intentional 인도적인, 계획된

☐ **coalition**   n. 합동, 연합

☐ **misgiving**   n. 불안, 걱정
v. misgive 염려되다, 걱정되다

☐ **equity**   n. 공평, 공명
a. equitable 공평한, 공정한

☐ **morbid**   a. 병적인, 무시무시한
n. morbidity 병적상태

☐ **ingenious**   a. 영리한, 재치 있는
n. ingenuity 발명의 재주, 독창력

☐ **lucrative**   a. 득이 되는, 이익이 남는
n. lucre 이득

☐ **inapt**   a. 적합하지 않은
n. inaptitude 적당하지 않음, 부적당

☐ **extrinsic**   a. 외부의, 비본질적인

☐ **enigmatic**   a. 알 수 없는, 불가사의한
n. enigma 수수께끼   v. enigmatize 수수께끼로 만들다

☐ **stagnant**   a. 고여있는, 발전 없는
v. stagnate 흐르지 않다, 썩다   n. stagnation 침체, 불경기

☐ **mundane**   a. 평범한, 일상적인
n. mundanity 현세, 속세

☐ **constrain**   v. 강요하다, 억지로 ~하게하다
n. constraint 강요, 압박   a. constrained 강압적인, 강제적인

☐ **curtail**   v. 줄이다, 생략하다
n. curtailment 단축, 삭감

☐ **reiterate**   v. 반복하다, 되풀이 하다
n. reiteration 반복   a. reiterant 되풀이 하여 말하는, 반복하는

☐ **deceptive**   a. 속이는, 믿을 수 없는
n. deception 속임, 사기

☐ **comprehend**   v. 이해하다, 파악하다
n. comprehension 이해, 이해력   a. comprehensive 이해력 있는

☐ **comprise**   v. 구성되다, 이루어지다
n. comprisal 포함, 함유

☐ **defer**   v. 미루다, 연기하다

☐ **confine**   v. 제한하다, 한정하다
n. confinement 감금, 한정

☐ **conscript**   v. 징집하다   n. 신병, 징집 병
n. conscription 징병제도

☐ **disregard**   v. 무시하다, 경시하다   n. 무시, 경시
a. disregardful 무관심한

☐ **differentiate**   v. 구별하다, 차별하다
n. differentiation 차별, 구별   ad. differently 다르게, 같지않게

☐ **convince**   v. 확신하다, 설득하다
n. conviction 확신

☐ **etaliate**   v. 복수하다, 보복하다
n. retaliation 보복, 앙갚음   a. retaliatory 보복의, 복수심이 강한

Day 15

☐ **hybrid**　　　　　n. 잡종, 혼성물　a. 잡종의
　n. hybridity 잡종성

☐ **subsidy**　　　　　n. 보조금, 장려금, 보상금
　a. subsidiary 보조의, 부수적인　n. subsidiarity 보조적임, 보완성

☐ **guile**　　　　　n. 교활, 책략
　a. guileless 악의가 없는, 성실한　a. guileful 교활한, 음험한

☐ **posture**　　　　　n. 자세, 몸가짐, 형태
　v. posturize 포즈를 취하다　a. postural 자세의, 마음가짐의

☐ **extrovert**　　　　　n. 사교적인 사람, 외향적인 사람　a. 사교적인
　a. extroverted 외향성이 강한

☐ **maneuver**　　　　　n. 책략

☐ **immaculate**　　　　　a. 깨끗한, 순결한, 결점 없는
　n. immaculateness 청결함, 티없음　ad. immaculately 청결하게, 티없이

☐ **hectic**　　　　　a. 몹시 바쁜, 열광적인
　n. hecticness 광적임　ad. hectically 광적으로, 격앙되어

☐ **imminent**　　　　　a. 긴박한, 급박한
　ad. imminently 임박하여

☐ **sanitary**　　　　　a. 위생의, 청결한
　ad. sanitarily 위생상, 위생적으로

☐ **equivocal**　　　　　a. 불확실한, 모호한
　n. equivocality 다의성, 애매함　ad. equivocally 분명하지 않게, 수상하게

☐ **intricate**　　　　　a. 복잡한, 난해한, 얽힌
　n. intricateness 얽힘, 복잡함　ad. intricately 얽혀, 복잡하여

☐ **incorporate**　　　　　v. 합치다, 법인으로 만들다
　n. incorporation 법인, 회사　a. incorporated 법인조직의

☐ **ameliorate**　　　　　v. 개선하다, 향상시키다
　n. amelioration 개량, 개선　a. ameliorative 개선의

☐ **incriminate**　　　　　v. 죄를 씌우다, 연루 시키다
　n. incrimination 죄를 씌움

☐ **coagulate**　　　　　v. 응고하다, 딱딱해지다
　n. coagulation 응고, 응고물

☐ **forsake**　　　　　v. 버리다
　a. forsaken 버림받은, 고독한

☐ **allege**　　　　　v. 단언하다, 우기다, 진술하다
　n. allegation 주장, 진술　ad. allegedly 주장한 바에 의하면

☐ **allure**　　　　　v. 매혹하다, 꾀다
　n. allurement 유혹

☐ **enervate**　　　　　v. 약하게 하다, 기운을 빼앗다
　n. enervation 원기상실, 쇠약

☐ **allude**　　　　　v. 암시하다, 넌지시 말하다
　n. allusion 암시　a. allusive 암시적인, 넌지시 말하는

☐ **denote**　　　　　v. 뜻하다, 의미하다
　n. denotation 표시, 지시

☐ **detach**　　　　　v. 떼어놓다, 분리하다
　n. detachment 분리, 이탈　a. detachable 분리할 수 있는

☐ **subside**　　　　　v. 가라앉다, 진정되다
　n. subsidence 함몰, 침전

☐ **covet**　　　　　v. 탐내다
　a. covetous 몹시 탐내는

☐ **breakthrough**　　n. 약진, 도약, 돌파구

☐ **cessation**　　n. 중단, 정지
v. cease 그치다, 멈추다

☐ **innumerable**　　a. 무수한, 수많은
n. innumeracy 헤아릴 수 없음

☐ **systematic**　　a. 조직적인, 체계적인
v. systematize 조직화하다

☐ **monetary**　　a. 금전상의, 돈의
n. monetarism 통화주의　v. monetize 화폐로 주조하다

☐ **incredulous**　　a. 믿지 않는, 의심 많은
a. incredible 대단한, 믿기 어려운　n. incredulity 믿기 어려움

☐ **mortal**　　a. 죽음을 면할 수 없는, 치명적인
n. mortality 죽음을 면할 수 없는 운명

☐ **gullible**　　a. 잘 속는
a. gullish 바보 같은　n. gullibility 잘 속음

☐ **circumspect**　　a. 조심성 있는, 신중한
a. circumspective 주의 깊은, 신중한

☐ **allocate**　　v. 배분하다, 할당하다
n. allocation 배당, 배급, 할당

☐ **alleviate**　　v. 완화시키다, 경감시키다
n. alleviation 경감, 완화

☐ **prosecute**　　v. 기소하다, 고소하다
n. prosecution 기소, 고발

☐ **transient**　　a. 일시적인, 덧없는
ad. transiently 일시적으로, 단기 체류로　n. transience 일시적임, 덧없음

☐ **exquisite**　　a. 아름다운, 훌륭한, 정교한
ad. exquisitely 절묘하게, 정교하게

☐ **infirm**　　a. 약한, 우유부단한
n. infirmity 허약, 쇠약

☐ **obstinate**　　a. 완고한, 고집 센
ad. obstinately 완고하게, 완강하게　n. obstinacy 완고함, 완강함

☐ **exuberant**　　a. 열광적인
ad. exuberantly 풍성하게, 생기에 가득 차게　n. exuberance 충만

☐ **latent**　　a. 잠재의, 잠복의, 숨어있는
ad. latently 숨어 있어, 잠재하여　n. latency 숨어 있음, 잠재, 잠복

☐ **insolent**　　a. 오만한, 무례한, 건방진
ad. insolently 건방지게, 무례하게　n. insolence 오만, 무례

☐ **extravagant**　　a. 낭비하는, 사치스러운
ad. extravagantly 낭비적으로, 사치스럽게

☐ **parallel**　　a. 평행의, 같은 방향의

☐ **eradicate**　　v. 제거하다, 근절하다
n. eradication 근절, 박멸　a. eradicative 근절시키는

☐ **incense**　　v. 매우 화나게 하다, 격노하다
n. incensement 몹시 화나게 함, 격분 시킴

☐ **meditate**　　v. 명상하다, 숙고하다, 생각하다
n. meditation 명상, 숙고　a. meditative 명상적인

☐ **divulge**　　v. 폭로하다, 누설하다
n. divulgence 누설, 폭로

Day 16

☐ **deterrent** — n. 방해물, 억제력

☐ **commotion** — n. 동요, 소동, 폭동
a. commotional 격동[동란]의   v. commove 동요하다, 선동하다

☐ **connoisseur** — n. 감정가, 감식가, 전문가
n. connoisseurship 감식안, 감정업

☐ **detour** — n. 우회, 우회길   v. 우회하다, 돌아가다

☐ **adversary** — n. (시합의) 적, 상대자
n. adversaryism 적대주의   a. adversarial 적대 관계에 있는

☐ **detrimental** — a. 해로운, 불리한
ad. detrimentally 손해를 입히게, 해롭게

☐ **comprehensive** — a. 포괄적인, 넓은, 이해가 빠른
ad. comprehensively 포괄적으로, 광범위하게

☐ **archaic** — a. 구식의, 고대의, 원시의
ad. archaically 고풍으로, 옛 말투로

☐ **dexterous** — a. 손재주가 있는, 영리한, 민첩한
ad. dexterously 솜씨 좋게, 교묘하게

☐ **aquatic** — a. 물의, 물속의
ad. aquatically 물 속에서, 물 속에 살면서

☐ **discreet** — a. 분별있는, 사려 깊은, 신중한
ad. discreetly 분별 있게, 사려 깊게   n. discreetness 분별 있음, 사려깊음

☐ **dubious** — a. 의심스러운, 모호한
ad. dubiously 수상하게, 의심스럽게   n. dubiousness 수상함, 의심스러움

☐ **miniscule** — a. 매우 작은, 하찮은

☐ **subordinate** — n. 하급자   v. 하위에 두다

☐ **agonize** — v. 괴로워하다, 고뇌하다
n. agony 고통, 고뇌

☐ **mimic** — v. 흉내내다, 모방하다
n. mimicry 흉내   n. mimicker 흉내내는 사람

☐ **rejuvenate** — v. 원기를 회복하다[시키다]
n. rejuvenation 회춘, 원기회복

☐ **dismiss** — v. 떠나게 하다, 해고하다
n. dismissal 해산, 해고

☐ **encompass** — v. 포함하다, 둘러싸다

☐ **submerge** — v. 잠기다, 가라앉다
n. submergence 침수, 침몰

☐ **dismantle** — v. 분해하다, 떼어내다
n. dismantlement 분해

☐ **perish** — v. 멸망하다, 죽다
a. perishable 죽기 쉬운, 썩기 쉬운

☐ **strain** — v. 잡아당기다, 긴장시키다
a. strained 팽팽한, 긴장된

☐ **subdue** — v. 정복하다, 억제하다
a. subdued 정복된, 억제된

☐ **stumble** — v. 넘어지다, 비틀거리다

□ **philanthropist**　　n. 박애주의자
n. philanthropy 박애, 인류애

□ **perjury**　　n. 위증, 거짓말
v. perjure 위증하다　n. perjurer 위증자

□ **ordeal**　　n. 시련, 고난

□ **antipathy**　　n. 혐오, 반감
a. antipathetic 반감을 가진

□ **tumult**　　n. 소란, 소동
a. tumultuous 소란스러운, 거친

□ **momentous**　　a. 중요한, 중대한
n. momentum 추진력, 힘

□ **turbulent**　　a. 거친, 휘몰아치는
n. turbulence 소란, 난기류

□ **picturesque**　　a. 그림같이 아름다운
n. picture 그림

□ **frugal**　　a. 검소한, 간소한
n. frugality 절약, 검소

□ **trite**　　a. 진부한, 흔한

□ **regressive**　　a. 퇴화하는, 회귀하는
n. regression 퇴화, 퇴보

□ **subsequent**　　a. 다음의, 수반하는
n. subsequence 다음, 결과　ad. subsequently 그 후에, 다음에

□ **deteriorate**　　v. 악화시키다, (질을) 저하시키다
a. deteriorative 악화되는, 타락적인　n. deterioration 악화, 타락

□ **concede**　　v. 인정하다, 승인하다, 양보하다
n. concession 양보　a. concessive 양보의

□ **appease**　　v. (사람을) 달래다, 진정시키다
n. appeasement 진정, 타협

□ **conjecture**　　v. 추측하다, 짐작하다　n. 짐작, 추측

□ **console**　　v. 위로하다, 위문하다
a. consolable 위안할 수 있는

□ **augment**　　v. 증가하다, 증가시키다
n. augmentation 증가, 증가율　a. augmented 증가된

□ **devastate**　　v. 파괴하다, 황폐시키다
a. evastative 유린하는, 황폐시키는　n. devastation 파괴, 황폐

□ **detract**　　v. 가치를 떨어뜨리다
n. detraction 욕설, 비난　a. detractive 욕을 하는, 비난하는

□ **dwindle**　　v. 작아지다, 감소되다
n. dwindler 발육이 나쁜 사람

□ **breach**　　v. (법, 약속을) 위반하다, ～을 깨뜨리다
　　n. 위반, 불이행, 파손, 돌파구

□ **emancipate**　　v. 해방하다, 자유롭게 하다
a. emancipated 해방된, 자주적인　n. emancipation 해방, 자유, 이탈

□ **appall**　　v. 섬뜩하게 하다, 질리게 하다
a. appalling 소름끼치는, 무서운　ad. appallingly 소름끼치도록, 형편없이

□ **deviate**　　v. 벗어나다, 빗나가다
n. deviation 벗어남, 탈선

Day 17

☐ **patron**   n. 후원자, 보호자, 고객
v. patronize 후원하다, 보호하다   n. patronization 후원, 지원

☐ **nuance**   n. 미묘한 차이, 함축성

☐ **foliage**   n. 잎, 잎 무늬
a. foliaged 잎이 있는

☐ **volition**   n. 결단, 의지력
a. volitional 의지의, 의지에 관한   ad. volitionally 의지로, 의욕적으로

☐ **pedagogue**   n. 교사, 학자
n. pedagogy 교육학, 교육

☐ **mediocre**   a. 보통의, 평범한
n. mediocrity 평범, 보통   v. mediocritize 평범하게 하다

☐ **menace**   n. 협박, 위협, 공갈   v. 협박하다, 위협하다
ad. menacingly 위협[협박]적으로

☐ **noxious**   a. 해로운, 유해한, 불건전한
n. noxiousness 유해

☐ **emaciated**   a. 야윈, 쇠약한, (땅이) 메마른
v. emaciate 쇠약하게 하다, (토지를) 메마르게 하다

☐ **impromptu**   a. 즉흥적인, 즉석의

☐ **improvised**   a. 즉흥의, 즉석의
v. improvise 즉석에서 하다

☐ **grotesque**   a. 기괴한, 이상한
n. grotesquery 기괴한 성질[것]   ad. grotesquely 기괴하게, 우스꽝스럽게

☐ **opulent**   a. 풍부한, 호사스러운
n. opulence 풍요, 풍부

☐ **pathological**   a. 병적인, 병리상의
n. pathology 병리학

☐ **integral**   a. 절대 필요한, 없어서는 안될

☐ **indomitable**   a. 불굴의

☐ **induce**   v. 유발하다, 야기하다
n. induction 유도, 유발   a. inductive 귀납의

☐ **exert**   v. 쓰다, 노력하다
n. exertion 노력, 분발   a. exertive 노력하는

☐ **embed**   v. 끼워넣다

☐ **trespass**   v. 불법 침입하다, 침해하다
n. trespasser 침입자

☐ **emulate**   v. 모방하다, ~에 필적하다, 경쟁하다
n. emulation 경쟁

☐ **loiter**   v. 어슬렁거리다

☐ **mitigate**   v. 줄이다
n. mitigation 경감, 완화   a. mitigative 완화하는

☐ **reinforce**   v. 강화하다
n. reinforcement 보강, 강화

☐ **dispose**   v. 처리하다, 처분하다
a. disposal 처분, 처리   a. disposable 처분할 수 있는

☐ **denunciation**　　n. 비난, 탄핵
v. denounce 비난하다, 고발하다

☐ **zenith**　　n. 천정, 절정
a. zenithal 천정의, 정점의

☐ **census**　　n. 인구조사

☐ **grudge**　　n. 원한
a. grudging 원한을 품은, 싫어하는

☐ **delusion**　　n. 망상, 허상
v. delude 속이다　a. delusive 기만적인, 거짓의

☐ **mishap**　　n. (가벼운)사고, 불행한 일

☐ **fracture**　　n. 골절　v. 뼈가 부서지다
a. fractural 골절의

☐ **limber**　　a. 유연한

☐ **incontrovertible**　　a. 명백한
n. incontrovertibleness 명백함

☐ **adverse**　　a. 불리한, 반대의
n. adversity 역경, 불운　n. adversary 적, 반대자

☐ **peripheral**　　a. 중요하지 않는, 주변적인
n. periphery 주위, 주변

☐ **frail**　　a. 약한, 깨지기 쉬운
n. frailty 약함, 단점

☐ **pecuniary**　　a. 재정상의, 금전상의
ad. pecuniarily 금전상으로, 재정상으로

☐ **volatile**　　a. 휘발성의, 증발하기 쉬운
v. volatilize 휘발[증발]하다

☐ **gregarious**　　a. 사교적인
ad. gregariously 떼지어, 군거하여　n. gregariousness 군거성, 군생

☐ **voluminous**　　a. 권수가 많은, 부피가 큰
ad. voluminously 권수가 많아, 저서가 많아

☐ **lethargic**　　a. 혼수상태의, 졸리는, 둔한
ad. lethargically 혼수 상태로, 둔감하게　v. lethargize 혼수 상태에 빠지게 하다

☐ **flounder**　　v. 허우적거리다, 허둥대다
ad. flounderingly 허둥대며, 실수를 저지르며

☐ **patronize**　　v. ~와 거래하다, ~를 후원하다
n. patron 후원자, 고객　a. patronizing 후원하는, 은인인 체하는

☐ **bewilder**　　v. 당황하다, 어리둥절하다
n. bewilderment 당황, 당혹　a. bewildering 당혹케 하는

☐ **inaugurate**　　v. 취임하다
n. inauguration 개시, 취임　a. inaugural 취임(식)의, 개회의

☐ **elucidate**　　v. 자세히 설명하다
n. elucidator 설명자, 해설자　a. elucidative 설명적인, 해명적인

☐ **admonish**　　v. 충고하다, 훈계하다
n. admonishment 충고, 훈계　ad. admonishingly 충고하는 투로, 훈계조로

☐ **cede**　　v. (권리를) 양도하다, 양보하다

☐ **dehydrate**　　v. 탈수하다, 건조시키다
n. dehydration 탈수, 건조　n. dehydrator 탈수기

☐ **melancholy**　　n. 우울함, 의기소침
a. melancholic 우울한, 침울한　ad. melancholically 우울하게, 침울하게

☐ **peril**　　n. 위험, 모험
a. perilous 위험한, 모험적인　ad. perilously 위험하게, 모험적으로

☐ **verdict**　　n. 판결, 심판

☐ **tenacious**　　a. 단단히 잡고 있는, 집요한, 완강한
ad. tenaciously 집요하게, 끈질기게　a. tenaciousness 집요함, 끈질김

☐ **blunt**　　a. 무딘, 퉁명스러운
ad. bluntly 무디게, 무뚝뚝하게　n. bluntness 무딤, 뭉툭함, 무뚝뚝함

☐ **celestial**　　a. 하늘의, 천국의

☐ **dejected**　　a. 낙담한, 기가 죽은
ad. dejectedly 기가 죽어, 낙담하여　n. dejectedness 기가 죽음, 낙담

☐ **therapeutic**　　a. 치료의, 치료법의
ad. therapeutically 치료상으로, 치료법으로　n. therapeutics 치료학, 치료법

☐ **terrestrial**　　a. 지구상의, 육지의
ad. terrestrially 지구(상)에, 육지로

☐ **tepid**　　a. 미지근한, 미온의
n. tepidness 미지근함　ad. tepidly 미지근하게

☐ **inadvertent**　　a. 부주의 한, 우연한
ad. inadvertently 부주의하게, 무심코　n. inadvertence 부주의, 실수

☐ **vulgar**　　a. 상스러운, 천한
ad. vulgarly 상스럽게, 천하게　n. vulgarity 속됨, 상스러움

☐ **vigilant**　　a. 조심성 있는, 경계하는
n. vigilance 경계, 조심

☐ **prodigal**　　a. 낭비하는
n. prodigality 방탕, 낭비

☐ **adjacent**　　a. 가까운, 근접한
n. adjacency 인접, 인근

☐ **resilient**　　a. 회복하는, 되돌아가는
n. resilience 탄력, 복원

☐ **frivolous**　　a. 사소한, 천박한
n. frivolity 천박, 경박

☐ **figurative**　　a. 비유적인
n. figure 숫자, 모습　n. figuration 비유적 표현, 형상

☐ **contemplate**　　v. 숙고하다, 생각하다
n. contemplation 묵상, 명상

☐ **castigate**　　v. 혹평하다, 벌주다
n. castigation 혹평

☐ **erode**　　v. 침식하다, 부식하다
n. erosion 부식, 침식

☐ **repel**　　v. 막다, 쫓아버리다
a. repellent 불쾌한, 반발하는

☐ **dissemble**　　v. 숨기다, 가장하다

☐ **premeditate**　　v. 미리 계획하다
n. premeditation 미리 계획함

☐ **exemplify**　　v. 예가 되다
n. exemplification 예증, 사례　a. exemplary 모범적인

☐ **monopoly**   n. 독점
v. monopolize 독점권을 얻다, 독점하다   a. monopolistic 독점적인

☐ **placebo**   n. 위약

☐ **alliance**   n. 연합, 동맹
v. ally 동맹하다, 제휴하다

☐ **monotone**   n. 단조로움
a. monotonous 단조로운   v. monotonize 단조롭게 하다

☐ **conventional**   a. 전통적인, 틀에 박힌
n. convention 집회, 협정, 관습

☐ **cosmopolitan**   a. 세계적인, 국제적인
n. cosmopolis 국제도시

☐ **imperative**   a. 필수적인, 긴요한
n. imperator 전제군주

☐ **supple**   a. 유연한, 유연성 있는
n. suppleness 유연

☐ **counterfeit**   a. 위조의   v. 위조하다
n. counterfeiter 위조자

☐ **exemplary**   a. 훌륭한, 모범적인
v. exemplify 예시하다, 예증하다

☐ **futile**   a. 헛된, 효과 없는
v. futility 무가치, 무익

☐ **deflated**   a. 자신감 잃은, 공기가 빠진
v. deflate 공기를 빼다, 수축시키다

☐ **sedate**   a. 조용한, 침착한, 냉정한
ad. sedately 조용히, 침착하게   a. sedative 진정시키는, 누그러뜨리는

☐ **pedantic**   a. 현학적인, 박식한 체하는
ad. pedantically 현학적으로, 박식한 체하여   n. pedanticalness 현학적임

☐ **penitent**   a. 뉘우치는, 후회하는
a. penitentiary 후회의, 참회의

☐ **sedentary**   a. 앉아 있는, 앉아서 일하는
ad. sedentarily 앉아 있으면서, 앉아 일하며

☐ **timid**   a. 겁많은, 소심한
n. timidity 겁, 소심, 내성적임   ad. timidly 겁많게, 소극적으로

☐ **belligerent**   a. 용감한, 호전적인
n. belligerence 호전성, 전쟁을 좋아함   ad. belligerently 호전적으로

☐ **delegate**   v. ~을 대표로 임명하다
n. delegation 대표로 임명하기

☐ **vacillate**   v. 흔들리다, 비틀거리다
n. vacillation 흔들림, 동요

☐ **recur**   v. 다시 일어나다, 재발하다
a. recurrent 빈발하는, 재발하는

☐ **elude**   v. ~를 교묘히 피하다, ~를 벗어나다
n. elusion 회피, 도피

☐ **reconcile**   v. ~를 중재하다, 만족시키다
n. reconciliation 조정, 화해   a. reconciliatory 화해의, 조화의

☐ **verify**   v. …을 검증하다, 입증하다
a. verifiable 확인할 수 있는   n. verifiability 실증할 수 있음

☐ **adulterate**   v. ~를 떨어뜨리다, 절하하다
a. adulterated 품질을 떨어뜨린   n. adulteration 섞음질, 불량품

☐ **blot**　　　n. 얼룩, 오점

☐ **benediction**　　　n. 축복, 기도
a. benedictional 축복의, 감사 기도의

☐ **fidelity**　　　n. 충실, (약속) 엄수

☐ **fervor**　　　n. 열정, 열렬
a. fervent 열렬한, 강렬한　a. fervid 열렬한, 열정적인

☐ **hierarchy**　　　n. 계층, 서열
a. hierarchical 계급 제도의

☐ **faculty**　　　n. 능력, 교수단
a. facultative 권한을 주는

☐ **lavish**　　　a. 풍부한, 사치스러운
n. lavishness 낭비, 헤픔　ad. lavishly 아낌없이, 낭비적으로

☐ **capricious**　　　a. 변덕스런, 불안정한
n. caprice 변덕, 일시적 기분　ad. capriciously 변덕스럽게, 불규칙적으로

☐ **ignoble**　　　a. 품위가 없는, 천한
n. ignobleness 품위가 없음, 비열함

☐ **paramount**　　　a. 최고의, 최고 권력을 쥔
n. paramountcy 최고권, 탁월

☐ **scrupulous**　　　a. 견실한, 양심적인, 정확한
ad. scrupulously 양심적으로, 용의주도하게　n. scrupulousness 양심적임, 용의주도함

☐ **immutable**　　　a. 바꿀 수 없는, 불변의
n. immutability 불변　ad. immutably 불변하게

☐ **distraught**　　　a. 정신이 혼란한, 산만한

☐ **obsolete**　　　a. 구식의, 진부한
v. obsolesce 쇠퇴해가다　a. obsolescent 쇠퇴해가는, 구식의

☐ **compulsory**　　　a. 의무적인, 강제적인
n. compulsion 강박현상, 강제

☐ **conspicuous**　　　a. 눈에 띄는, 뚜렷한
n. conspicuousness 눈에 띔

☐ **voracious**　　　a. 게걸스레 먹는, 탐욕적인
n. voracity 폭식, 탐욕

☐ **consolidate**　　　v. 통합하다, 합병하다
n. consolidation 합병

☐ **dissuade**　　　v. 그만두게 하다, 못하게 하다
n. dissuasion 설득, 만류

☐ **condense**　　　v. 압축하다, 응축하다
a. condensed 응축한, 간결한　n. condensation 응축, 압축

☐ **fathom**　　　v. 헤아리다, 간파하다
a. fathomable 추측할 수 있는

☐ **conspire**　　　v. 음모를 꾸미다
n. conspiracy 음모, 공모

☐ **quench**　　　v. 해소하다, (갈증 등을) 가시게 하다
a. quenchless 억누를 수 없는

☐ **compress**　　　v. 압축하다, 압박하다
a. compressed 압축된, 간결한

☐ **disperse**　　　v. 흩뜨리다, 분산시키다
n. dispersion 살포, 분산

☐ **decadence**　　　n. 타락
a. decadent 퇴폐적인

☐ **nomad**　　　n. 유목민, 방랑자
a. nomadic 유목의, 방랑의

☐ **staple**　　　n. 주요산물, 주요품

☐ **gist**　　　n. 요점, 요지

☐ **drawback**　　　n. 결점, 단점

☐ **nutrition**　　　n. 영양분
a. nutritious 영양이 많은　n. nutrient 영양분

☐ **constellation**　　　n. 성운, 성좌
v. constellate 성좌를 이루다, 떼를 짓다

☐ **sterile**　　　a. 불임의, 불모의
n. sterility 불임, 불모

☐ **complacent**　　　a. 만족하는
n. complacence 자기 만족

☐ **languid**　　　a. 나른한, 기운 없는
v. languish 기운이 없어지다, 약해지다

☐ **lucid**　　　a. 분명한
n. lucidity 명료, 밝음

☐ **agile**　　　a. 기민한, 재빠른
n. agility 민첩, 명민함

☐ **astute**　　　a. 빈틈없는, 기민한
ad. astutely 날카로운 통찰력으로, 빈틈없이　n. astuteness 빈틈없음

☐ **versatile**　　　a. 다재 다능한, 만능의
n. versatility 융통성, 다재다능

☐ **deficient**　　　a. 부족한, 불충분한
n. deficiency 부족, 결핍　n. deficit 부족액, 부족

☐ **impeccable**　　　a. 흠이 없는, 죄를 저지르지 않은
a. impeccant 죄가 없는, 결백한　ad. impeccably 결점이 없게

☐ **inept**　　　a. 부적당한, 서투른
ad. ineptly 서투르게, 적합치 않게　n. ineptness 서투름, 적합치 않음

☐ **captivate**　　　v. 매혹하다, 사로잡다
n. captivation 매혹, 매료　a. captivating 매혹적인

☐ **nullify**　　　v. 무효로하다, 취소하다
n. nullification 무효(화), 파기, 취소

☐ **veto**　　　v. 거부권을 행사하다　n. 거부권
a. veto-proof 거부권에 대항하는

☐ **glisten**　　　v. 반짝 빛나다, 번쩍거리다
ad. glisteningly 반짝반짝

☐ **vex**　　　v. 괴롭히다, 성나게하다
n. vexation 짜증내기, 괴롭히기　a. vexed 속타는, 짜증나는

☐ **tantalize**　　　v. 남을 애태우다, 감질나게 하다
a. tantalizing 남의 기대를 부추기는, 감질나는

☐ **manipulate**　　　v. 잘 다루다, 조정하다
a. manipulative 손으로 다루는, 솜씨 있게 다루는

☐ **antagonize**　　　v. 대항하다, 적대하다
n. antagonist 적대자, 경쟁자　a. antagonistic 적대하는, 대립하는

Day 20

☐ **hygiene**   n. 위생, 위생학
a. hygienic 위생적인, 청결한   n. hygienist 위생학자

☐ **snare**   n. 덫, 올가미

☐ **sprout**   n. 새싹, (식물의) 눈   v. 싹트다, 발생하다
n. sproutling 작은 싹, 새싹

☐ **deluge**   n. 대홍수, 범람

☐ **siege**   n. 포위, 포위공격
a. siegeable 포위[공격]할 수 있는

☐ **latency**   n. 숨어있음, 잠복
a. latent 숨은, 잠재한

☐ **tremor**   n. 떨림, 전율
a. tremorous 떨리는, 진동하는

☐ **sphere**   n. 구, 구체, 지구의
a. spherical 구형의, 구면의

☐ **chubby**   a. 토실토실한, 살찐
n. chubbiness 오동통함

☐ **adroit**   a. 손재주가 있는, 재치가 있는
ad. adroitly 능숙하게, 영리하게   n. adroitness 솜씨있음, 영리함

☐ **sullen**   a. 무뚝뚝한, 시무룩한
n. sullenness 시무룩함, 뚱함   ad. sullenly 시무룩하게, 뚱하게

☐ **corpulent**   a. 뚱뚱한, 비만의
ad. corpulently 뚱뚱하게, 비대하게   n. corpulence 비만, 비대

☐ **palpable**   a. 명백한
n. palpability 명백함

☐ **wholesome**   a. 건강에 좋은, 유익한

☐ **somber**   a. 침울한, 흐린

☐ **malicious**   a. 악의 있는
n. malice 악의, 원한

☐ **congruent**   a. 일치하는, 조화된
n. congruity 조화, 일치

☐ **solicitous**   a. 걱정하는, 염려하는
n. solicitude 걱정, 근심

☐ **sanction**   v. 허가하다

☐ **congregate**   v. 모이다, 군집하다
n. congregation 모임, 집회   a. congregative 집합적인

☐ **seep**   v. 새다, 누출되다
n. seepage 누출(액)   a. seepy 물이 스며 나오는

☐ **distort**   v. 왜곡하다, 비틀다
n. distortion 왜곡, 뒤틀림   a. distorted 비뚤어진, 왜곡된

☐ **persecute**   v. 박해하다, 괴롭히다
n. persecution 박해, 학대

☐ **diverge**   v. 다르다, 갈라지다
n. divergence 분기, 일탈

☐ **persevere**   v. 참다, 인내하다
n. perseverance 인내, 참을성

☐ **configuration**　　n. 도구, 기구
v. configure 형성하다, 배열하다

☐ **congestion**　　n. 혼잡, 정체
v. congest 혼잡하다, 정체시키다

☐ **condolence**　　n. 애도
v. condole 위로하다, 문상하다　a. condolent 위로하는

☐ **sovereign**　　n. 통치자

☐ **candor**　　n. 솔직함, 정직
a. candid 솔직한, 숨김없는

☐ **sober**　　a. 술 취하지 않은, 냉정한
n. sobriety 술 취하지 않음, 맑은 정신

☐ **incessant**　　a. 끊임없는
ad. incessantly 끊임없이

☐ **meticulous**　　a. 세심한, 신중한
ad. meticulously 꼼꼼하게

☐ **indignant**　　a. 화난, 분개한
n. indignity 모욕, 경멸　n. indignation 분개, 분노

☐ **indigenous**　　a. 토착의, 원산의

☐ **translucent**　　a. (반)투명한
a. translucid 반투명의

☐ **treacherous**　　a. 위험한, 믿을 수 없는
n. treachery 배반

☐ **dismal**　　a. 음산한, 침울한
ad. dismally 음울하게, 쓸쓸하게　n. dismalness 음울, 쓸쓸함

☐ **downcast**　　a. 의기소침한, 풀이죽은
ad. downcastly 의기소침하게, 풀이 죽어　n. downcastness 의기소침함

☐ **static**　　a. 정적인, 고정된　n. 소음
ad. statically 정적으로

☐ **prolific**　　a. 다산의, 비옥한
n. prolificity 다산성, 다산력　n. prolificacy 다산, 다작

☐ **despotic**　　a. 독재의, 절대군주의
ad. despotically 독재적으로, 절대 군주로

☐ **sluggish**　　a. 느린, 둔한, 기능이 활발하지 못한
ad. sluggishly 게으르게, 나태하게　n. sluggishness 게으름, 나태

☐ **loathsome**　　a. 싫은, 기분 나쁜
a. loath 싫어서, 질색하여

☐ **copious**　　a. 많은, 대량의, 풍부한
ad. copiously 풍부[풍성]하게　n. copiousness 풍부함, 풍성함

☐ **congruous**　　a. 일치하는, 조화하는
n. congruity 적합, 조화

☐ **coax**　　v. 달래어 ~시키다
n. coaxing 감언으로 꾀기, 달래기

☐ **mortify**　　v. 분하게 하다, 굴욕을 느끼다
n. mortification 굴욕, 치욕

☐ **reckon**　　v. 계산하다, 생각하다, 기대하다
n. reckoning 계산, 셈　a. reckonable 계산할 수 있는, 짐작할 수 있는

☐ **propagate**　　v. 보급하다, 선전하다, 번식시키다
n. propagation 번식, 증식　a. propagational 번식의, 증식의

Day 21

☐ **punctuality**   n. 시간 엄수
a. punctual 시간을 지키는   ad. punctually 시간을 엄수하여, 정확하게

☐ **abode**   n. 주소, 주거

☐ **hindrance**   n. 방해, 장애
v. hinder 방해하다, 훼방놓다

☐ **lineage**   n. 혈통, 계통

☐ **fortitude**   n. 인내, 강건함
a. fortitudinous 불굴의 정신이 있는

☐ **forfeit**   n. 벌금, 위약금   v. 상실하다, 몰수당하다
n. forfeiture 몰수, 벌금, 과료

☐ **elastic**   a. 탄력의, 탄력 있는
v. elasticate (옷감·옷 따위에) 신축성을 지니게 하다   a. elasticity 탄력, 신축성

☐ **arduous**   a. 고된, 힘든
ad. arduously 힘들게, 정열적으로   n. arduousness 불요불굴, 끈기

☐ **titanic**   a. 거대한, 강력한
ad. titanically 거대하게

☐ **tactile**   a. 촉각의
n. tactility 감촉성

☐ **meager**   a. 메마른, 빈약한
ad. meagerly 빈약하게 결핍되어   n. meagerness 빈약함, 결핍됨

☐ **haughty**   a. 건방진, 도도한
ad. haughtily 건방지게, 오만하게   n. haughtiness 건방짐, 오만

☐ **lethal**   a. 치명적인, 죽음의
n. lethality 치명적임

☐ **elongate**   v. 늘이다, 늘어나다
n. elongation 연장, 늘어남

☐ **beleaguer**   v. 포위하다, 괴롭히다

☐ **flinch**   v. 움츠리다, 움찔하다

☐ **implement**   v. 이행하다, 실행하다   n. 도구, 기구
n. implementation 이행, 실행

☐ **denounce**   v. 비난하다, 비방하다
n. denunciation 비난

☐ **smother**   v. 불을 끄다, 숨 막히게 하다
a. smothery 질식시키는, 숨막히는

☐ **smuggle**   v. 밀수출하다
n. smuggler 밀수입자

☐ **berate**   v. 호되게 꾸짖다

☐ **implore**   v. 간청하다, 애원하다
a. imploring 애원하는

☐ **fortify**   v. 강화하다
n. fortitude 굳건함, 강건함   n. fortification 방어시설

☐ **capitulate**   v. 굴복하다, 항복하다
n. capitulation 무조건 항복

☐ **indict**   v. 기소하다, 비난하다
n. indictment 기소, 고발

☐ **condescend**   v. 겸손하게 행동하다
n. condescension 겸손, 겸양

☐ **buffer**　　　　n. 완충지　v. 완화시키다

☐ **hypocrite**　　　　n. 위선자
n. hypocrisy 위선

☐ **metaphor**　　　　n. 은유, 비유
a. metaphoric 은유의

☐ **anarchist**　　　　n. 무정부주의자
n. anarchy 무정부 상태　n. anarchism 무정부주의

☐ **sly**　　　　a. 교활한, 은밀한
n. slyness 교활함　ad. slyly 교활하게

☐ **articulate**　　　　a. 분명한, 명료한
n. articulation 또렷한 발음　a. articulated 똑똑히 발음되는

☐ **vivacious**　　　　a. 활발한, 생기 있는
n. vivacity 생기, 활달

☐ **eminent**　　　　a. 유명한, 뛰어난
n. eminence 저명, 명성

☐ **secluded**　　　　a. 격리된
v. seclude 차단하다, 격리하다　n. seclusion 격리

☐ **tedious**　　　　a. 지루한, 따분한
n. tedium 권태, 지겨움

☐ **aesthetic**　　　　a. 미의, 미학적인
n. aesthete 유미주의자, 심미가　n. aesthetics 미학

☐ **perfunctory**　　　　a. 형식적인, 마지못한
ad. perfunctorily 형식적으로

☐ **manifold**　　　　a. 다양한, 다수의
ad. manifoldly 다양하게, 복합적으로　n. manifoldness 다양함, 복합적임

☐ **obliterate**　　　　v. 지우다, 제거하다
n. obliteration 말소, 제거

☐ **efface**　　　　v. 지우다, 제거하다
n. effacement 지움, 삭제　a. effaceable 지울 수 있는

☐ **sprinkle**　　　　v. ~을 뿌리다, 끼얹다
n. sprinkler 물뿌리개, 살수차　n. sprinkling 흩뿌림

☐ **reprehend**　　　　v. 비난하다, 꾸짖다
a. reprehendable 책망할 수 있는

☐ **exterminate**　　　　v. 박멸하다, 몰살하다
n. extermination 멸종, 전멸　a. exterminatory 근절[박멸]적인

☐ **wane**　　　　v. 작아지다, 쇠약해지다
a. waney 쇠퇴해 가는, 감소한

☐ **cleave**　　　　v. 쪼개다, 틈을 내다
n. cleavage 분열, 갈라진 틈

☐ **feign**　　　　v. ~인 체하다, 가장하다
ad. feigningly 가장하여, 꾸며내어　a. feigned 가장한, 겉치레의

☐ **revoke**　　　　v. (약속, 면허 등을) 취소하다, 철회하다
n. revocation 폐지, 축소

☐ **disseminate**　　　　v. (씨를) 뿌리다, 퍼트리다
a. disseminative 살포하는, 보급하는　n. dissemination 살포, 보급

☐ **ascribe**　　　　v. ~의 탓으로 하다
a. ascribable ~에 돌릴 수 있는, ~ 탓인

Day 22

☐ **advent**　　　　n. 출현, 도래

☐ **antecedent**　　　n. 선조, 전례
ad. antecedently 앞서, 선행하여   n. antecedence 앞섬, 선행

☐ **gleam**　　　　n. 미광, 희미한 빛   v. 어슴푸레 빛나다
a. gleamy 빛나는, 희미하게 빛나는   a. gleaming 반짝반짝 빛나는

☐ **quest**　　　　n. 탐구, 추구
n. question 물음, 질문   a. questing 탐색[탐구]하는

☐ **impetus**　　　　n. 힘, 자극, 충동

☐ **impulse**　　　　n. 추진력, 자극, 충동
n. impulsion 추진, 강제   a. impulsive 충동적인, 추진적인

☐ **custody**　　　　n. 보호, 감금
n. custodian 관리인, 보관자   a. custodial 보관[보호]의

☐ **paranoia**　　　　n. 편집 증, 망상증
a. paranoiac 편집광의

☐ **residue**　　　　n. 잔여, 나머지
a. residual 나머지의, 찌꺼기의   a. residuary 잔여의, 나머지의

☐ **prestige**　　　　n. 위신, 명성
a. prestigious 명성이 있는, 유명한   ad. prestigiously 유명하게, 일류로

☐ **requisite**　　　　a. 필수의, 필요한
ad. requisitely 필요하게, 필수적으로   n. requisiteness 필수적임, 필요 불가결함

☐ **combustible**　　　　a. 타기 쉬운, 흥분하기 쉬운
n. combustibility 연소성, 가연성

☐ **severe**　　　　a. 엄한, 엄격한
n. severity 격렬, 혹독   ad. severely 심하게, 엄하게

☐ **amorphous**　　　　a. 무정형의, 비결정질의

☐ **reciprocal**　　　　a. 호혜적인, 상호간의
v. reciprocate 보답하다, 답례하다

☐ **atrocious**　　　　a. 극악한, 지독한
n. atrocity 잔악, 포악

☐ **ample**　　　　a. 충분한, 풍부한
v. amplify 확대하다, 확장하다

☐ **vile**　　　　a. 몹시 나쁜, 지독한
v. vilify 비방하다, 중상하다

☐ **lenient**　　　　a. 자비로운
n. lenience 관용, 관대함

☐ **ominous**　　　　a. 불길한
n. omen 전조, 징조

☐ **replenish**　　　　v. 보충하다

☐ **stammer**　　　　v. 더듬거리다
a. stammering 말을 더듬는

☐ **rehabilitate**　　　　v. 원상 복구하다, 사회 복귀시키다
n. rehabilitation 사회 복귀, 갱생

☐ **ascend**　　　　v. 올라가다, 상승하다
a. ascendant 상승하는, 떠오르는   n. ascendancy 우세, 패권

☐ **elicit**　　　　v. 이끌어내다, 유도하다

☐ **misconception**　　a. 오해
v. misconceive 잘못 생각하다, 오해하다

☐ **novice**　　n. 초보자, 풋내기

☐ **standpoint**　　n. 관점, 시각

☐ **slander**　　n. 비방　V. 비방하다
a. slanderous 중상적인, 비방하는

☐ **pertinent**　　a. 적절한, 관련된
n. pertinence 적절, 적당

☐ **coarse**　　V. 조잡해지다

☐ **inanimate**　　a. 생명이 없는, 활기가 없는
n. inanimation 무기력

☐ **benevolent**　　a. 인정 많은, 너그러운
n. benevolence 자비심, 박애

☐ **pervasive**　　a. 널리 퍼져있는, 만연한
v. pervade 널리 퍼지다, 보급하다　n. pervasion 보급, 침투

☐ **ornate**　　a. 화려한, 잘 꾸민
n. ornamentation 장식

☐ **imperious**　　a. 권위적인, 거만한

☐ **perpetual**　　a. 끊임없는
v. perpetuate 불멸하게 하다, 영속시키다

☐ **inquisitive**　　a. 질문을 좋아하는, 탐구적인
ad. inquisitively 연구를 좋아하여　n. inquisition 조사[탐구]하는 일

☐ **naive**　　a. 순진한, 천진난만한

☐ **obscure**　　a. 분명치 않은, 어두컴컴한
ad. obscurely 애매하게, 희미하게

☐ **colossal**　　a. 거대한, 엄청난
ad. colossally 거대하게

☐ **vicious**　　a. 나쁜, 잔인한, 악의 있는
n. viciousness 사악함, 심술궂음

☐ **facilitate**　　V. 용이하게 하다, 쉽게 하다
a. facilitative 촉진하는　n. facilitation 용이하게 하기, 촉진, 조장

☐ **glaze**　　V. 판유리를 끼우다, 유약을 칠하다
a. glazed 유약을 바른, 유리를 끼운　n. glazer 윤내는 기계

☐ **invigorate**　　V. 기운나게 하다, 고무하다
a. invigorative 기운을 북돋우는, 격려하는　ad. invigoratingly 격려하여

☐ **interrogate**　　V. 심문하다, 질문 하다
a. interrogative 의문의, 묻고 싶은 듯한　n. interrogation 질문, 심문

☐ **inflame**　　V. 불태우다, 흥분시키다, 노하게 하다
ad. inflamingly 불을 붙여, 불태워　a. inflammable 가연성의

☐ **overstate**　　V. 과장하다
n. overstatement 과장한 말, 허풍

☐ **retreat**　　V. 물러나다, 후퇴하다, 은퇴하다

☐ **discharge**　　V. 짐을 내리다, (총을) 발사하다
n. discharger 짐 부리는 사람

Day 23

☐ **gratitude** n. 감사
v. gratify ～에게 고맙게 하다 a. gratifying 만족을 주는

☐ **hypothesis** n. 가설, 전제
a. hypothetical 가설의

☐ **imposter** n. 협잡꾼, 사기꾼

☐ **mutiny** n. 반항, 폭동 v. 반란을 일으키다
a. mutinous 반항적인 n. mutineer 모반자

☐ **affinity** n. 애호, 호감
a. affinitive 혈연의

☐ **euphemism** n. 완곡어법
a. euphemistic, euphemistical 완곡한 ad. euphemistically 완곡하게

☐ **forage** n. 사료, 식량 수집
n. forager 징발자, 약탈자 n. foraging 채집, 수렵

☐ **reign** n. 치세, 통치기간
a. reigning 군림하는, 정권을 잡고 있는

☐ **innocuous** a. 해가 없는, 악의가 없는
ad. innocuously 무해하여, 지루하여

☐ **notorious** a. 유명한, 악명 높은
ad. notoriously 유명하게

☐ **prodigious** a. 거대한, 놀랄만한
ad. prodigiously 터무니 없이, 경이적으로

☐ **apathetic** a. 무감동한, 냉담한
ad. apathetically 냉담하게

☐ **pious** a. 종교적인, 신앙심 깊은
n. piety 경건, 신앙심

☐ **relentless** a. 끊임없는, 가차없는

☐ **renowned** a. 유명한, 저명한
n. renown 명성

☐ **mock** v. 조롱하다, 흉내내다
n. mockery 조롱, 놀림 a. mocking 조롱하는

☐ **remunerate** v. 보상하다, 보답하다
n. remuneration 보수, 보상 a. remunerative 보수가 있는, 수지 맞는

☐ **ingest** v. 먹다, 섭취하다
n. ingestion 섭취

☐ **relinquish** v. 포기하다, 그만두다

☐ **saturate** v. 흠뻑 적시다, 담그다
a. saturated 속속들이 스며든

☐ **loathe** v. 몹시 싫어하다
a. loathsome 싫은 n. loathing 혐오, 질색

☐ **effervesce** v. 거품이 일다
a. effervescent 거품이 이는

☐ **enact** v. 제정하다, 규정하다
n. enactment 법령, 법규

☐ **ratify** v. 승인하다, 비준하다
n. ratification 비준, 인가, 승인

☐ **indulge** v. 빠지다, 탐닉하다
n. indulgence 관대, 탐닉 a. indulgent 멋대로 하는, 관대한

□ **symmetry**　　　　n. 균형, 좌우대칭

a. symmetrical 균형이 잡힌, 대칭의　　v. symmetrize 균형을 잡다

□ **parable**　　　　n. 우화, 비유담

□ **frenzy**　　　　n. 흥분, 격분, 열광

a. frenetic 열광적인, 미친

□ **remorse**　　　　n. 양심의 가책

a. remorseful 후회의, 양심의 가책을 받은

□ **plumage**　　　　n. 깃털

□ **placid**　　　　a. 조용한, 고요한

□ **mandatory**　　　　a. 강제의, 필수의

n. v. mandate 명령, 명령하다

□ **ambivalent**　　　　a. 양면적인, 상반하는 감정을 가진

n. ambivalence 양면의 가치

□ **charitable**　　　　a. 자비로운, 관용적인

n. charity 자선, 자비

□ **exorbitant**　　　　a. 터무니없는

n. exorbitance 엄청남, 과대

□ **susceptible**　　　　a. 영향 받기 쉬운

n. susceptibility 감수성　a. susceptive 감수성이 강한, 민감한

□ **pliant**　　　　a. 유연한, 유순한

a. pliable 유연한, 유순한　n. pliancy 유연, 유순

□ **verbose**　　　　a. 장황한, 용장 한

n. verbosity 장황함　ad. verbosely 장황하게

□ **luminous**　　　　a. 빛나는, 밝은

n. luminary 발광체, 인공 조명

□ **condone**　　　　v. 용서하다

n. condonation 용서, 묵과

□ **gasp**　　　　v. 헐떡거리다, 숨이 막히다

ad. gaspingly 헐떡거리며

□ **connive**　　　　v. 묵인하다, 음모를 꾸미다

n. conniver 묵인자　n. connivery 묵인

□ **dilapidate**　　　　v. 파손시키다

a. dilapidated 황폐한, 파손된

□ **equivocate**　　　　v. 말끝을 흐리다, 얼버무리다

n. equivocation 애매한 말씨　a. equivocal 미적지근한, 불안정한

□ **exalt**　　　　v. 승진시키다, 칭찬하다

a. exalted 고귀한　ad. exaltedly 의기 양양하게, 과장되게

□ **deplete**　　　　v. 감소시키다, 다 써버리다

n. depletion 감소, 고갈

□ **perjure**　　　　v. ~에게 위증시키다

a. perjured 위증한, 위증죄를 범한　n. perjury 위증죄

□ **reproach**　　　　v. 비난하다　n. 질책, 수치

a. reproachful 나무라는, 책망하는

□ **tarnish**　　　　v. 흐리게 하다, 녹슬게 하다

a. tarnishable 흐려지기 쉬운

□ **impede**　　　　v. 방해하다, 지연시키다

n. impediment 방해, 훼방

☐ **proponent**   n. 제안자, 지지자
v. propone 제안하다, 제의하다

☐ **anguish**   n. 고통

☐ **enmity**   n. 적의, 반목

☐ **upheaval**   n. 대변동, 격변
v. upheave 밀어 올리다

☐ **longevity**   n. 장수, 장기근속
a. longevous 장수의

☐ **overt**   a. 명백한, 공개적인
n. overture 제안, 예비교섭

☐ **liable**   a. 책임을 져야 할, 의무가 있는
n. liability 책무, 의무

☐ **intrinsic**   a. 본질적인, 내재된
ad. intrinsically 본질적으로

☐ **intrepid**   a. 용기 있는, 대담한
n. intrepidity 용맹, 대담

☐ **devoid**   a. 빠진, 없는

☐ **intact**   a. 완전한, 손대지 않은
ad. intactly 원래대로

☐ **serene**   a. 조용한, 화창한
ad. serenely 잔잔하게

☐ **quarantine**   v. 격리하다

☐ **coalesce**   v. 하나가 되다
n. coalescence 합병, 연합

☐ **ventilate**   v. 환기하다
n. ventilation 환기, 통풍

☐ **endeavor**   v. 노력하다

☐ **endorse**   v. 인정하다, 시인하다
n. endorsement 배서, 보증

☐ **absolve**   v. 면제하다, 사면하다
n. absolution 면제, 방면

☐ **barter**   v. 물물교환하다   n. 물물교환
n. barterer 물물교환자

☐ **endow**   v. 기부하다, 기증하다
n. endowment 기증, 기부

☐ **spawn**   v. 낳다   n. 알
n. spawning (물고기의) 산란

☐ **squander**   v. 낭비하다, 마구 쓰다

☐ **mourn**   v. 슬퍼하다, 한탄하다
n. mourner 애도자   n. mourning 슬픔, 비탄   a. mournful 슬픔에 잠긴

☐ **stagger**   v. 비틀거리다   n. 비틀거림
a. staggering 비틀거리는

□ **debris**　　n. 파편

□ **knack**　　n. 솜씨, 요령
a. knacky 솜씨가 좋은, 교묘한

□ **edifice**　　n. 대건축물, 조직

□ **remnant**　　n. 나머지

□ **symbiosis**　　n. 공생관계
n. symbiont 공생자

□ **haphazard**　　a. 우연의, 계획성 없는
n. haphazardry 우연성

□ **ludicrous**　　a. 우스운, 바보 같은

□ **sporadic**　　a. 때때로 일어나는
ad. sporadically 드물게, 산발적으로

□ **inimical**　　a. 해로운, 불리한

□ **tactful**　　a. 재치 있는, 세련된
n. tact 재치　a. tactless 재치 없는, 무뚝뚝한

□ **nocturnal**　　a. 야행성의, 밤의
n. nocturne 야상곡　ad. nocturnally 야간에, 매일밤

□ **eccentric**　　a. 별난
n. eccentricity 남다름, 별남

□ **hamper**　　v. 방해하다, 막다

□ **equivalent**　　a. 동등한　n. 동의어
n. equivalence 같음

□ **compound**　　a. 혼합의, 복합의

□ **reprove**　　v. 비난하다, 잔소리하다
n. reproof 책망, 꾸지람

□ **precipitate**　　v. ~를 촉진하다
a. precipitative 촉진시키는　ad. precipitately 거꾸로, 다급하게

□ **constrict**　　v. 압축하다, (발육을) 저해하다
a. constrictive 단단히 죄는

□ **disdain**　　v. 멸시하다　n. 경멸, 오만한 태도
a. disdainful 오만한

□ **dissolve**　　v. 용해시키다, 녹이다
a. dissolvent 용해력이 있는

□ **exhilarate**　　v. 기운을 북돋우다, 고무시키다
a. exhilarative 명랑한　n. exhilaration 활기 불어 넣기

□ **contrive**　　v. 발명하다, 연구하다
n. contrivance 발명품

□ **despise**　　v. 경멸하다, 몹시 싫어하다
a. despicable 경멸할 수 있는

□ **evict**　　v. 쫓아내다, ~를 되찾다
n. eviction 축출

□ **adhere**　　v. 부착하다
a. adherent 접착성의, 부착력이 있는

□ **disassemble**　　v. 분해하다, 해체하다
ad. disassembly 분해된 상태

☐ **discrepancy**　　n. 불일치, 모순
a. discrepant 일치하지 않는　ad. discrepantly 모순되게

☐ **discretion**　　n. 결정권, 분별, 신중
a. discretionary 자유재량의

☐ **descent**　　n. 하강, 하산
a. descendent 내려가는　n. descendant 후기 형태

☐ **predicament**　　n. 곤경, 궁지

☐ **coherent**　　a. 응집성의, 일치한
n. coherence 일관성

☐ **erratic**　　a. 별난, 이상한
a. erratical 괴상한

☐ **tenable**　　a. 주장할 수 있는, 조리 있는

☐ **desolate**　　a. 황폐한
n. desolation 무인상태

☐ **engrossed**　　a. 열중하는
n. engrossment 열중, 정서　ad. engrossingly 열중하게 하도록

☐ **incompatible**　　a. 모순된
n. incompatibility 양립불가

☐ **valiant**　　a. 용감한, 씩씩한
ad. valiantly 용감하게

☐ **tangible**　　a. 유형의, 실체가 있는
n. tangibility 명확함, 확실　ad. tangibly 명백히

☐ **debilitate**　　v. 약하게 하다
n. debilitation 허약, 노쇠

☐ **venerate**　　v. 존경하다
a. venerable 존경할만한　n. veneration 존경, 숭배

☐ **abide**　　v. 머물다, 살다, 준수하다
n. abode 주소, 거주　n. abidance 지속, 거주

☐ **entail**　　v. 수반하다, 부과하다
n. entailment 세습 재산

☐ **lament**　　v. 슬퍼하다, 한탄하다
a. lamentable 슬픈　n. lamentation 슬픔, 애도

☐ **obstruct**　　v. 방해하다, 막다
n. obstruction 방해물　a. obstructive 방해하는

☐ **hallucinate**　　v. 환각을 일으키다
n. hallucination 환각, 환상

☐ **ignite**　　v. 불 붙이다
n. ignition 점화, 발화

☐ **pacify**　　v. 진정시키다
a. pacifistic 평화론적인, 평화주의자의　n. pacifism 평화주의

☐ **radiate**　　v. 발산하다, 방출하다
n. radiation 방사, 방사물

☐ **abdicate**　　v. 포기하다, 버리다
n. abdication 사직, 권고

☐ **daunt**　　v. 위압하다
a. dauntless 불굴의, 꿈쩍도 하지않은

□ **sabotage**	n. 파괴, 방해 v. 고의로 방해하다, 파괴하다
□ **taboo**	n. 금기, 꺼림
□ **magnitude** v. magnify 확대하다	n. 중대함, 크기
□ **qualm**	n. 양심의 가책, 불안
□ **calamity**	n. 재난, 불행
□ **obdurate** n. obduracy 고집, 완고	a. 완고한, 냉혹한
□ **earnest** ad. earnestly 진지하게	a. 진지한, 진심의
□ **taciturn** n. taciturnity 말없음, 과묵	a. 말 없는
□ **salient**	a. 두드러진, 눈에 띄는
□ **judicious** a. judicial 사법의, 재판의 n. judiciary 사법부, 사법제도	a. 사려 깊은, 현명한
□ **wary** v. ware 주의하다, 조심하다	a. 조심스러운
□ **vehement** ad. vehemently 격렬하게	a. 열정적인, 격렬한
□ **quaint**	a. 예스럽고 정취있는, 색다르고 재미있는

□ **callow** n. callowness 미숙함	a. 미숙한, 경험이 없는
□ **aggravate** n. aggravation 중대화	v. ~를 악화 시키다
□ **diffuse** n. diffuser 보급자	v. 발산하다, 보급하다
□ **contend** n. contention 말다툼, 논쟁 .	v. 주장하다
□ **repudiate** n. repudiation 거부	v. 거절하다, ~을 부인하다
□ **plunge**	v. 담그다, 밀어 넣다
□ **sojourn** n. sojourner 일시 체류자	v. 묵다, 체류하다 n. 체류
□ **annihilate** n. annihilation 멸종	v. 몰살시키다
□ **crumble** n. crumbling 부스러기	v. 부수다
□ **renovate** n. renovation 개혁 n. renovator 혁신자	v. 혁신하다
□ **preside** a. presiding 통솔하는 n. presidium 이사회	v. 사회를 보다, 통솔하다
□ **deter** n. determent 방해물	v. 주저하게 하다
□ **dilute** n. dilution 희석	v. 희석시키다

MEMO

The VOCA+^{PLUS}

BULARY

완전 개정판

7

넥서스영어교육연구소 지음

NEXUS Edu

The VOCA⁺ BULARY

완전 개정판

난이도	대상	특징
Level 1	예비중 ~ 중등 1	
Level 2	중등 1 ~ 중등 2	★ 학년별로 꼭 알아야 하는 교육부 권장 표제어 선별
Level 3	중등 2 ~ 중등 3	★ 문어발도 부럽지 않은 핵심 파생어 확장 어휘
Level 4	중등 3 ~ 고등 1	★ 학교 내신까지 확실하게 대비하는 유의어/반의어/참고 어휘
Level 5	고등 1 ~ 고등 2	★ 완벽한 마무리를 위한 어휘 3종 테스트
Level 6	고등 2 ~ 수험 대비	★ 생생한 단어 MP3 듣기용 QR 코드 제공
Level 7	수험 대비	

Test   MP3

온라인 어휘 테스트 학습 제공 www.nexusEDU.kr
MP3 음원 다운로드 www.nexusbook.com

단어 바로 듣기

The VOCA⁺ BULARY 7

넥서스영어교육연구소 지음

교육부 권장 어휘 완벽 반영 + 학년별 심화 어휘
예비중부터 특목고·수능 대비까지 7단계 어휘 학습

완전 개정판

NEXUS Edu